T0331889

Demystifying
Computation
A Hands-On Introduction

Demystifying Computation
A Hands-On Introduction

Apostolos Syropoulos
Greek Molecular Computing Group, Greece

World Scientific

NEW JERSEY · LONDON · SINGAPORE · BEIJING · SHANGHAI · HONG KONG · TAIPEI · CHENNAI · TOKYO

Published by

World Scientific Publishing Europe Ltd.

57 Shelton Street, Covent Garden, London WC2H 9HE

Head office: 5 Toh Tuck Link, Singapore 596224

USA office: 27 Warren Street, Suite 401-402, Hackensack, NJ 07601

Library of Congress Cataloging-in-Publication Data
Names: Syropoulos, Apostolos, author.
Title: Demystifying computation : a hands-on introduction / by Apostolos Syropoulos,
   (Greek Molecular Computing Group, Greece).
Description: [Hackensack] New Jersey : World Scientific, [2017] |
   Includes bibliographical references and index.
Identifiers: LCCN 2016045892| ISBN 9781786342652 (hc : alk. paper) |
   ISBN 9781786342669 (pbk : alk. paper)
Subjects: LCSH: Data processing. | Coding theory.
Classification: LCC QA76 .S965 2017 | DDC 004--dc23
LC record available at https://lccn.loc.gov/2016045892

British Library Cataloguing-in-Publication Data
A catalogue record for this book is available from the British Library.

Copyright © 2017 by World Scientific Publishing Europe Ltd.

All rights reserved. This book, or parts thereof, may not be reproduced in any form or by any means, electronic or mechanical, including photocopying, recording or any information storage and retrieval system now known or to be invented, without written permission from the Publisher.

For photocopying of material in this volume, please pay a copying fee through the Copyright Clearance Center, Inc., 222 Rosewood Drive, Danvers, MA 01923, USA. In this case permission to photocopy is not required from the publisher.

Desk Editors: Ram Mohan K/Mary Simpson

Typeset by Stallion Press
Email: enquiries@stallionpress.com

Printed in Singapore

To my son Demetrios-Georgios
and to…Koula

Preface

Today billions of people own and use smartphones, tablets, smart TVs and other such devices. Yet most of these users do not realize that all these devices are actually computers. In addition, most people do not realize that when they listen to an MP3 audio file or when they view videos, somehow a computer transforms computer data to sounds and/or images. Of course, one should not forget semi-autonomous cars, that is, a device that is driving the car for us. To put it simply, computers are everywhere and can do amazing things. But computers are programmable, so why are these devices called computers?

Intuitively speaking, all such devices are (specialized) computers because they do things automatically or mechanically. This is certainly a basic characteristic of computing devices but this is not the only one. In particular, one can say that digital audio and video files contain data (symbols) that are processed by a *computer program*. However, there are other cases where this is not that obvious. Thus, in order to fully justify our answer, we need to have a deep understanding of computing and its various expressions. The aim of this book is two-fold: first, to explain that computing is about the mechanical solution to certain kinds of problems and, second, to show that there are many and different approaches to computing.

Chapter 1 is a brief historical account of computing devices. In particular, it starts with a discussion of numbering systems and then proceeds with a discussion of early computing devices. These include all devices that appeared before the first electronic computer. Next, there is a general discussion about the different generations electronic computers that includes a presentation of Japan's fifth generation computers project. The chapter concludes with a discussion about the future of computing.

Chapter 2 is an introduction to computability theory, which forms the core of the theory of computation. The chapter contains a description of the scientific environment that led to the formulation of a number of problems. More specifically, attempts to solve or, better, to give answers regarding the solvability of these problems led to the formulation of mathematical systems and conceptual computing devices that provided the answer sought. Later on, these mathematical tools were used to develop computability theory and complexity theory.

The limits of computation are discussed in the Chapter 3. In addition, this chapter serves as an introduction to hypercomputation, which is the idea that we can go beyond the barrier imposed by the "classical" theory of computation. The chapter discusses objections against the theory of computation and against hypercomputation. In addition, there is a brief discussion on the computational abilities of the human mind.

Chapter 4 contains presentations of various forms of natural computing, that is, "devices" that can be found in nature or mimic natural phenomena. The text discusses DNA computing, membrane computing, amorphous computing, cellular automata, physarum machines, swarm intelligence, chaos computing, analog computing, and neural networks. Certainly, there are other forms of natural computing but I have decided not to present all since this is not an encyclopedia of computing.

Chapter 5 is a presentation of quantum computing, the most promising new approach to computing. In a way this approach makes use of basic quantum phenomena. Since I do not expect all readers to be familiar with quantum mechanics, I have included a "crash course" on quantum mechanics. Readers should use this material only to understand the basic principles, which are needed in order to understand how quantum computing work. Next, there is a discussion of quantum circuits, cluster-state quantum computers, topological quantum computers, and adiabatic quantum computers. The discussion is far from being complete, but the aim of the book is to introduce readers to various forms of computing so that they understand what computing is. Also, this chapter is quite demanding for someone who wants to fully grasp all relevant ideas.

Today, many people are talking about fuzzy sets and fuzzy logic mainly because these concepts have found so many applications. Fuzzy sets are a mathematical description of vagueness and they are very popular among computer scientists and engineers. The aim of the Chapter 6 is to introduce the relevant ideas from a mathematical as well as philosophical points of view. In particular, one of the goals of this chapter is to explain what vagueness is and how fuzzy sets model it. Then, there is a discussion of fuzzy computing that is followed by an introduction to rough set theory, an alternative mathematical model of vagueness. Rough automata are also presented although their theory is not mature enough.

Chapter 7 is a short one and discusses various ideas proposed by modern approaches to the problem of gravity quantization and their relation to the limits of computing. In particular, the chapter discusses three controversial ideas: the universe as a computer, space–time discreteness, and ultimate computing devices.

Instead of providing a "normal" bibliography, at the end of each chapter, there is an annotated bibliography that describes only the books that have been used in the writing of this book. Other citations appear as footnotes in the main text.

This book is neither a textbook nor a coffee-table book. It is a book that should be read by anyone who really wants to get a taste of the theory of computation. Although the book is self-contained, in the sense that the reader is first introduced to certain mathematical ideas and/or notation and then how they are used, the book is also suitable for people who have knowledge in mathematics. Mathematics is a language that can express many things compactly and rigorously. So instead of saying many things it is better to describe something mathematically, even if the reader will not fully grasp everything. The point here is to give readers a basic understanding and not to make them experts.

Acknowledgments

Writing a book is not an easy task. Of course, many other tasks are not easy either. For example, designing or digitizing a computer font and creating a new piece of software are not easy tasks. In my own experience, there are always people and/or organizations that help an author in various and, sometimes, unexpected ways. First of all, I would like to thank Alice Oven who believed in this project and helped me to realize it until the day she left Imperial College Press (ICP). Also, I would like to thank Mary Simpson, my new ICP editor, for her support and help. In addition, I would like to thank the Laboratorio delle Macchine Matematiche dell'Università di Modena e Reggio Eilia and the Museo Galileo, Florence for allowing me to freely include in this book, the images of devices they keep in their collection. Moreover, I would like to thank the National Archaeological Museum, Athens, Greece, for ignoring my requests to allow me to include an image of the Antikythera mechanism in this book. This prompted me to draw Figure 1.1(b)! In addition, I really must express my gratitude to the following people who read parts of the book and helped me to both improve the presentation and eliminate a number of errors and/or omissions: Andromahi Spanou (Ανδρομάχη Σπανού), Theophanes Grammenos (Θεοφάνης Γραμμένος), Vasilis Evangelidis (Βασίλης Ευαγγελίδης), Pablo García Risueño, Anastasia Pechtelidou (Αναστασία Πεχτελίδου), and Ioannis Kanellos (Ιωάννης Κανέλλος). In addition, I would like to thank Yiannis Kontovos (Γιάννης Κοντοβός) for his drawings.

Apostolos Syropoulos
Xanthi, Greece
May 2016

About the Author

Apostolos Syropoulos holds a B.Sc. in Physics from the University of Ioannina, Ioannina, Greece, an M.Sc. in Computer Science from the University of Göteborg, Göteborg, Sweden, and a Ph.D. in Theoretical Computer Science from the Democritus University of Thrace, Xanthi, Greece. He is mainly interested in the limits of computation and on non-conventional models of computation. In particular, he is interested in models of computation that use vagueness (e.g., fuzzy models of computation). Also, he is interested in categorical models of fuzzy sets and multisets. In addition, he has a strong interest in digital typography. In particular, he has published a number of software tools and computer fonts. He has authored or co-authored nine books and over 60 papers and articles.

Contents

Chapter 1

A Brief History of Computing

Since the dawn of civilization, humans have been developing increasingly sophisticated methods of calculation and computation. The transition from simple, numerical systems to fully electronic machines takes us through a fascinating journey of knowledge and discovery in history. The design and construction of computing devices used today differ substantially from former models, and here, we will explore the progression of innovation within this complex field.

1.1 From Numbers to Calculating

Numbers and their properties have remained my fascination ever since my early school years. What really intrigued me the most was how new kinds of numbers have been introduced to deal with problems. I learned that *negative* numbers were introduced to solve problems like this equation, $4 = 4 \cdot x + 20$, *irrational* numbers (i.e., numbers that cannot be expressed as fractions) are the solutions of equations like $x^2 - 2 = 0$, and *imaginary* numbers (i.e., numbers that are multiples of i, the imaginary unit, a number whose square, $i \cdot i$, is equal to -1) were devised to solve equations like $x^2 + 4 = 0$. Although I learned many things about numbers and the problems they solved, still I had no idea who invented numbers and how people started using numbers. It seems there are no records that can be used to tell the history of the invention of numbers. So let us assume that there was a time when humans did not know how to count. At that time, they only used concepts like single, pair, and many when talking about quantities. In fact, nouns in ancient European languages had three numbers, that is, singular, dual, and plural. It is quite possible that they started to feel the need for counting when they began to domesticate wild animals. Shepherds needed to know how many animals were in their flocks so they had to know their exact number. These shepherds soon realized that a flock of six sheep and a flock of six goats have something in common: the quantity

1

of animals is the same. Farmers realized the same when they counted fruits, vegetables, and so on. The conclusion was that it does not matter what one counts, but how many objects one counts. This simple remark is the essence of mathematical abstraction. And I suppose the first human being who realized this simple fact is probably the father of mathematics.

It is more than clear that early humans have used their hands as an aid to counting and calculation. Since our hands have 10 fingers, humans in most parts of the planet have used this number as a basis for counting. In other words, the *decimal* numeral system that we use today was invented by the first people who used their fingers to count. However, humans did not write numbers as we do today. For example, the Romans used the "digits" I (1), V (5), X (10), L (50), C (100), D (500), and M (1000) to write down numbers. When they had to write a number, they "decomposed" the number into parts corresponding to quantities equal to the available "digits" and then they simply wrote down the corresponding "digits". Thus, the number 2017 was written as MMXVII. The alphabetic numeral system of Ancient Greeks was similar. The table below shows the modern form of its "digits".

α'	1	ι'	10	ρ'	100	͵α	1000	͵ι	10000	͵ρ	100000
β'	2	κ'	20	σ'	200	͵β	2000	͵κ	20000	͵σ	200000
γ'	3	λ'	30	τ'	300	͵γ	3000	͵λ	30000	͵τ	300000
δ'	4	μ'	40	υ'	400	͵δ	4000	͵μ	40000	͵υ	400000
ε'	5	ν'	50	φ'	500	͵ε	5000	͵ν	50000	͵φ	500000
ϛ'	6	ξ'	60	χ'	600	͵ϛ	6000	͵ξ	60000	͵χ	600000
ζ'	7	ο'	70	ψ'	700	͵ζ	7000	͵ο	70000	͵ψ	700000
η'	8	π'	80	ω'	800	͵η	8000	͵π	80000	͵ω	800000
θ'	9	ϟ'	90	ϡ'	900	͵θ	9000	͵ϟ	90000	͵ϡ	900000

Thus, the number 2017 is rendered as ͵βιζ'. The so-called acrophonic numbering system was another system that was used by Ancient Greeks. Its set of "digits" is shown below:

I	1	Γ	5	Δ	10	Γᐞ	50
H	100	Γᴴ	500	X	1000	Γˣ	5000
M	10000	Γᴹ	50000				

In this system the number 2017 is written as XXΔΓII.

Interestingly, not all humans have been using the decimal numeral system. Many people, including the Mayas and the Aztecs, have been using a numeral system that had the number 20 as its basis. This numeral system is called *vigesimal*. It is quite possible that the Mayas and the Aztecs have been using the fingers of both their hands and their feet for counting and this might explain why they have opted to use the number 20 as basis for their numeral system. The table that follows shows the various "digits" used to write numerals.

°	1	° °	2	° ° °	3	° ° ° °	4
⸺	5	⸺	6	⸺	7	⸺	8
⸺	9	⸺	10	⸺	11	⸺	12
⸺	13	⸺	14	⸺	15	⸺	16
⸺	17	⸺	18	⸺	19	⸺	0

Numbers in this system are written from top to bottom, and the most significant digit is always at the top. For example, the number 2017 would be rendered as follows:

These are not the only numeral systems people have ever used. The Ancient Sumerian people had used a numeral system with 60 as its basis (such a system is called *sexagesimal*). Unfortunately, there is no reasonable explanation, just speculations, for this peculiar choice. This system is unique such that the numbers 2, 120, 7200, and 1/30 were all written in an identical manner. Moreover, this number system is still in some use even today. The fact that 1 hour has 60 minutes and 1 minute has 60 seconds has its roots to the Sumerian numeral system. Since humans had used the numbers 10, 20, and 60 to specify numeral systems, it makes sense to say that any number can be used as a basis for a numeral system. For example, one can use the numbers 2, 8, and 16 as bases for numeral systems that are called *binary*, *octal*, and *hexadecimal*. It is possible to use a negative number or even an imaginary number as a basis for a numeral system! Nevertheless, these exotic numeral systems will not concern us in what follows.

In ancient Egypt, agriculture had been developed by making use of the dry and rainy seasons. It was very important to know when these seasons were to arrive. Initially, they might have used some rules of thumb to predict these seasons. Later on, they developed a calendar to precisely predict the seasons. Developing a calendar means that one is able to record numbers and text, that is, one has a writing system at her disposal. The writing system should also provide some means so as to perform some, if not all, arithmetical operations. After all, it is not easy to work difficult operations "in your head". The Egyptians developed such methods but they were adequate only for additions and subtraction while there was provision for fractions. All civilizations that developed a writing system also developed notations for numbers and methods to perform arithmetical operations with these notations. Sooner or later, merchants, astronomers, and all the people who heavily used numbers in their everyday business discovered that they needed faster and easier ways to do arithmetical operations and so the demand for devices that could assist humans in such operations was presumably high.

The first device that could assist humans to perform arithmetical operations fast is the abacus. An abacus consists of beads that can be moved up and down on a series of sticks or strings within a wooden frame usually. The abacus is found in almost any nation in every part of the planet. An abacus can be used to perform additions and subtractions easily, while it is not very difficult to perform multiplications. Divisions are much harder.

The Greek mathematician Eratosthenes of Cyrene ('Ερατοσθένης) is best known for being the first human to calculate the circumference of the Earth. In addition, Eratosthenes built a calculating device, which was called *mesolabio* [see Figure 1.1(a)], for easing the labor involved in solving a particular problem. The mesolabio consisted of three rectangular frames of equal size that could slide on a rail at their base so they could be partially superimposed on one another. Each frame had a string stretching over the diagonal. The mesolabio was invented in order to solve the Delian problem, that is, the construction of a cube with twice the volume of a given cube using only a straightedge and compass. In the 19th century, mathematicians showed that this problem could not be solved using the tools originally specified. However, Eratosthenes solved the problem using the mesolabio. In a sense, he did not solve the problem but gave an answer to the first part of the problem, that is, whether it is possible to construct a cube with twice the volume of a given cube. The important lesson to learn here is that it might be possible to solve problems by relaxing some initial constraints and/or conditions (see Section 3.1 for a detailed discussion of problems and their solutions).

Without doubt, the most impressive device of antiquity is the Antikythera mechanism,[1] which was recovered from an ancient shipwreck in 1901 and was probably built sometime between 150 BC and 60 BC. More than a century has passed since the mechanism was recovered, yet there is no real consensus regarding its purpose. However, one can say that the device encompasses what was known about the Universe [or "Cosmos" (Κόσμος) as this word is inscribed on the mechanism] at the time of its construction. Thus, it is not an exaggeration to say that the mechanism was some sort of mechanical encyclopedia of astronomy. The device was probably enclosed in a wooden box whose height was 320–330 mm, its width 170–180 mm, and its depth 80 mm. The box was found inside more than 30 toothed wheels. On one side of the box, there was a handle and the user had to turn it in order to operate the mechanism. Figure 1.1(b) shows a reconstruction of the front display of the Antikythera mechanism. The front

---

[1]Mike G. Edmunds. *The antikythera mechanism and the mechanical universe.* Contemporary Physics, 55(4), pp. 263–285, 2014.

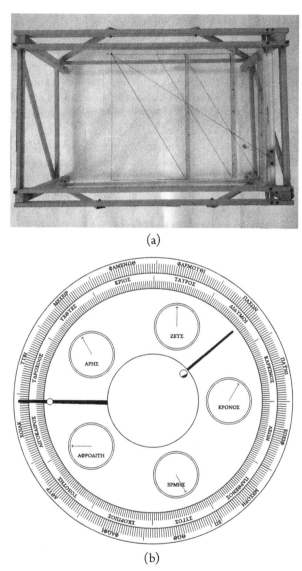

(a)

(b)

Figure 1.1: Eratosthenes's mesolabio and the front display of the Antikythera mechanism. (a) A replica of Eratosthenes's mesolabio. Image courtesy of Laboratorio delle Macchine Matematiche dell'Università di Modena e Reggio Emilia. (b) This front display of the Antikythera mechanism is based on its latest reconstruction (see text for a description of its various parts). Image created by the author using the LaTeX TikZ package from a drawing that appeared on Nature, Vol. 468, pp. 496–498 (2010).

display contained two large pointers — the bigger one showed the date in the Greek–Egyptian calendar (the outer annulus showed Egyptian month names) and the smaller one showed the position of the moon on the zodiac scale (inner annulus showed the name of the 12 zodiac signs). The little ball on the smaller pointer showed the phases of the moon. In addition, there are fine planetary dials (little circles). Each dial corresponds to one of the known planets at the time: Saturn (ΚΡΟΝΟΣ), Jupiter (ΖΕΥΣ), Mars (ΑΡΗΣ), Venus (ΑΦΡΟΔΙΤΗ), and Mercury (ΕΡΜΗΣ). It is quite possible that these dials could have shown key events in each planet's cycle. Naturally, one could infer that when the two big pointers overlapped, then an eclipse should happen. Thus, the device could predict eclipses, among others.[2] Strictly, the mechanism is not a calculating device, but it does have the capability to perform multiplication and division. All these prove that technology was quite advanced in antiquity and not so much primitive as we typically think.

The next milestone in the development of calculating devices is the Rabdologia, or Napier's Bones, as they are more commonly known, after their inventor John Napier, who was a Scotsman whose main discovery is the logarithm. Rabdologia is based on the use of Gelosia, a method for doing multiplication, which was most likely developed in India. This is not a device like the Antikythera mechanism, which had gears and worked much like a clock, but something similar to the abacus. The Jesuit Athanasius Kircher implemented the idea of incorporating Rabdologia into some form of mechanical assembly. This device is known as *Organum Mathematicum* (see Figure 1.2). The slide rule was another device that was inspired by Napier's work. It was developed by William Oughtred and others.

1.2   Mechanical Calculating Devices

In a sense, Organum Mathematicum (see Figure 1.2) was a precursor to the mechanical calculating devices that were developed in the 16th century and afterwards. Wilhelm Schickard, who was a Professor of Hebrew, Astronomy, Mathematics, and Geodesy at the University of Tübingen, Germany, designed and built a device, the *Rechen Uhr* (calculating clock), in 1623. The calculating clock was the first mechanical calculating device. Unfortunately, no copy of the machine has survived. What we know about this machine is contained in three documents: two letters between Schickard and his close friend Johannes Kepler, and a sketch of the machine with instructions to a workman. The sketch is not so elaborate, but the hints provided in the letters were useful enough to reconstruct the machine.

The French mathematician and philosopher Blaise Pascal is the second person who designed and constructed a mechanical calculating machine. Using the *Pascaline*

[2]Christián C. Carman and James Evans. *On the epoch of the antikythera mechanism and its eclipse predictor*. Archive for History of Exact Sciences, 68, pp. 693–774, 2014.

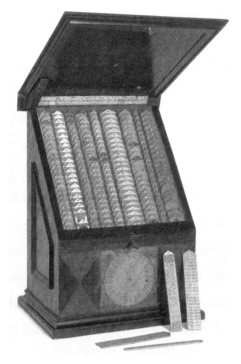

Figure 1.2: A replica of Organum Mathematicum. Image courtesy of Museo Galileo, Florence, Photo Franca Principe.

[see Figure 1.3(a) on page 8], as the machine is known, was quite easy. In fact, one could perform additions and subtractions. Multiplications were possible by repeatedly performing additions while divisions were not out of question. Pascal tried to put his invention into production. Although this was not a profitable move, still this is the reason why a large number of Pascalines survived till today.

Gottfried Wilhelm Leibniz was a German philosopher and mathematician who is primarily known to be one of the two people who devised the differential calculus. The other one is Isaac Newton. In 1671, Leibniz designed a calculating device, the *Step Reckoner*, which was built three years later. The most important feature of this device was its stepped drum [see Figure 1.3(b) on page 8], that is, a cylinder bearing nine teeth of different lengths, which increase in equal amounts around the drum. Variations of the stepped drum were in use until recently. Leibniz's *Instrumentum Arithmeticum*, as he actually called his machine, differs significantly from Pascaline, in that it allows multiplication and division to be done directly, without making consecutive additions or subtractions. It is worth noting that Leibniz "invented" the binary system for philosophical reasons, which should not concern us here.

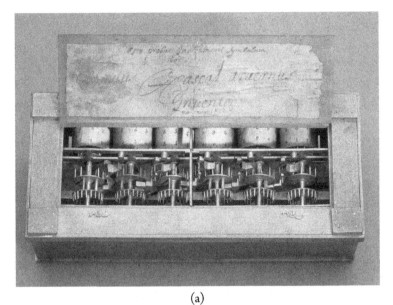

(a)

(b)

Figure 1.3: Two important mechanical calculating devices: the Pascaline and the Instrumentum Arithmeticum. (a) A Pascaline is opened up so one can see the gears and cylinders that are rotating to display the numerical result. © Musée des arts et métiers-Cnam, Paris, photo J-C Wetzel. (b) An Instrumentum Arithmeticum whose stepped drums can be clearly seen in the middle of the image. © Photo Deutsches Museum.

After the introduction of the step reckoner and for almost 200 years, calculating machines were considered as toys since there was no real use for them. In addition, it was not possible to advance the calculating capabilities of these machines since the technology of the time could not produce the fine parts needed for the construction of such precise mechanisms. However, at the beginning of the 19th century, there was an increase in commercial transactions that gave the required thrust for production of *effective* calculating devices. Indeed, in 1820, the French insurance executive Charles Xavier Thomas de Colmar build a mechanical calculating device, which he called the *Arithmometer* (see Figure 1.4). This machine was a modification of Leibniz's machine though he was not aware of Leibniz's work. This may sound like an oxymoron, but Thomas de Colmar built his machine using the idea of a stepped drum and, in this respect, it is a modification of the earlier machine. The machine was put into production, but it was not popular. This changed in 1867 when the Arithmometer was exhibited in the Paris Exposition and earned praise from the judges. Thereafter, the machine became very popular. However, people were trying to improve the machine by replacing the stepped drum with a gear that could quickly change the number of

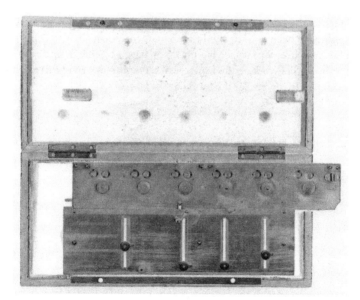

Figure 1.4: The Arithmometer calculating device (in inverted color). Image courtesy of Division of Medicine & Science, National Museum of American History, Smithsonian Institution.

teeth coming out from their surface. In 1873, Frank S. Baldwin solved this problem by inventing a variable-toothed gear. And in 1875, he used this technology to construct the "Baldwin's 1875 machine". In 1878, Willgodt T. Odhner, a Swedish national who was working in Russia, constructed almost the same machine in Europe. Later on, the variable-toothed gear was used by different companies that produced calculating devices and one of the most famous was the one produced by the German company Brunsviga.

The machines described so far could be used to perform a number of consecutive operations in order to compute something. In particular, a human operator had to make a plan and use the machines to execute it so as to find the result needed. Clearly, it would be far more useful to have a machine that would accept both the numbers and the plan and deliver the result sought after some time. At the first quarter of the 19th century, there were devices that could follow a plan to perform a particular task. For example, the Jacquard loom, which was invented by Joseph Marie Jacquard, is a loom where a number of interchangeable punched cards, attached one at the end of another, control the weaving of the cloth so that any desired pattern can be obtained automatically. Subsequently, the punched cards were used by the American statistician Herman Hollerith to feed data to his census machine. Later on, they were used to input data to early digital computers but soon they were replaced by electronic devices. A form of punched cards have been used by the English mathematician Charles Babbage in the designs of his *Analytical Engine* (see Figure 1.5 on page 11). The design of this device was based on his earlier work on the *Difference Engine*. This design of this machine was based on a simple idea. Consider the formula

$$T = x^2 - 2x + 4$$

This formula can be used to generate a sequence of values for T as shown below:

Δ^2	Δ	T	x
		4	0
	−1	3	1
2	1	4	2
2	3	7	3
2	5	12	4
2	7	19	5

The column designated with the letter Δ contains the differences between successive values of Ts and the column designated with Δ^2 contains the differences between successive values of Δs. Clearly, the numbers in the column designated with Δ^2 are the same and they will remain the same if one goes further. Thus, one can use this remark to find any value of T. This particular case is about the values of a polynomial of degree 2. In case one needs to find the values of a polynomial of degree 3, 4, or higher, then

Figure 1.5: The Analytical Engine. Image courtesy of Science Museum/Science & Society Picture Library.

it is necessary to introduce the columns designated with Δ^3, Δ^4, etc., with the expected meaning. Based on this remark, one can calculate the value of any polynomial. Babbage use this idea to partially build his Difference Engine. In fact, he built only a part of the calculating mechanism. In 1833, he abandoned the project in favor of the Analytical Engine.

The Analytical Engine project started when Babbage realized that his previous design is not general enough since it could not perform multiplications and divisions. In 1833, he realized that instead of performing multiplications or divisions, a machine could perform repeated additions or subtractions, provided it was possible to control the total number of additions or subtractions. Especially for divisions, he needed a mechanism to check the result of each subtraction in order to determine what should be done next. In addition, he found a substantially faster method of curry propagation. These findings were, in essence, the reason why he abandoned his previous project and started the Analytical Engine.

The real innovation common to the many designs of the Analytical Engine was the inclusion of a basic storage and calculating units. The characteristic of these designs is their ability to process numbers with many digits; — to be precise. Here I must stress that we are talking about integer numbers, positive or negative, but not decimal numbers. But this is not a severe restriction as one can always simulate computations of decimal numbers with computations of whole numbers (e.g., the IEEE Standard

754 specifies how to represent a specific range of decimal numbers as binary numerals with no decimal point). Another important aspect of these designs is the inclusion of provision for loops and branching. This simply means that the machine could repeatedly perform a number of instructions and that it could take one or another course or action depending on some arithmetic value. What is really interesting is how one could specify a *plan* of action to be performed by the machine.

The plan, or *program* as it called nowadays, was feed to the machine by two strings of Jacquard punched cards. The first one was used to specify the arithmetic operations to be performed and, loosely speaking, the second one was used to specify the location of the operands. Both strings of cards are important and using only one is meaningless as, for example, an arithmetic operation without operands makes no sense. In 1840, Babbage visited Turin, Italy, to make a presentation on the Analytical Engine. Luigi Federico Menabrea (who became later Prime Minister of Italy) was among the audience and took notes of the presentation. These notes were later on published in French in *Bibliothèque Universelle de Genève*, October, 1842, No. 82. This paper was then translated into English by Augusta Ada Byron, countess of Lovelace and was published in 1843 in the *Scientific Memoirs*, Vol. 3, pp. 666–731. Ada, as she is commonly known, appended extensive notes to her translation. The notes were prepared with guidance from Babbage. In these notes she states:

> The operating mechanism can even be thrown into action indepen-
> dently of any object to operate upon (although of course no result
> could then be developed). Again, it might act upon other things
> besides number, were objects found whose mutual fundamental
> relations could be expressed by those of the abstract science of
> operations, and which should be also susceptible of adaptations to
> the action of the operating notation and mechanism of the engine.
> Supposing, for instance, that the fundamental relations of pitched
> sounds in the science of harmony and of musical composition were
> susceptible of such expression and adaptations, the engine might
> compose elaborate and scientific pieces of music of any degree of
> complexity or extent.

This excerpt from Ada's publication is visionary since the author speculates that a calculating machine should be able to deal not only with numbers but with other things too (e.g., sounds). This is the reason why Ada has a special place in the history of computers. It is quite possible that some readers may have heard that Ada was the "world's first programmer" (i.e., a person that specifies a plan that has to be carried out by machine). Unfortunately, there is nothing to support this view. Although Ada received tutoring in mathematics and music, still it seems highly unlikely that she knew how to program the Analytical Engine. As a matter of fact, all but one of the programs cited in her notes had been prepared by Babbage a few years earlier. Ada got involved with the Analytical Engine project because Babbage hired her. And he had done so because he wanted independent people to convey knowledge of the project to the wider public. This was something he did also for his earlier project.

Babbage argued that the Analytical Engine was a *universal* calculating machine since it could perform any arithmetic calculation, provided there was sufficient time. Babbage's argument is based on three simple remarks. When one wants to perform arithmetic operations on numbers with more than 40 digits, then one can always break the numbers in segments consisting of 40 digits and use these segments for the calculations. Programs are specified by strings of punched cards whose length has theoretically no limit, that is, there is no limit to what the machine can perform. Since the machine can write numbers by punching cards, which can be read later on, the machine has practically no storage limits.

Babbage's machines are certainly a major milestone in the history of computing, nevertheless, they had little or no impact on the development of the field. The reason is mainly that he had chosen not to publish an account of his ideas and mechanisms. The Menabrea–Ada paper does not contain a description of how the machine operated. Instead, it focused on the mathematical principles embodied in the machine and nothing more.

1.3   Modern Computers

Computers as we perceive them today are machines that are able to manipulate sequences of binary digits (i.e., sequences of the digits 0 and 1). In a way, this was dictated by the fact that electronic equipment can be easily set up representing the two binary digits. For example, early computers used vacuum tubes because these devices could either block or allow the flow of electric current and thus one could encode the digits 0 or 1, respectively. But this was not enough. In order to be able to do useful things, one had to use circuits that would allow the computer to perform additions, subtractions, multiplications, divisions, and so on. In order to perform an arithmetic operation, we must ensure that both operands have at most a specific number of binary digits (e.g., 8, 16, 32, 48, and so on). If an operand has fewer digits, then we add leading zeros. The various operations can be implemented by circuits that consist of *logic gates*. These are devices that implement various logical operations. These are operations between *truth values* (e.g., *true* and *false*) of some *logic* (i.e., a set of rules and principles that allow one to "correctly" reason). In *Boolean*[3] or *bivalent* logic, there are two truth values — true and false. That is, each statement in this logic is either true or false. It is customary to represent true with 1 and false with 0. The basic logical

---

[3] Named after George Boole an English mathematician and philosopher who systematized Aristotle's logic (i.e., the logic we usually employ in our everyday reasoning).

operations (or Boolean connectives) between truth values are *negation* ($\neg$), *conjunction* ($\wedge$), *disjunction* ($\vee$), and *exclusive disjunction* ($\underline{\vee}$). These operations are implemented as a NOT gate, an AND gate, an OR gate, and a XOR gate. The following tables, which are called *truth tables*, show what value these logical operators yield for the various combinations of input values:

$$
\begin{array}{cccc}
 & 0 \wedge 0 = 0 & 0 \vee 0 = 0 & 0 \underline{\vee} 0 = 0 \\
\neg 1 = 0 & 0 \wedge 1 = 0 & 0 \vee 1 = 1 & 0 \underline{\vee} 1 = 1 \\
\neg 0 = 1 & 1 \wedge 0 = 0 & 1 \vee 0 = 1 & 1 \underline{\vee} 0 = 1 \\
 & 1 \wedge 1 = 1 & 1 \vee 1 = 1 & 1 \underline{\vee} 1 = 0
\end{array}
\tag{1.1}
$$

Thus, a logic gate for any of the three basic operations should implement the corresponding truth table. It is possible to have more complex operations such as the NAND operation:

$$\neg(a \wedge b) = (\neg a) \vee (\neg b)$$

It has been proved that one needs only NAND logical gates in order to perform any kind of operation, including arithmetic. In different words, the NAND gate is a *universal* gate. So it should not surprise us the fact that modern computers are built using only NAND logical gates. Thus, in a sense, the history of electronic computers is an account of progress in the technology that accelerated the encoding of binary digits and the operations between sequences of binary digits.

First, it is crucial to say that truth values are realized as electromagnetic signals. Thus, any NAND logical gate inputs two such signals and outputs only one. Clearly, both input signals are carrying some *energy*[4] while only one signal comes out, so the problem is what happened to the energy corresponding to the lost signal? Landauer's principle, which has proposed by Rolf William Landauer, explains that this energy is dissipated. The erasure of a single bit generates heat of $k_B T \ln 2$, where k_B is the Boltzmann constant (approximately 1.380650×10^{-23} Joule per Kelvin), T is the temperature of the circuit in Kelvin degrees, and $\ln 2$ is approximately 0.69315. This simply means that even if one could manage to eliminate all energy losses, still the gate would dissipate energy at every operation. Furthermore, this implies that any further improvements to computer technology cannot be implemented unless this problem is addressed. In the 1970s, Charles Henry Bennett argued that if computation could be *reversible*, the heat dissipation could be limited to the effects of erasure only. This idea can be realized by gates that associate a unique input with a unique output and vice versa. A trivial example of a reversible logic gate is the NOT gate, which, unfortunately,

---

[4]Simply put, energy is the capacity of a physical body or a physical system to perform work. There are several forms of energy. For example, heat (thermal energy) is energy produced from the movement of atoms or molecules. Kinetic energy is energy of motion and potential energy is the energy due to a body's position (on a table or on a mountain).

is not a universal gate. Another example of a reversible logic gate is the TOFFOLI gate, which had been invented by Tommaso Toffoli. The TOFFOLI gate is a universal one. Physical models of reversible gates show high sensitivity to errors and this is the reason they are not widely used. On the other hand, "just replacing" one kind of gate with another is not that simple but the general idea is that this is feasible and therefore it should be tried. The TOFFOLI gate receives three signals corresponding to binary digits and yields three signals. If the first two input digits are 1s, it yields them and the negation of the third digit. In all other cases, it yields its input intact. Mathematically, this can be expressed by $(a, b, c) \rightarrow \left(a, b, c \veebar (a \wedge b)\right)$.

Although most people think that the *Electronic Numerical Integrator And Computer*, or just ENIAC (see Figure 1.6), is the first digital computer and, therefore, its designers are the inventors of the electronic computer, still there is substantial dispute as to who was the first true inventor of the electronic computer. In 1943, John Vincent Atanasoff with the help of his graduate student Clifford Berry completed the Atanasoff-Berry Computer (ABC). This machine was designed to solve systems of linear algebraic equations and it was the first machine to use vacuum tubes. The ABC was not a *programmable* computer (i.e., one could not "feed" it with a plan specifying all the actions it should perform), so it cannot be classified as the first general purpose electronic computer.

Figure 1.6: The ENIAC.

ENIAC was developed by the Ballistics Research Laboratory in Maryland to assist in the preparation of artillery firing tables. It was completed at the University of Pennsylvania in November 1945. And it was conceived and designed by John Mauchly and John Adam Presper Eckert, Jr. ENIAC was a programmable computer. Nevertheless, Alice Rowe Burks and Arthur Walter Burks argued in a book they coauthored that ENIAC had used technology that was invented by Atanasoff. Thus, according to the Burks, the ABC was the first electronic computer. Regardless of what engineers and scholars think, on October 19, 1973 the U.S. District Judge Earl R. Larson ruled out that the ENIAC derived many basic ideas from the Atanasoff–Berry Computer. Nevertheless, this did not solve the problem!

Konrad Zuse was a German civil engineer who built the first programmable electric, but not electronic, computer in 1941. Zuse's Z3 used internally the binary number system. Zuse used electromechanical relays for the construction of his computer because it was difficult to find vacuum tubes in wartime Germany. Note that it was shown that Z3 was a universal machine. Zuse developed the world's first real computer programming language, that is, a sort of artificial language by whose help one can create a program, specifying the actions the computer should perform. Zuse's programming language was called *Plankalkül* (plan calculus). Later on, he worked on the Z4 computer. This machine was completed at the Federal Technical Institute (ETH) in Zürich, Switcherland, in 1950. Many people assume that the Z3 is the world first *digital* computer. Technically, this is true, however, it is not known if Zuse's work had affected in any way the development of modern computers. So, the jury is still out on this matter. Regardless of the final verdict, all these people have shaped the field of computing in one way or another.

Computer technology has evolved much since the 1950s and the 1960s and today we are using machines that are extremely fast when compared to these "ancient" machines. Despite this speed up, all these machines function in a way that is fundamentally similar to the way the early machines operated. What has changed is the building blocks we are using today to build computers. In different words, today we are using far more advanced electronic circuits compared to those that were in use in the 1950s. More specifically, the first generation of computers used vacuum tubes to control the "flow" of electric current through the computer's circuits. Computers of this first generation were typically controlled by plug board wiring or by a series of directions encoded on a paper tape. Transistors, which are semi-conductor devices and have roughly the same functionality as vacuum tubes, were used in the construction of computers that belong to the second generation computer. Since transistors are much smaller than vacuum tubes, computers of this generation were much smaller than their first generation counterparts. These computers used magnetic disks and tapes for data storage. The ATLAS computer is a typical example of a second generation computer. In the third computer generation, the transistors became part of an integrated circuit, which is a set of electronic circuits on one small plate ("chip") of semi-conductor

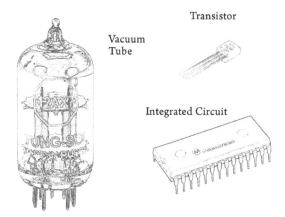

Figure 1.7: Building blocks used in the circuitry of the first three computers generations.

material. Typically, thousands of transistors and other components (e.g., resistors and capacitors) are packed inside integrated circuits. Figure 1.7 shows the size difference between the building blocks used in the circuitry of the first three computer generations. The IBM System/360 is probably the best known third generation computer system. The fourth and current computer generation uses Very-Large-Scale Integration (VLSI). Thus, it is now possible to pack large numbers of integrated circuits into a single chip. The fourth generation of computers started roughly when the first microprocessors appeared, that is, sometime in the 1970s. In fact, the hearts residing inside modern commodity computers are VLSI chips.

In October 1981, Japan announced its plans to develop highly innovative computers. The computers were supposed to be the first models of the fifth generation of computers. These computers should be able to process non-numeric data at very high speeds. More specifically, these machines were supposed to combine knowledge information processing (to introduce some sort of intelligence in computers) and large-scale parallel processing. In general, this means that these machines should be able to perform many tasks simultaneously. Most people would agree that modern computers actually do perform many tasks at the same time. However, the truth is that even today some computers are not able to perform even two tasks at the same time. Instead, they "serve" each task for a very small amount of time and this cycle repeats very fast so that the user gets the impression that tasks are performed simultaneously. In 1981, this method of operation was the norm and not the exception for most computational systems. In order to achieve the first task, it was thought that computers should be programmable in *logic programming* languages. As there are different groups of spoken languages that have some characteristics in common (e.g., think of the Germanic and the Romance languages), there are computer programming languages that have common origins and characteristics. In particular, logic programming languages are systems where users specify facts and general relationships between them and "ask" the system specific questions that can be deduced from the facts and their relationships. For example, here is how one could specify the computation of the sum of the integers between 0 and some number n. There is only one fact: the sum of the numbers between 0 and 0 is 0. And there is only one relationship: the sum of the numbers between 0 and n is equal to n plus the sum of the numbers between 0 and $n - 1$. Thus, the sum of the numbers 0, 1, 2, 3, and 4 is equal to 4 plus the sum of the numbers 0, 1, 2, and 3. This, in turn, is equal to 3 plus the sum of the numbers 0, 1, and 2, etc. Surprisingly, this method of computing can be used to compute many different things. In fact, this is the definition of a *recursive* function and I will say more about this in Section 2.2.

It is a fact that the project for the creation of a fifth generation computer failed. One of the reasons the project failed was the choice of the programming language. From the very beginning, the project used the *Prolog* programming language. However, this language did not provide facilities for the expression of non-sequential computation. In different words, the language allowed users to express sequences of computational tasks that should be performed in this particular order. When this became clear, project members tried to design new logic programming languages that would allow users to express non-sequential computation with them; nevertheless, they never managed to succeed in designing the project language. Another problem with this project was that soon computers became very powerful and the computational speed up promised by the project had been reached by conventional hardware. In essence, this meant that there was no future for the project. More about this project and its failure can be found in the literature (see the annotated bibliography at the end of this chapter).

1.4   The Future of Computing

Sunday, April 19, 2015 marked the 50th anniversary of Moore's Law, a law that has transformed industry and society in unexpected ways.[5] On that date, Gordon Earle Moore, initially an employee of Fairchild Semi-conductor and later Intel's cofounder, published an article in *Electronics* magazine[6] that predicted that the number of transistors per square inch (1 inch is about 2.54 cm) on integrated circuits would double every 18 months. In 1975, he updated his prediction to once every two years. This prediction is commonly known as Moore's law.

This law is so significant because progress in micro-chip technology has led to personal computers, smartphones, and many other electronic products. One should

---

[5]It is of course a coincidence, but this section was written on April 19, 2015.
[6]Gordon E. Moore, *Cramming more components onto integrated circuits*. Electronics, 38(8), pp. 114–117, 1965.

also not forget the many companies that provide products and services that make sense just because of this progress. However, this progress will come to an end sooner or later, even if we forget Landauer's principle whose consequence would be the generation of heat that would possibly melt parts of a computer. Some predict that by 2020 Moore's Law will collapse. Unfortunately, one cannot go against the laws of nature and this poses the important question: When computer technology will reach this limit, will it stop evolving? The answer is that probably the technology we use today will stop evolving but computer technology will not stop evolving. Naturally, one may wonder how computer technology could evolve when its core elements cannot be improved. If one uses new and different core elements or uses these core elements in a radically different way, then it is possible to improve computer technology. For example, there is a whole field of research that seeks to find unconventional computational methods that include quantum computing [i.e., use of the quantum properties of matter to compute (see Chapter 5)], membrane computing [i.e., a model of computation that is based on the functionality of cells (see Section 4.2.1)], DNA computing [i.e., DNA strands are used to encode and solve problems (see Section 4.1)], vague computing [i.e., computation is not strict but rather vague (see Chapter 6)], and chaos computing [i.e., the idea of using chaotic systems for computation (see Section 4.5)]. It is not enough to formulate a theory for a new model of computation: one needs to build at least a prototype to show that the ideas do work and that they can produce some of the expected results. Fortunately, there are many prototypes and in some cases even commercial products. For example, D-Wave Systems, Inc., is a Canadian computer company that currently sells quantum computers. On the other hand, there are laboratory prototypes of chemical reaction–diffusion processors, extended analogue computers, microfluidic circuits, gas-discharge systems, chemo-tactic droplets, enzyme-based logical circuits, crystallization computers, geometrically constrained chemical computers, and molecular logical gates and circuits. However, all these prototypes cannot be mass produced at this moment.

When computers with different core elements will be widely available, probably not as consumer goods, how can we be sure that these alternative computers will be able to solve more problems? Will we see one day truly intelligent machines? The established view is that there are limits to what can be achieved with computers; nevertheless, there is no universal agreement on where this limits lies. As for truly intelligent machines, humans and animals are such machines! But, of course, we are interested in the creation of artificial intelligent machines. Since there are intelligent machines created by natural selection, one can expect to see artificial intelligent machines sooner or later. And this means that we need to understand the real "computational" power of the human mind, in particular, and how animal brains function, in general. However, before doing so, we need to understand what computation is. Certainly, most people think they know the answer to this question, but reality shows otherwise.

Annotated Bibliography

- William Aspray, editor. *Computing Before Computers*. Iowa State University Press, Ames, Iowa, 1990.

This book provides a wealth of information about calculating devices. The discussion of most pre-computer machines that are described in Section 1.2 is based on the corresponding presentations of this book. I have noticed that the book includes a discussion about a device that the authors call *Schott's device*, which is supposed to be the invention of Gaspar Schott. However, most sources agree that Schott did only describe in his writings the Organum Mathematicum and nothing more.

- Alice Rowe Burks and Arthur Walter Burks. *The First Electronic Computer: The Atanasoff Story*. The University of Michigan Press, Ann Arbor, MI, 1989.

This is the book where the Burks put forth their arguments in favor of the ABC as the first electronic computer. I think this is an interesting book that presents a "heretic" view of things.

- John H. Conway and Richard K. Guy. *The Book of Numbers*. Springer, New York, 1996.

This book discusses the various elementary forms of numbers (e.g., integers, reals, etc.) as well as other forms of numbers (e.g., surreal numbers, infinitesimal numbers, etc.). I think it is a very interesting book.

- Georges Ifrah. *The Universal History of Numbers*. John Wiley & Sons, New York, 1998. Translated by David Seltos, E. F. Harding, Sophie Wood, and Ian Monk.

An excellent account of all kinds of numbering systems and numerals that had been used in various parts of the planet. The book includes also a detailed explanation of the possible origin of the sexagesimal numbering system.

- Donald E. Knuth. *An imaginary number system*. Communications of the ACM, 3(4), pp. 245–247, 1960.

The computer science legend Donald E. Knuth described in this paper a number system whose basis is the number $2i$. This system is called "quater-imaginary" and every complex number can be represented with the digits 0, 1, 2, and 3 without a sign. A *complex number* is one that is a real and an imaginary part. Thus $3 + 4i$, $2 - 2i$ are complex numbers and the real part of $3 + 4i$ is 3 and its imaginary part is $4i$. The magnitude of a complex number $z = x + yi$ is $|z| = \sqrt{x^2 + y^2}$. Given a complex number $z = x + yi$, its conjugate is the complex number $z^* = x - yi$.

- Andrew Pollack. *'Fifth Generation' Became Japan's Lost Generation*. New York Times, pp. D1–D3, June 5, 1992.

The author of this article describes why the fifth generation computer project failed. This newspaper article is written for people without any background in science and technology.

- Cesare Rossi, Flavio Russo, and Ferruccio Russo. *Ancient Engineers' Inventions*, volume 8 of *History of Mechanism and Machine Science*. Springer, Heidelberg, 2009.

This book describes a number of ancient machines and devices and, to the best of my knowledge, it is the only one that contains a detailed description of the Mesolabio.

- Arnold Thackray, David Brock, and Rachel Jones. *Moore's Law: The Life of Gordon Moore, Silicon Valley's Quiet Revolutionary*. Basic Books, New York, 2015.

This book tells Moore's story as well the story of his law. In fact, it tells the story of the Moore family from the time they settled to California and goes on to describe the life of Gordon Moore until today.

Chapter 2

From Hilbert to Gödel to Turing

The word *computation* derives from the Latin word *computo* and means "to settle things together". From the etymology of the word, it is clear that its meaning is not precise. Although even today there is no universally accepted definition of computation, still it is widely accepted that a computational process is an *effective* process. In the 1930s, three seemingly different mathematical models of computation were put forth as an attempt to solve this problem. How and why these models emerged as well as their impact on the development of the theory of computation is discussed in this chapter.

2.1 Hilbert's Dream

David Hilbert

All the machines and devices presented in the previous chapter have the ability to produce a numerical result. Furthermore, all these machines can add up the same numbers and produce the same result, although the methods employed to produce the result are not the same. Surprisingly, the notion of a method or *algorithm*[1] by which one carries out a computation is vague and not precisely defined. In the 1930s, logicians (i.e., specialists in mathematical logic) tried to give precise meaning to the word computation by introducing *conceptual* computing devices (i.e., devices that "live" in our minds but do not "violate" any physical law) and special mathematical systems capable of presenting the steps required to perform a

---

[1]The term algorithm derives from a mangled transliteration of Arabic Al-Khwarizmi, "native of Khwarazm", surname of the Persian mathematician Muhammad ibn Musa al-Khwarizmi whose works introduced sophisticated mathematics to the West.

computation. In fact, these logicians devised these conceptual computing devices and mathematical systems while trying to give answers to specific problems. In turn, these problems were posed by the famous German mathematician David Hilbert in the beginning of the 20th century. Hilbert's problems were about the very nature or the *foundations* of mathematics.

Most people know Hilbert for his many contributions to mathematics [e.g., Hilbert spaces (see Section 5.3)], but his work on the philosophy and the foundations of mathematics is equally important. The research project known as *Hilbert's program* has its roots in Hilbert's work on plane geometry. In 1903, Hilbert published a book titled *Grundlagen der Geometrie* (*The Foundations of Geometry*), which was based on a course on Euclidean geometry that he gave at the University of Göttingen during the winter semester of 1898–1899. In this work, Hilbert tried to remedy some problems that were evident in Euclid's (Εὐκλείδης) Στοιχεῖα (*Elements*). This is a collection of 13 books in which the ancient Greek mathematician Euclid presented a number of *axioms* (i.e., self-evident truths) and using them and the proof techniques he was aware of, he showed the validity of other statements about plane geometry. Unfortunately, Euclid's proofs contained some gaps and appeals to intuition. Thus, Hilbert rewrote the axioms and reworked Euclid's proofs using these new axioms. Euclid's work is fascinating because he managed to show many things about plane geometry by starting from a few simple principles. Interestingly, the Dutch philosopher Baruch Spinoza wrote his *Ethics* by applying Euclid's presentation in the Elements. The success of Hilbert's project made him ponder whether it would be possible to use the same principles to develop any scientific subject.

Without taking the following definition too literally, one might say that intuition is the ability to know something without deduction or reasoning. Although intuition plays an important role in the scientific method, Hilbert believed that the scientific method should not rely on it. Instead, he proposed that a theory should be developed by using the *axiomatic* method, that is, the method where one lays down a set of axioms and some *derivation rules* and uses the axioms and the rules to derive any truth in a particular discipline. Hilbert went a step further and proposed that the axioms should be represented by sequences of symbols (i.e., strings in modern parlance) and a proof would be identified with a string transformation process. However, he did not insist on the form of the strings. Instead, he thought that any collection of symbols can be used to create these strings. Thus, Hilbert considered that the strings were meaningless. The collection of all strings produced by a specific set of axioms using specific transformation rules makes up a *formal language*. For instance, the collection of all binary numerals make up a trivial formal language. Previously, we talked about "mathematical systems" but in mathematics they are called *calculi* or *formal systems*. Such a system is a collection of axioms expressed as string transformation rules (or *rewriting rules*, as they are also known) that can be used to derive strings from the axioms.

Typically, string transformation rules look like the following rules that describe binary numerals:

$$\text{BinaryNumeral} \longrightarrow \text{BinaryNumeral Digit}$$
$$\text{BinaryNumeral} \longrightarrow \text{Digit}$$
$$\text{Digit} \longrightarrow \text{"0" | "1"}$$

The first rule specifies that a binary numeral is another binary numeral that is followed by a digit while the second rule specifies that a binary numeral is just a digit. And, of course, digit is either the digit zero or the digit one. We could say that for this simple system "Digit" is an axiom and "BinaryNumeral" the derivation rule. Of course, Hilbert was not interested in binary numerals but on how to express theorems (i.e., mathematical statements) and their proofs. For example, Hilbert might be interested in expressing in symbolic form the following theorem:

Theorem. *There are two irrational numbers, q and r, such that q^r is rational.*

This theorem can be proved by considering the number $\sqrt{2}^{\sqrt{2}}$. Obviously, this number is either rational or irrational. If it is rational, then $q = \sqrt{2}$ and $r = \sqrt{2}$ and so the theorem has been proved. However, if this number is irrational, then by setting $q = \sqrt{2}^{\sqrt{2}}$ and $r = \sqrt{2}$ one gets

$$q^r = \left(\sqrt{2}^{\sqrt{2}}\right)^{\sqrt{2}} = \sqrt{2}^{\sqrt{2}\cdot\sqrt{2}} = \left(\sqrt{2}\right)^2 = 2,$$

which means that we have found the two irrational numbers we were looking for. In order to express this theorem in symbolic form, one should realize that it asserts that two numbers are *not rational* while the first raised to the power of the second is a *rational* number. So, let the expression $R(n)$ mean that n is a rational number. Also, suppose that the symbol $\neg$ means "not". Thus the expression $\neg R(n)$ should be pronounced as *n is not a rational number*. Also, let $\exp(x, y)$ pronounced as *x is raised to power of y*. In addition, let the symbols $\wedge$ and $\exists$ be pronounced as "and" and "exists", respectively. Then, one can express the theorem above in symbolic form as follows:

$$\exists x \exists y \Big(\neg R(x) \wedge \neg R(y) \wedge R\big(\exp(x, y)\big)\Big)$$

Someone who does not know this theorem and who is provided with the information above should read this formula as follows:

> *There exists an x, there exists a y such that not rational x and not rational y and rational x raised to power of y.*

Of course, this is wrong English but it is a sort of "mechanical" translation of the mathematical formula.

In order to prove this theorem using the axiomatic method, one needs to set up a formal system. Then, starting from the axioms, one should mechanically follow the various derivation rules in order to come up with a string that proves the theorem. Typically, one goes backwards by trying to identify the axioms that may lead to the theorem. The word *mechanically* means that one should follow the rules without thought and volition. When a particular *path* does not lead to the desired result, then one can *backtrack* and follow a different one. If no path leads to the desired string, there is no proof of the theorem.

Previously, I stated that the symbols of a formal system are meaningless. This simply implies that one can assign any meaning they want to any symbol. For example, if the intended meaning of R is "prime number" (i.e., a number that can be divided by one and itself only) and exp denotes the multiplication function, then the theorem above could be interpreted as "the product of two prime numbers is also a prime number". This statement is obviously false, since the product of two primes is obviously divisible by the two primes. Thus, one needs to impose certain restrictions on a formal system just to avoid the embarrassing situation where one proves something that obviously does not hold. A possible way to prevent this from happening would be the introduction of additional axioms that would express the required properties of a specific theorem. On the other hand, there is nothing special about the symbols $\exists$, $\neg$, and $\wedge$ and so one could rewrite the theorem using Cherokee letters as follows:

$$\text{h} \, x \text{h} \, y \Big(\omega R(x) \, \mho \, \omega R(y) \, \mho \, R \big(\exp(x, y) \big) \Big)$$

And this is the reason why replacing $\neg$ with ω, $\exists$ with h, and $\wedge$ with $\mho$ will have no effect on a formal proof, provided, of course the change is also done to the formal system.

Although it is not a trivial task to set up a formal system that would prove the theorem above, nevertheless, one can try to discuss what might be needed in order to achieve this particular goal. First, one should not forget that the rules of a formal system transform one or more strings (called premises) to another string (called conclusion). For example, consider the following rule:

$$a(t) \longrightarrow \exists x a(x)$$

Here the string $a(t)$ is transformed to the string $\exists x a(x)$. A typical use of such a rule would be to transform premises of the form "John is tall" or "Mary is smart" to conclusions of the form "there is someone who is tall" and "there is someone who is smart". Obviously, there are more complex transformation rules. A very simple example of such a complex rule is the following one:

$$\alpha, \beta \longrightarrow \alpha \wedge \beta$$

This rule assumes that both α and β are true and "concludes" that $\alpha \wedge \beta$ is also true. For example, if α stands for "John left" and β for "Carol arrived", then $\alpha \wedge \beta$ is the conclusion that "John left and Carol arrived". It would be possible to show the validity of the theorem above by using at least these transformation rules and these two axioms: $\neg R(a)$ and $R(\exp(\exp(a, a), a)$. In fact, there is a modern branch of computer science called *automated theorem*, proving that is about the development of computer programs that are able to show that some statement is true using axioms and transformation rules, which are called *inference* rules. This, in turn, uses ideas and results from *proof theory*, that is, the area of mathematics which studies the concepts of mathematical proof and mathematical provability. In a sense, proof theory is a descendant of Hilbert's program! So far we have seen what is the essence of Hilbert's program, however, nothing has been said about the formalization of his program.

During the *Second International Congress of Mathematicians*, which was held in Paris in 1900, Hilbert was invited to deliver one of the main lectures. In fact, Hilbert presented 10 problems to his audience and later in the printed form of his lecture he added 13 more. These problems were designed to serve as examples for the kind of problems whose solutions would lead to furthering of disciplines in mathematics. From this collection of problems, Hilbert's second problem is about the *consistency* of the axioms of a simple system that was devised to reason about positive integers and their properties. In particular, with this problem, Hilbert asked if the axioms of the system are independent and, more importantly, not contradictory. In his own (translated) words:

> Upon closer consideration the question arises: Whether, in any way, certain statements of single axioms depend upon one another, and whether the axioms may not therefore contain certain parts in common, which must be isolated if one wishes to arrive at a system of axioms that shall be altogether independent of one another.
>
> But above all I wish to designate the following as the most important among the numerous questions which can be asked with regard to the axioms: To prove that they are not contradictory, that is, that a finite number of logical steps based upon them can never lead to contradictory results.

In different words, Hilbert insisted that the axioms should not be contradictory to one another. This simply means that it should not be possible to deduce a "truth" that invalidates any other proved "truth". For example, it should not be possible to derive from the axioms of a system two formulas such as $3 < 2$ and $3 > 2$. This is the consistency requirement and it is not the only requirement as will be revealed below. Hilbert used the term *calculus* to refer to what we have called the formal system. Although the axiomatic method is about the transformation of a discipline into a collection of strings representing its axioms and a collection of transformation rules, it is quite possible to go the opposite way. That is, it is possible to construct a formal system and then to (try to) find an interpretation of it. This way one arrives at the idea behind Hilbert's *meta-mathematics*. So, if it is possible to use arbitrary formal systems to solve mathematical problems, we have at our disposal a method by means of which we could solve all mathematical problems!

At the 1928 International Congress of Mathematicians in Bologna, Italy, Hilbert introduced a new problem that is known as the 10th problem that asked for the following:

> **Determination of the solvability of a Diophantine equation.** Given a Diophantine equation with any number of unknown quantities and with integral numerical coefficients: To devise a process according to which it can be determined by a finite number of operations whether the equation is solvable in integers.

A Diophantine equation is any equation in unknown $x, y, \ldots$ that can be raised to integer powers and have integer coefficients. For instance, the equations $4x + 5y + 5z - 9 = 0$ and $x^3 + y^3 - z^3 = 0$ are Diophantine equations while $\frac{1}{3}\sqrt[3]{x} + 8 = 0$ is not. Diophantine equations have to be solved over the integers. For example, the equation $x^3 + y^3 - z^3 = 0$ has many real solutions (e.g., $x = 1$, $y = 1$, and $z = \sqrt[3]{2}$) but no non-zero integer solution. On the other hand, the equation $-3x + 4y - 4 = 0$ has one integer solution, that is, $x = 0$ and $y = 1$. Diophantine equations were named after the Greek mathematician Diophantus of Alexandria (Διόφαντος ὁ Ἀλεξανδρεύς), who is often called the "father of algebra".

There are many and different methods to solve Diophantine equations, but there is no single method to solve all these equations. Also, although it is possible to solve some Diophantine equations, most of them cannot be solved by any means. What Hilbert actually asked for was a *universal* and rigorous method (i.e., an algorithm) for recognizing the solvability of Diophantine equations. In different words, Hilbert asked for a general solution to a *decision problem* or *Entscheidungsproblem* in German, which is a finite-length question that can be answered with *yes* or *no*. In addition, Hilbert asked whether formal systems are *finitely describable* (i.e., whether the axioms and inference rules are constructible in a finite number of steps, while, also, theorems should be derivable in a finite number of steps), *complete* (i.e., whether every true statement that can be expressed in a given calculus can be derived from the axioms of the system), and consistent. In order to better understand the last three requirements, let us examine closely the "formal system" of binary numerals. Obviously, the system is finitely describable since one needs less than one hundred symbols to describe them. The system is complete since all binary numerals can be derived from the transformation rules. The system is also consistent because each binary numeral is derived by a specific sequence of transformations and these cannot yield another binary numeral. Nevertheless, let me say that binary numerals is an almost useless "formal system" and not the kind of system that one could use to check the validity of Hilbert's ideas.

2.2   Hilbert's Nightmare

One could say that logic is the study of correct reasoning and formal logic is the abstract study of statements and rules for making deductions. Aristotle (Ἀριστοτέλης) was the first thinker who made a systematic study of logic in his *Organon* ("Οργανον), a collection of six works on logic. The Organon, Friedrich Ludwig Gottlob Frege's *Grundgesetze der Arithmetik* (*Basic Laws of Arithmetic*), and Alfred North Whitehead and Bertrand Russell's *Principia Mathematica* are the most influential books on logic ever written, according to Andrew David Irvine's article in *Principia Mathematica* in the Stanford Encyclopedia of Philosophy. *Principia Mathematica* is a three-volume work that was first published in 1910, 1912, and 1913. Frege, Whitehead, and Russell were proponents of *logicism*, that is, the idea that all of mathematics can be reduced to logic. Notice that the theorem presented in the previous section is proved in a system where one starts from the axioms and using the transformation rules finds the proof. In particular, one rearranges, inserts, and/or deletes symbols using the transformation rules whereas in logic one assumes the truth of axioms and using inference rules tries to find the proof. The differences between the two approaches are subtle, nevertheless, it is not my intention to present these differences. Instead, I want to make clear why using the system presented in *Principia Mathematica* as a formal system makes perfect sense. Indeed, the Austrian Kurt Friedrich Gödel, the foremost mathematical logician of the 20th century, used a formal system that is based on the logical system from *Principia Mathematica* to describe a very important discovery that invalidated Hilbert's program.

Kurt Friedrich Gödel

In 1931, Gödel published a paper where he described his discovery. This paper is entitled *Über formal unentscheidbare Sätze der Principia Mathematica und verwandter Systeme I* (*On formally undecidable propositions of Principia Mathematica and related systems I*).[2] Gödel's work is important mainly for two reasons. First, he showed that given some formal system, it contains theorems that cannot be proved or disproved within the system. And second, in order to arrive to this result, he defined an *arithmetization* of a formal system, that is, he found a method by which each expression in a formal system can be represented by a unique natural number.

---

[2] The paper was published in *Monatshefte für Mathematik und Physik*, 38(1), pp. 173–198, 1931. The original paper is available in the SpringerLink web site. The paper's title gives the impression that a second part had been published, nevertheless, a second part was never published.

Therefore, statements about strings can be expressed as numbers. Thus Gödel assigned numbers to constant symbols as follows:

1	3	5	7	9	11	13	17	19	23	...
↑	↑	↑	↑	↑	↑	↑	↑	↑	↑	
0	s	¬	∨	∀	(	)	a	b	c	...

The symbol ∀ is "pronounced" *for all*. In addition, *variables* (i.e., usually letters that stand for some value) are associated with a number of the form p^n, where p is a prime number and n depends on what the variable stands for. In particular, when a variable stands for a number, it is a variable of type one and then $n = 1$. Variables of type two refer to collections of numbers (i.e., expressions like *Prime, Odd*, etc.) and then $n = 2$. Type three variables refer to collections of numbers and then $n = 3$, and so on. Variables of type one are written as $a_1, b_1, \ldots$; variables of type two are written as $a_2, b_2, \ldots$, and so on. [On page 74 of *Gödel's Proof*, the authors identify type two variables with *sentential* variables and type three variables with *predicate* variables. A sentential variable stands for an expression that contains constant symbols and variables (e.g., $p \vee q$) and a predicate variable stands for an expression that contains constants and non-constant symbols and variables (e.g., $x = sy + z$).] A sequence of symbols is associated with a sequence of numbers and this sequence is associated with a unique number. In particular, a sequence of numbers $n_1, n_2, \ldots, n_k$ is associated with the number $2^{n_1} \times 3^{n_2} \times \cdots \times p_k^{n_k}$, where p_k is the kth prime number. As an example, consider the sequence $\neg b_2 \vee c_2$. The symbols of the sequence are associated with the number 5, 17^2, 7, and 23^2. Thus the string $\neg b_2 \vee c_2$ is associated with the number

$$2^5 \times 3^{289} \times 5^7 \times 7^{529} = 2202144384151235831866638834965809178071132 0298$$

2391662504186001011040330751237896390039088 0825

2566777623783560951675651524487082515767836 7756

1479334931232555175370031274576987912282130 0574

5696807694151192853645055372091011514531590 2084

9469755346443156523990027332078739750234977 2807

1724717349495680042994845588418167480666602 9817

2065596815918566859943135568262412280141016 1290

3845056199632243863132364279652041327397907 3094

7680139172347115815067959708308378801841006 5809

7656447408355551699613618488569453872232788 3135

6390151448500840616648771506768947231935658 3216

4966005903238586470452500000

This number is the Gödel number of the expression. Internally, modern computers employ also an arithmetization. Each symbol (or character in computer science parlance) is assigned a number and each string is viewed as a sequence of numbers but the similarity stops here. Another difference between the two arithmetizations is that Gödel used decimal numbers while characters are mapped to binary numerals.

A paradox is a logical conundrum that contradicts itself in a confusing way. For example, Russell's paradox, which was discovered by Russell, is about some weird *set*. Roughly, a set is any collection, group, or conglomerate of things of any kind that are called *elements*. Clearly, a set can have as elements other sets. Here are some examples of sets:

— the set of all students in the class;
— the set of all odd numbers;
— the set of all letters of the English alphabet.

Russell's paradox is about the set of all sets that are not elements of themselves. In different words, it is about the existence of the following set:

$$R = \{x \mid x \notin x\}$$

Note that what appears on the right of the symbol | is the property that the each element of the set (i.e., what appears on the left of the | symbol) must satisfy. The expression $x \in Y$ means that x belongs to set Y. The expression $x \notin Y$ means that x does not belong to set Y. The symbol $\in$ was introduced by Giuseppe Peano and is a stylized lowercase Greek letter epsilon ("ε"), the first letter of the word ἐστί, which means "is". Now, the question is if R is a member of itself? Suppose that $R \in R$. Then, it must satisfy the condition of not being a member of itself, which means that $R \notin R$. Conversely, if $R \notin R$, then it satisfies the condition of not being a member of itself and so $R \in R$! Since these arguments lead to contradictions, it means that there is no such set. The paradox exists mainly because set theory was naïvely formulated. Eubulides of Miletus (Εὐβουλίδης ὁ Μιλήσιος) is known for a number of paradoxes he proposed. For example, the liar paradox is about the truth of the statement "This statement is false". This sentence cannot be true because if it is true, it has to be *false*, which is a contradiction. By a similar argument, one can show that this sentence cannot be false. So this statement is neither true nor false. Note that paraconsistent logics allow statements that are both true and false, nevertheless, we are using classical logic here. Gödel showed that there is a flaw in Hilbert's program by showing the existence of a paradoxical statement, similar to the liar paradox, in a specific formal system. In particular, Gödel first constructed the formal system P. As was noted above, this system is basically the formal system of *Principia Mathematica* augmented with axioms and inference rules borrowed from Peano arithmetic (i.e., a formal system that can be used to reason about natural numbers and their properties). Then, he showed that the statement "This sentence is unprovable" is expressible in system P but it is neither provable nor refutable in it. A "sketch" of Gödel's proof is based on the fact that there are statements that are false but cannot be proved in the system. For example, such a statement is "False statements are unprovable". The statement "This sentence is unprovable" cannot be false because that would mean that it is not unprovable (i.e., it is provable), thus it would contradict the statement "False statements are unprovable". But the statement "This sentence is unprovable" can be true, provided it is unprovable. If we assume that this statement is provable, then the statement is false and therefore is unprovable. By a not so mathematically rigorous *reductio ad absurdum*,[3] one concludes that the statement is indeed unprovable and true. So Gödel showed that the system P is not complete since there is no proof for every true statement. The negation of the statement "This sentence is unprovable" is also unprovable. Since the original statement is true, this statement is false and so it is unprovable because we assumed that "False statements are unprovable". Gödel went further and proved that all formal systems contain true statements that cannot be proved. Gödel's results are known in the literature as *incompleteness theorems*.

In a way, Gödel's result was a death blow to Hilbert's program. However, the so-called Gödel's second theorem was the last nail in the coffin of Hilbert's program. This theorem stated that one cannot prove the consistency of a formal system in the system itself. So when we have any formal system that is powerful enough to reason about natural numbers, then the system contains true yet unprovable statements and it is impossible to prove its consistency! Physical systems are also describable by formal systems as Newton Carneiro Affonso da Costa and Francisco Antônio Dória have shown.[4] Ideally, economic systems should be also describable by formal systems and obviously these system should be also incomplete. Intuitively, one could argue that this is (one of) the reason why when following a specific economic recipe, quite often the results are not the ones that one would expect. Of course, there are other reasons that affect the development of an economic system, but this book is not about economics. On the other hand, the fact that one cannot prove the consistency of a formal system in the system itself does not exclude the possibility to have another more powerful formal system where one can prove the consistency of the former formal system. Another important aspect of the first theorem is that it makes clear that belief is stronger than truth.

A *function* (or *mapping*) is a correspondence between two sets that associates with each element of the first set one and only one element of the second set. Usually, functions have names like f, g, h, etc. Typically, these correspondences are expressed by some rules. An example of one such rule would be: "add two and then square the

---

[3]A form of argument in which a statement is disproved by illustrating how it leads to an absurd consequence.
[4]Newton Carneiro Affonso da Costa and Francisco Antônio Dória. *Undecidability and incompleteness in classical mechanics*. International Journal of Theoretical Physics, 30(8), pp. 1041–1073, 1991.

result". Typically, a function having this rule would be written in mathematical notation as follows: $f(x) = (x + 2)^2$. Here the name of the function is f and x stands for the number (or value) that is mapped, while the expression on the right, when evaluated, is the number that x is mapped to. Thus, the number 3 is mapped to the number 25 and the expression $3 + 1$ is mapped to the number 36. When defining a function, it is quite possible to use another function. For example, consider the function $g(x) = 3x$, then the function $f(x) = g(x) + 45$ is defined in terms of function g. When a function is defined in terms of itself, it is called a *recursive* function. There is no question that a reader who knows nothing about recursive functions may think that it is almost impossible to have a function that is defined in terms of itself. Thus, it is necessary to give an example of a recursive function. Consider function $s(n)$ that maps n to the sum $0 + 1 + 2 + \cdots + n$. This function can be defined as follows:

$$s(0) = 0$$
$$s(1) = 0 + 1$$
$$s(2) = 0 + 1 + 2$$
$$s(3) = 0 + 1 + 2 + 3$$
$$s(4) = 0 + 1 + 2 + 3 + 4$$
$$s(5) = 0 + 1 + 2 + 3 + 4 + 5$$
etc.

After carefully inspecting these equations, one may note that $s(1) = s(0)+1$, since $s(0) = 0$ and $s(1) = 0 + 1$, $s(2) = s(1) + 2$, for similar reasons, etc. In summary,

$$s(0) = 0, \quad s(1) = s(0) + 1, \quad s(2) = s(1) + 2, \quad s(3) = s(2) + 3, \quad s(4) = s(3) + 4, \text{ etc.}$$

Thus, we observe that $s(n)$ is equal to $s(n - 1) + n$, when $n = 1, 2, 3, 4, 5$. Obviously, there is no reason to believe that this is not the general rule. So, we can safely conclude that the following equations can be used to compute the sum $0 + \cdots + n$ for any natural number n:

$$s(0) = 0$$
$$s(n) = s(n - 1) + n$$

Thus, we have *recursively* defined the function that computes the sum of all numbers up to a given number n. By following a very similar train of thought, one can easily define a recursive function that computes the product of the natural numbers up to a number n. Note that these functions *compute* numbers. Gödel used recursive functions in his proof, nevertheless, Stephen Cole Kleene[5] showed that recursive functions are actually

---

[5] Stephen Cole Kleene. *General recursive functions of natural numbers.* Mathematische Annalen, 112(1), pp. 727–742, 1936.

a mathematical model of computation equivalent to other models of computation that will be presented in this chapter. Kleene specified exactly how to define recursive functions using certain schemas and a few primitive functions.

2.3   The λ-calculus

It is a fact that Gödel's work paved a path that was followed by others who eventually shaped the field of computability theory. In particular, Alonzo Church and Alan Mathison Turing showed that certain decision problems are simply undecidable and they used these results to show that the Entscheidungsproblem is undecidable.

The λ-calculus is a formal system that was introduced in 1932–1933 by Church in the spirit of the axiomatic method. For this reason, the original system also had rules for logic. Thus Church devised the λ-calculus in the hope that all of mathematics could be derived from it. A few years later, Kleene and John Barkley Rosser showed that the original calculus was not consistent. This meant that the λ-calculus could not serve Church's initial purpose. However, the part of the calculus that dealt with functions was particularly interesting. Indeed, Church, while investigating the computational properties of this sub-calculus, managed to give an answer to the Entscheidungsproblem. In order to fully appreciate Church's results, it is necessary to have a very basic understanding of the λ-calculus and it properties.

The λ-calculus has a few basic symbols and an unlimited number of variables. The basic symbols are: "λ", ".", "(", and ")". The system is about λ-expressions and their *reduction*, that is, how one can transform an expression to a form that cannot be transformed any further. Any variable x forms the simplest λ-expression. If N and M are λ-expressions, so are $\lambda x.N$ and NM, where x stands for any possible variable. The expression $\lambda x.N$ is the way to defined (anonymous) functions (e.g., think of it as the equivalent of the definition $f(x) = N$ but without the "f" part...). In addition, the expression NM is the way to calculate a particular function value (e.g., think of it as the value $f(M)$, where $f(x) = N$) and it is called *application*. When N is an expression of the form $\lambda x.N'$, then the expression NM is transformed to the expression N'', which is obtained from N' by substituting each occurrence of x with M. For example, the expression $(\lambda x.ab(x))(cd)$ is reduced to the expression $ab(cd)$ by substituting each occurrence of x with cd. When we have expressions of the form $(\lambda x.\lambda y.xy)a$ one should try to "remove" the leftmost λ provided this is applicable. Otherwise, one should try to "remove" any other λ until it is not possible for any other reduction. There are cases where two or more expressions use the same variable name for different purposes. For example, consider the λ-expression $(\lambda b.b(a))(a)$. The reduction $a(a)$ is obviously wrong as the a in parentheses is not the same as the other one. A permissible way out is to replace all occurrences of a in $(\lambda b.b(a))$ with c or any other fresh variable name and only then to perform the reduction. Thus, the expression $(\lambda b.b(a))(a)$ will be reduced to $(\lambda b.b(c))(a)$, which will be reduced to

$a(c)$. In general, when working with the λ-calculus, one routinely uses this method to reduce expressions. Although there are many more details regarding transformations, still there is no need to delve into all details in order to understand Church's results.

In order to use the λ-calculus as a tool to perform calculations, one needs to be able to encode numbers and their operations as λ-expressions. Indeed, one can encode natural numbers and their operations while it is even possible to encode complex numbers. A possible encoding of whole numbers is the following one:

$$0 \rightarrow \lambda y.\lambda x.x$$
$$1 \rightarrow \lambda y.\lambda x.y(x)$$
$$2 \rightarrow \lambda y.\lambda x.y(y(x))$$
$$3 \rightarrow \lambda y.\lambda x.y(y(y(x)))$$
$$4 \rightarrow \lambda y.\lambda x.y(y(y(y(x))))$$
$$\text{etc.}$$

The symbol $\rightarrow$ is pronounced "is expressible as". The multiplication operator is encoded as the expression $\lambda a.\lambda b.\lambda c.a(bc)$. As an example, let us see how one can compute the product 2×2:

$$\times(2,2) \rightarrow \left(\lambda \underline{a}.\lambda \underline{b}.\lambda c.a(bc)\right)\left(\lambda y.\lambda x.y(y(x))\right)\left(\lambda z.\lambda w.z(z(w))\right)$$

$$\asymp \lambda c.\left(\lambda y.\lambda x.y(y(x))\right)\left(\left(\lambda \underline{z}.\lambda w.z(z(w))\right)c\right)$$

$$\asymp \lambda c.\left(\lambda y.\lambda x.y(y(x))\right)\left(\lambda w.c(c(w))\right)$$

$$\asymp \lambda c.\left(\lambda x.\left(\lambda w.c(c(w))\right)\left(\left(\lambda \underline{w}.c(c(w))\right)(x)\right)\right)$$

$$\asymp \lambda c.\left(\lambda x.\left(\lambda \underline{w}.c(c(w))\right)\left(c(c(x))\right)\right)$$

$$\asymp \lambda c.\left(\lambda x.c(c(c(c(x))))\right)$$

$$\asymp \lambda c.\lambda x.c(c(c(c(x))))$$

$$\rightarrow 4$$

Note that I have used the expression $\times(2,2)$ instead of 2×2 simply because here the operator is defined as a function. Also, the expression $a \asymp b$ means that a is equivalent to b. The underlined letters are those that are substituted in the expression. Of course, this example is included as a demonstration of the computation power of the λ-calculus and the reader should not pay much attention to the derivation details.

The operator for addition is encoded as the expression $\lambda w.\lambda x.\lambda y.\lambda z.wy(xyz)$ and there are encodings for the other common operators between natural numbers. Thus, one can encode any whole number in the λ-calculus and it is possible to perform ordinary arithmetical operations. In different words, the λ-calculus is yet another mathematical theory that makes precise the informal notion of computation. From the previous example, one can safely conclude that

$$(\lambda\underline{a}.\lambda\underline{b}.\lambda c.a(bc))\ (\lambda y.\lambda x.y(y(x)))\ (\lambda z.\lambda w.z(z(w)))\ \Rightarrow\ \lambda c.\lambda x.c(c(c(c(x))))$$

since there is a direct way to transform the expression on the left of the "$\Rightarrow$" symbol to the one on the right. Note that $A \Rightarrow B$ means that A can be transformed to B. An interesting question is this: Without applying any transformation, is there a way to tell whether the expression on the left stands for the expression on the right? More generally, given two arbitrary λ-expressions E_1 and E_2, is there an effective method to decide whether $E_1 \Rightarrow E_2$? The term "effective method" (or effectively calculable) is a synonym for *algorithm* and roughly means any clerical method which when applied to symbolic *input* would eventually yield some symbolic *output*. But I will say more on algorithms later in this chapter.

Church devised an arithmetization suitable for the λ-calculus and used a methodology that resembles closely Gödel's proof in order to prove his results. And this is the reason why Gödel's work is so important. The arithmetization used for the λ-calculus is described by the following table:

1	11	13	17	19	23	27	...
↑	↑	↑	↑	↑	↑	↑	
λ	(	)	a	b	c	d	...

Church managed to prove that there is no effective method capable of determining if $A \Rightarrow B$ for any two λ-expressions A and B. This discovery amounts to a negative answer to the Entscheidungsproblem for systems capable of expressing portions of arithmetic. In different words, Church showed that the Entscheidungsproblem is undecidable for systems like *Principia Mathematica*. Later on, Church showed that the Entscheidungsproblem is in *general* undecidable.

2.4   The Turing Machine

So far I have presented two mathematical models of computation: recursive functions and the λ-calculus. However, both these models are not some sort of machine that operates to compute a result. After all, computing devices are machines that perform calculations and deliver their results and not some weird mathematical formalism. In 1935, Alan Turing was attending lectures given by Maxwell Herman Alexander Newman. In the course of these lectures, Turing was introduced to the Entscheidungsproblem. He was immediately intrigued by this problem and decided to work on its solution. In 1936, Turing published a phenomenal paper titled "On computable numbers, with an application to the Entscheidungsproblem"[6] where he introduced a conceptual computing device, which now bears his name. Turing called these devices *automatic machines* or just *a-machines*. He used these machines to solve the Entscheidungsproblem. In fact, he showed that there is a problem that no Turing machine can solve it and, consequently, he used this result to show that the Entscheidungsproblem is undecidable, in general. But first let me explain what a Turing machine is and how it operates.

Alan Mathison Turing. Image courtesy of Sherborne School

A Turing machine consists of a *scanning head* and an infinite paper tape in both directions that is divided into printable cells. The machine is assumed to operate in *discrete time* (i.e., actions take place at each tick of the clock). The scanning head is able to read what is printed on cells and it can print a single symbol on a cell. How the scanning head reads and writes is not specified. Of course, one may assume that the scanning head performs some sort of optical character recognition in order to read a symbol while it is equipped with some special apparatus capable of erasing symbols from cells and/or printing symbols into them. Initially, the scanning head is placed atop the first cell that is non-blank. There is a special form of the Turing machine that is infinite in one direction. In this case, the scanning head is placed on the leftmost or rightmost cell, depending on which direction the tape extends. The scanning head is also able to move to the left or to the right of the cell its scans. Alternatively, one may say that the scanning head stands still while there is some sort of mechanism that moves the paper tape. Whether the scanning head will go to the left or to the right or whether the tape is moved to the right or to the left for that matter, whether the scanning head will erase a cell or print a symbol on a cell depends on the *controlling device*, which is actually a set of rules that specify what should be done for each particular case. In particular, before each tick of the clock, the machine is in a specific *state* (e.g., "sad", "happy", etc.) and the scanning head sits atop a specific cell that has printed on it some symbol s. The machine consults its controlling device and enters into a new state and the scanning head performs some action (e.g., prints a symbol, moves to the left, etc.) provided there is rule that specifies this action. Figure 2.1 is an artistic depiction of a Turing machine. In this depiction, the tape is moving and the scanning head stands still.

Turing insisted that the contents of the controlling device should be in a compact form. Instead of using words like "sad" for the various states of a machine, he used symbols of the form q_i, where i is an index that can assume a natural number as value.

---

[6] Alan M. Turing. *On computable numbers, with an application to the entscheidungsproblem.* Proceedings of the London Mathematical Society, 42, pp. 230–265, 1936.

Figure 2.1: An artist's impression of a Turing Machine. © Yiannis Kontovos.

For example, the symbols q_1 and q_2 may stand for two machine states. Also, the letters R and L should mean a move of the scanning head to the cell immediately to the right or to the left, respectively. Thus, a controlling device might contain expressions like this one $q_i S_j S_k L q_m$. This expression should be read as follows: if the machine

is in state	and scanning	then print	and move	and enter state
q_i	S_j	S_k	L	q_m

When it is necessary to print a symbol without moving the scanning head, one should use the symbol N. For example, the expression $q_i S_j S_k N q_m$ specifies that the scanning head should print the symbol S_k but the scanning head should not move. In most cases, the symbols S_k are assumed to be either the digit "1" or the digit "0", where "0" stands for a blank symbol. Thus, if one wants to erase a symbol, she can ask the machine to print the symbol "0". Numbers are written as sequences of ones separated by zeros. For example, the symbol "1" stands for the number 0, the sequence "11" stands for the number 1, the sequence "111" stands for the number 2, etc.

Emil Leon Post

In October 1936, Emil Leon Post proposed a machine that is similar to Turing's. Post's initial description was a bit vague, however, later on, he proposed a formulation whose controlling device contained expressions with only four symbols, instead of five. In this configuration, the expression $q_iS_jLq_m$ should be read as follows: if the machine

is in state	and scanning	then move	and enter state
q_i	S_j	L	q_m

Also, the expression $q_iS_jS_kq_m$ should be read as follows: if the machine

is in state	and scanning	then print	and enter state
q_i	S_j	S_k	q_m

The machine stops once there is no expression that is applicable. The result of its computation is the number of ones printed on the tape. Thus, if there are six ones, then the result of the computation is the number 6. Note, the difference between data entered before the machine is set in motion and after the machine has been terminated. It is not *trivial* to say beforehand how many clock ticks are needed for a Turing machine to deliver a result. Moreover, one cannot exclude the case of a machine that does not terminate. Before saying more about this subject, I will present a simple Turing machine that computes the sum of two natural numbers. The controlling device of this machine will contain the following expressions:

$$q_1\,1\,0\,q_1$$
$$q_1\,0\,R\,q_2$$
$$q_2\,1\,R\,q_2$$
$$q_2\,0\,R\,q_3$$
$$q_3\,1\,0\,q_3$$

Assume that we want to compute the sum 2 + 2. Then, the tape of the machine will contain the following symbols:

$$q_1 \quad \begin{array}{cccccccc} 1 & 1 & 1 & 0 & 1 & 1 & 1 \\ \uparrow \end{array}$$

The arrow points to the cell where the scanning head is placed and the machine is in state q_1. Obviously, the only applicable expression is the expression $q_1\,1\,0\,q_1$. After applying this expression, the tape will look as follows:

$$q_1 \quad \begin{array}{cccccccc} 0 & 1 & 1 & 0 & 1 & 1 & 1 \\ \uparrow \end{array}$$

Now the machine will apply the expression $q_1\,0\,R\,q_2$ and the scanning head will move to the right:

$$q_2 \quad \begin{array}{cccccccc} 0 & 1 & 1 & 0 & 1 & 1 & 1 \\ & \uparrow \end{array}$$

The machine will continuously apply the expression $q_2\ 1\ R\ q_2$ until the scanning head reaches the first zero:

$$q_2 \left|\ 0\quad 1\quad 1\quad 0\quad 1\quad 1\quad 1\right.$$
$$\uparrow$$

Now the machine will apply the expression $q_2\ 0\ R\ q_3$, that is, it will ignore the zero and it will move to the next cell while entering state q_3:

$$q_3 \left|\ 0\quad 1\quad 1\quad 0\quad 1\quad 1\quad 1\right.$$
$$\uparrow$$

It is not difficult to see that now the machine can apply only the expression $q_3\ 1\ 0\ q_3$:

$$q_3 \left|\ 0\quad 1\quad 1\quad 0\quad 0\quad 1\quad 1\right.$$
$$\uparrow$$

The scanning head is sitting atop a cell that has the symbol "0" printed on it while it has entered state q_3. This implies that no expression can be applied and so the machine stops. The result of the computation is the number of ones on the tape. There are four ones, thus the result is the number $4 = 2 + 2$. So the machine has managed to compute the sum of two numbers. The reader is invited to check that the machine can compute any other sum.

Sometimes the following quadruple is also considered:

$$q_i S_j q_k q_l \tag{2.1}$$

This quadruple is particularly useful if we want to construct a Turing machine that will compute *relatively computable functions*. These quadruples provide a Turing machine with a means of communicating with an external agency that can give correct answers to questions about a set A, which is a subset of $\mathbb{N}$. More specifically, when a machine is in state q_i and the cell that the scanning head scans contains the symbol S_j, then the machine can be thought of asking the question, "Is n an element of A?" Here n is the number of 1's that are printed on the tape at this particular moment. If the answer is "yes", then the machine enters state q_k; otherwise, it enters state q_l. Turing machines equipped with such an external agency are called *oracle machines*, and the external agency is called an *oracle*. I will say more about these machines in Section 3.2.

A *universal* Turing machine is a machine that is able to simulate the behavior of any other ordinary Turing machine. This is achieved by first printing on the tape of the universal machine a (unique) number that describes the ordinary machine as well as the number that is printed on the tape of the ordinary machine and then by processing these two numbers. The first number is actually a Gödel number, which is derived by associating each basic symbol of a Turing machine with an odd number greater than or equal to 3 as follows:

$$\begin{array}{ccccccccccc}
3 & 5 & 7 & 9 & 11 & 13 & 15 & 17 & 19 & 21 & 23 & \cdots \\
\uparrow & \uparrow & \uparrow & \uparrow & \uparrow & \uparrow & \uparrow & \uparrow & \uparrow & \uparrow & \uparrow \\
R & L & N & S_0 & q_0 & S_1 & q_1 & S_2 & q_2 & S_3 & q_3 & \cdots
\end{array}$$

This mapping is a general one and each machine has its own Gödelization map. For example, the Turing machine that computes the sum of two natural numbers has the following Gödelization map:

$$\begin{array}{ccccccc}
3 & 5 & 7 & 9 & 11 & 13 & 15 \\
\uparrow & \uparrow & \uparrow & \uparrow & \uparrow & \uparrow & \uparrow \\
R & 0 & q_0 & 1 & q_1 & q_2 & q_3
\end{array}$$

And here are the Gödel numbers for each expression of this machine:

$$q_1\ 1\ 0\ q_1 \rightarrow 2^{11} \times 3^9 \times 5^5 \times 7^{11} = 249,086,222,607,801,600,000$$

$$q_1\ 0\ R\ q_2 \rightarrow 2^{11} \times 3^5 \times 5^3 \times 7^{13} = 6,027,271,559,398,656,000$$

$$q_2\ 1\ R\ q_2 \rightarrow 2^{13} \times 3^9 \times 5^3 \times 7^{13} = 1,952,835,985,245,164,544,000$$

$$q_2\ 0\ R\ q_3 \rightarrow 2^{13} \times 3^5 \times 5^3 \times 7^{15} = 1,181,345,225,642,136,576,000$$

$$q_3\ 1\ 0\ q_3 \rightarrow 2^{15} \times 3^9 \times 5^5 \times 7^{15} = 9,568,896,327,701,306,265,600,000$$

The Gödel number of any machine is the number $2^{e_1} \times 3^{e_2} \times 7^{e_3} \times \cdots \times p_k^{e_k}$, where e_i is the Gödel number of each expression contained in the controlling device and p_i is the ith prime number. Thus the Gödel number, G_n, of the machine that computes the sum of two natural numbers is

$$G_n = 2^{249086222607801600000} \times 3^{6027271559398656000}$$
$$\times 5^{1952835985245164544000} \times 7^{1181345225642136576000}$$
$$\times 11^{9568896327701306265600000}$$

Obviously, this is an extremely large number! And, of course, one needs to print $G_n + 1$ 1's on the tape of the universal machine plus the presentation of its arguments. It seems that this is a task that requires centuries if not millennia to be accomplished!

Initially, Turing himself gave a complete description of a universal machine and later on some other researchers gave alternative description of universal machines. However, these machines are far too complex for newcomers. In 2002, Stephen Wolfram conjectured that a machine that uses three symbols (e.g., 0, 1, and 2) and has two states is a universal machine. Wolfram announced a $25,000 prize for determining whether or not that Turing machine is in fact universal. Alex Smith, an undergraduate student of the University of Birmingham, UK, presented a proof that this machine is universal and won the prize. I have followed a debate on a mailing list about the correctness to this proof but all I can say is that no one has actually examined Smith's proof thoroughly although it is publicly available, nevertheless, I assume that the proof is correct. The controlling device of this machine contains the following expressions:

$$q_1 \, S_2 \, S_1 \, L \, q_1$$
$$q_1 \, S_1 \, S_2 \, L \, q_1$$
$$q_1 \, S_0 \, S_1 \, R \, q_2$$
$$q_2 \, S_2 \, S_0 \, R \, q_1$$
$$q_2 \, S_1 \, S_2 \, R \, q_2$$
$$q_2 \, S_0 \, S_2 \, L \, q_1$$

Previously, I stated that a Turing machine may not terminate, which obviously means that it will run forever. Clearly, it would be really useful to be able to tell beforehand if a Turing machine with a specific input will terminate or not. This is known in the literature as the *halting problem*. In simple words, the halting problem asks if there is a computer program that got stalled, can we decide if the program works or not? Turing gave an answer to this problem by using a universal Turing machine. His proof is quite involved, nevertheless, one can give a description in layman's terms of this proof.[7]

It is not unheard of that there are apps (i.e., smartphone applications) that can freeze a smartphone. Although one cannot rule out malice, I think that negligence from the app developer is the main reason. Thus, an app might freeze because it tries to access some non-existent memory location. Sometimes such an operation may crash an app, but there are cases where the whole system freezes because of it. In the latter case, one needs to restart the smartphone. Clearly, it would be quite beneficial if there were an app that would examine apps in order to check whether they would freeze a phone or not. Let us call this app *Freeze*. This app would be really easy to use — select an app and print the verdict in a few minutes. As soon as this wonderful app would hit an app store, someone would create a new app out of sheer boredom. A possible name for such an app would be *Paradox*. This app would perform the following actions:

— Run Freeze and ask it to inspect Paradox.
— If Freeze returns *OK* then freeze the phone.
— If Freeze returned *Not OK* then print the message *Freeze detected that Paradox freezes* and terminate normally.

---

[7] The description that follows is due to Pål Grønås Drange and Jan Arne Telle and appeared in the Norwegian daily Morgenbladet. Since I do not speak Norwegian, I have used the exposition of this description by Thore Husfeldt in his blog.

One may suspect that this is a malicious app designed to freeze phones or that it is an app than can actually detect whether some app may freeze a phone. Let us see why none of this assumptions hold true.

Suppose that Paradox freezes the phone. Then, Freeze should have detected this and therefore Paradox should print the message "Freeze detected that Paradox freezes" and terminate normally. But this means that the phone did not freeze, although we assumed that it did freeze! Now suppose that Paradox does not freeze the phone. Then, Freeze will determine this and it will return "OK", which means that Paradox will freeze the phone although we assumed the opposite! Since we have ruled out that both initial assumptions are not valid, we can safely conclude that the Freeze app cannot exist. Of course, Turing did not use apps but he used his machine to show exactly the same: No Turing machine can determine whether another Turing machine will terminate or not. Of course, an app is far more complicated than a Turing machine since an app is an *interactive* system while a Turing machine is a closed system. However, I will say more on this in Chapter 3.

Roughly speaking, Turing used this result to show that the Entscheidungsproblem has no solution. In Turing's own words:

> ... there can be no general process for determining whether a given formula 𝔄 of the functional calculus K is provable, i.e., that there can be no machine which, supplied with any one 𝔄 of these formulas, will eventually say whether 𝔄 is provable.

In simple words, given an expression of some formal system, Turing concluded that there is no a-machine, and, more generally, not any other (computing) machine, that can determine whether this expression can be proved.

2.5   The Church–Turing Thesis

In the previous sections, it was noted that Gödel and Church considered recursive functions and the λ-calculus, respectively, as mathematical models of computation. Obviously, the Turing machine is also a model of computation. Strictly speaking, the Turing machine is not a mathematical model of computation, nevertheless, it is not difficult to define a function that can precisely describe the functionality of each Turing machine. Thus, one can roughly assume that the Turing machine is a mathematical model of computation.

The reader may naturally ask whether there is any relationship between these three models of computation. Let us try to compare the λ-calculus and the Turing machine. We have seen that a Turing machine can compute the sum of any two numbers. Although I have not demonstrated how to add two numbers using the λ-calculus, still I have demonstrated how to multiply two numbers and I have given the expression that can be used to compute the sum of any two numbers. Thus, both the Turing machine and the λ-calculus can be used to compute any sum. Obviously, the same can be said for multiplication and I think that no one would object that one can perform subtractions and divisions with both systems. Moreover, this same principle applies to other more complex mathematical expressions. In fact, Turing proved that anything expressible in the λ-calculus can be computed by a Turing machine and everything that can be computed by Turing machines is expressible in the λ-calculus. In addition, Church proved that all recursive functions can be expressed in the λ-calculus and all functions expressible in the λ-calculus are recursive. From these two results, one can deduce that all recursive functions can be computed by Turing machines and all functions computed by Turing machines are recursive. In different words, these three models of the notion of computation are equivalent.

I have briefly described three models of computation and I will discuss more models in the chapters that follow, still there is no precise definition of the notion of computation that is universally accepted. At the time Church and Turing made their proposals, it was widely accepted that a computational process should be an *effective* one. Unfortunately, there was and still there is no consensus as to what effective means! Marvin Minsky, in his classical book on computability theory, identified effective procedure with a "set of rules which tell us, from moment to moment, precisely how to behave", provided we have at our disposal a universally accepted way to interpret these rules. Minsky concluded that this definition is meaningful if the steps are actually steps performed by some Turing machine. This approach is not satisfactory since it should make no reference to an existing model of computation. Brian Jack Copeland[8] proposed four criteria that any sequence of instructions that make up a procedure or method should satisfy in order for it to be characterized as effective:

(i)   Each instruction should be expressible by finite means (i.e., a finite sequence of symbols).
(ii) The instructions produce the desired result in a finite number of steps.
(iii) They can be carried out by a human being unaided by any machinery save paper and pencil.
(iv) They demand no insight or ingenuity on the part of the human carrying it out.

What is even more confusing is that an *algorithm* is considered to be an effective procedure! The following is a phrasing of what an algorithm is[9]:

[8]Brian Jack Copeland.   *The Church–Turing thesis*.   In The Stanford Encyclopedia of Philosophy, Edward N. Zalta, ed. Fall 2002. http://plato.stanford.edu/archives/fall2002/entries/church-turing/.
[9]This definition is borrowed from Ellis Horowitz and Sartaj Sahni. *Fundamentals of Data Structures in Pascal*. Computer Science Press, 1984.

Definition 2.5.1 An algorithm is a finite set of instructions that if followed, accomplish a particular task. In addition, every algorithm must satisfy the following criteria:

(i) *input*: there are zero or more quantities that are externally supplied;
(ii) *output*: at least one quantity is produced;
(iii) *definiteness*: each instruction must be clear and unambiguous;
(iv) *finiteness*: if we trace out the instructions of an algorithm, then for all cases the algorithm will terminate after a finite number of steps;
(v) *effectiveness*: every instruction must be sufficiently basic that it can, in principle, be carried out by a person using only pencil and paper. It is not enough that each operation be defined as in (iii), but it must also be feasible.

A rather different idea regarding effectiveness has been put forth by Carol Cleland[10] who argues that even everyday procedures can be rendered as effective. For example, she argues that if a recipe for a sauce is to be carried out by an expert chef, then the whole procedure can be classified as effective. Mostly computer scientists and mathematicians would agree that cooking recipes are not rigorously defined (e.g., what exactly is a pinch of salt or pepper?) and therefore are not algorithms. However, in a vague world (i.e., the world we actually live in), a pinch of salt is a vague quantity and the final result is vague or, more precisely (!), a dish to some degree. This idea and its applicability to computation will be examined in Chapter 6.

Church proposed the use of his λ-calculus as a realization of the notion of *effectively calculable*. From the previous discussion, it should be clear that this is an arbitrary assumption although one can justify it. Similarly, Turing identified computable numbers with those numbers that can be computed by a Turing machine, which is again something completely arbitrary. And since recursive functions are Turing computable, one can "conclude" that if a function is recursive, then it is computable and vice versa. The next logical step is to make the following bold statement:

Thesis 2.5.1 *Every effectively computable function is Turing computable, that is, there is a Turing machine that realizes it. Alternatively, the effectively computable functions can be identified with the recursive functions.*

This statement is known in the literature as the *Church–Turing Thesis* (or CTT, for short). Although the CTT is an hypothesis, many researchers and thinkers assume it is valid. Nevertheless, not everyone believes that this statement is true. For example, the Hungarian mathematicians László Kalmár and Rózsa Péter and the French mathematician Jean Porte questioned the equivalence between recursive functions and computable functions. However, these ideas and other similar will be examined in Chapter 3.

---

[10] Carol E. Cleland. *On effective procedures*. Minds and Machines, 12, pp. 159–179, 2002.

Gábor Etesi and István Németi[11] describe as effectively computable any function of natural numbers for which there is a *physical computer* realizing it. Given some function describing how some natural numbers function, then a physical computer realizes it when some imaginary observer can do the following with the computer: The observer can "start" the computer with some number as input and later on (according to the observer's clock) "receives" a number from the computer as output such that this number is the actual value of the function. Etesi and Németi, after introducing the notion of *artificial computing systems*, that is, thought experiments relative to a fixed physical theory that involve computing devices, rephrased the Church–Turing thesis as follows[12]:

Thesis 2.5.2 *Every function realizable by an artificial computing system is Turing computable.*

Since artificial computing systems are thought experiments relative to a fixed physical theory, the thesis can be rephrased as follows:

Thesis 2.5.3 *Every function realizable by a thought experiment is Turing computable.*

According to Etesi and Németi, a thought experiment relative to a fixed physical theory is a theoretically possible experiment, that is, an experiment that can be carefully designed, specified, etc., according to the rules of the physical theory, but for which we might not currently have the necessary resources.

David Elieser Deutsch[13] has reformulated the Church–Turing thesis as follows:

Thesis 2.5.4 *Every finitely realizable physical system can be perfectly simulated by a universal model computing machine operating by finite means.*

If one considers that the human mind is a physical system, this thesis can be rephrased as follows.

Thesis 2.5.5 *The human brain realizes only Turing-computable functions.*

This thesis is the core of *computationalism*, the philosophical theory that claims that a person's mind is actually a Turing machine. Consequently, one may go a step ahead

---

[11] Gábor Etesi and István Németi. *Non-Turing computations via malament-hogart space-times*. International Journal of Theoretical Physics, 41(2), pp. 341–370, 2002.
[12] Actually, they call this "updated" version of the Church–Turing thesis the *Church–Kalmár–Turing* thesis, named after Church, Kalmár, and Turing.
[13] David Deutsch. *Quantum theory, the Church–Turing principle and the universal quantum computer.* Proceedings of the Royal Society of London A, 400, pp. 97–115, 1985.

and argue that since a person's mind is a Turing machine, then it will be possible one day to construct an artificial person with feelings and emotions. The mind is indeed a machine, but one that transcends the capabilities of the Turing machine and operates in a profoundly different way. But I will say more about this in Chapter 3.

2.6   Easy and Difficult Problems

Nowadays, the established view is that there are problems that are either solvable or unsolvable. Given some problem P it is assumed that the term "solvable" means that it is possible to devise an algorithm to solve (instances of) P or, *equivalently*, to construct a Turing machine that solves (instances of) P regardless of the time required to actually solve P. Furthermore, when a problem is solvable, then the problem is either easy or difficult. The classification does not depend on how easy it is to have the problem solved by a human being but it does depend on how much time it takes to solve the problem with a machine (usually a Turing machine). More specifically, it depends on the total number of instructions that a machine has to execute in order to deliver a result, which also depends on the length of the input.

The easiest way to calculate the number of instructions required to solve a particular problem is to define a function that takes as an argument the length of an algorithm's input. For example, when an algorithm is able to sort n numbers, then the length of its input is n. Also, if an algorithm solves quadratic equations, then the length of its input is 3. As regards functions that measure instructions, when a function is a constant one, then the time required is constant no matter how long is the input. Therefore, such an algorithm is fast and so it is definitely easy. When the value of the function is n^2, where n is the length of the input, then the corresponding algorithm is relatively fast and is also classified as easy. However, when the value of the function is 2^n, then the algorithm is slow. For example, if n is equal to 6, then it takes 64 instructions to deliver a result while when n is equal to 7, it takes 128 instructions and so on. A typical example of a function whose computation is slow is the following one:

$$F(0) = 0$$
$$F(1) = 1$$
$$F(n) = F(n-1) + F(n-2)$$

This function is known in the literature as the Fibonacci function, named after the Italian mathematician Leonardo Fibonacci. This function is actually a model of population growth. In particular, it solves the following problem:

Assume that a pair of rabbits are released in the wild. After one month, the rabbits mate and the end of the second month, the female gives birth to another pair of rabbits. Let's assume that the rabbits never die and each female gives birth to one pair with one male and one female, every month from the second month. How many pairs will there be in X months?

Here is how one can compute the value $F(5)$:

$$F(5) = F(4) + F(3)$$
$$= \big(F(3) + F(2)\big) + \big(F(2) + F(1)\big)$$
$$= \Big(\big(F(2) + F(1)\big) + \big(F(1) + F(0)\big)\Big) + \Big(\big(F(1) + F(0)\big) + F(1)\Big)$$
$$= F(1) + F(0) + F(1) + F(1) + F(0) + F(1) + F(0) + F(1)$$
$$= 1 + 0 + 1 + 1 + 0 + 1 + 0 + 1$$
$$= 5$$

Note that the number of function *expansions* (i.e., by what each function call is replaced) is $2^{n-2} - 1$. Thus, the number of expansions grows exponentially and this is exactly the reason, this is a difficult problem.

In general, when for some algorithm the number of instructions required to solve an instance of a problem is *polynomial*, then the algorithm is called easy. Recall that a polynomial is an algebraic expression of the form $a_0 + a_1 x_1 + a_2 x_2^2 + \cdots + a_k x_k^k$ (e.g., the expressions $x^2 + 4$, $1 + x$, and x^3 are polynomials). Thus, if $p(n)$ is a polynomial whose only variable is n, then an algorithm is easy when it takes $p(n)$ instructions to solve an instance of the problem whose input length is n. The class of problems that are easy is denoted by $\mathcal{P}$.

Turing was the first who described an extension to his "standard" model of computation. He called these extended Turing machines *c-machines* and described them as follows:

> For some purposes we might use machines (choice machines or c-machines) whose motion is only partially determined by the configuration [controlling device] (hence the use of word "possible" in §1). When such a machine reaches one of these ambiguous configurations, it cannot go on until some arbitrary choice has been made by an external operator. This would be the case if we were using machines to deal with axiomatic systems.

In a sense, c-machines correspond to machines that function in a non-deterministic way. This means that the course of action is not determined from the input. Similarly, a non-deterministic Turing machine is one whose course of action is not determined entirely by its input and its controlling device; rather as each execution step, the machine can chose from a set of possible actions. When there is a non-deterministic Turing machine that solves some problem and the number of instructions required to solve an instance of a problem is *polynomial*, then the problem is called difficult.

The class of problems that are difficult is denoted by $\mathcal{NP}$. Note that the number of instructions required to verify that an answer is actually an answer to an $\mathcal{NP}$ problem is polynomial.

One of the unsolved problems of the theory of computation is the relation between these two classes: $\mathcal{P} \overset{?}{=} \mathcal{NP}$. The established view is that $\mathcal{P} \neq \mathcal{NP}$ because one assumes that the Church–Turing thesis is valid. At first, it seems that this question is not really important. After all, problems that belong to $\mathcal{P}$ are solvable and so are problems that belong to $\mathcal{NP}$. However, in order to fully understand the difference between easy and difficult problems, let us see another interesting problem—The Towers of Hanoi puzzle. This problem was invented by the French mathematician François Édouard Anatole Lucas around 1883. The puzzle can be stated as follows: There are three needles and a tower of disks on the first one, with the smaller on the top and the bigger at the bottom. The purpose of the puzzle is to move the whole tower from the first needle to the second, by moving only one disk every time and by observing not to put a bigger disk atop of a smaller one. Figure 2.2 shows a typical set up of the puzzle. Assume that on the first needle there is a tower of n rings. Then, the "easy" way to solve this puzzle is to move a tower of height $n - 1$ to the third needle, move the last ring to the second needle, and finally move the tower from the third needle to the second one.[14] It can be shown that when one starts with a tower of height n, then one has to perform $2^n - 1$ moves in order to solve the puzzle. For example, when one has a tower of 64 disks, then it is necessary to perform 18,446,744,073,709,551,615 moves in order to solve the problem. Now, contrast this with the binary search algorithm that is used to find the position of a number in a sorted sequence of numbers. In order to find the position of the number, one asks whether the number in the middle is equal, greater, or less than the number we seek. If it is equal to the number, we stop. If it is less than the number, we compare our number with the number that is located in the middle of the

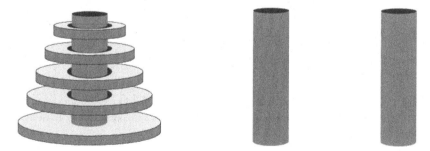

Figure 2.2: A typical set up of the Towers of Hanoi puzzle.

---

[14]See the author's web page at http://asyropoulos.eu for a thorough presentation of the puzzle and a number of different solutions.

lower part of the sequence, otherwise, we compare our number with the number that is located in the middle of the upper part of the sequence, etc. Obviously, if there is a very long sequence, it will take some time to find our number, but this amount of time is insignificant to the amount of time needed to solve the Towers of Hanoi puzzle. If $\mathcal{P} = \mathcal{NP}$, then this would mean that there is a way to solve the Towers of Hanoi puzzle with a speed that is comparable to the speed needed to find a number in a sorted sequence. There are proposals aiming at solving difficult problems easily. I will say more on this in the chapter that follows.

Annotated Bibliography

• Henk Barendregt. *The Lambda Calculus. Its Syntax and Semantics*. College Publications, London, 2012.

This is the most complete presentation of the λ-calculus. Anyone who wants to study the calculus should use this book. However, I do not think this is the ideal book for anyone who seeks a tutorial introduction to the λ-calculus. This particular edition is a cheap one and not the expensive one published by Elsevier.

• George S. Boolos, John P. Burgess, and Richard C. Jeffrey. *Computability and Logic*. Cambridge University Press, Cambridge, 4th edition, 2002.

This is a classic book on mathematical logic and the theory of computation. The book is more suitable for people interested in mathematical logic. It covers a wide range of subjects in an accessible way.

• David A. Duffy. *Principles of Automated Theorem Proving*. Wiley Professional Computing. John Wiley & Sons, Chichester, 1991.

This is a book on automated theorem proving that I found particularly useful during my graduate studies. It presents the basic ideas and explores systems that were state of the art at that time. I think it is still worth reading.

• Kurt Gödel. *On Formally Undecidable Propositions Of Principia Mathematica and Related Systems*. Dover Publications, New York, 1992. Translated by B. Meltzer, preface introduction by R.B. Braithwaite.

This booklet is a translation into English of Gödel's original paper. The included introduction is quite helpful in order to understand the notation used as well as some subtle points in the paper itself.

- David Hilbert. *Mathematical problems.* Bulletin of the American Mathematical Society, 8(10), pp. 437–479, 1902.

This article includes all of Hilbert's problems. The text is a translation of Hilbert's original article. The translator was Mary Winston Newson and the author's original work that appeared in the Göttinger Nachrichten, 1900, pp. 253–297, and in the Archiv der Mathernatik und Physik, 3d ser., vol. 1 (1901), pp. 44–63 and 213–237.

- Andrew Hodges. *Alan Turing: The Enigma.* Vintage, London, 2014.

This book is a biography of Alan Turing and in a sense it is interesting to read what motivated Turing to invent his machine. In my own opinion, the book at certain points presents things in an exaggerated way. To me, Turing was a great thinker but certainly not a rock star...

- Stephen Cole Kleene. *Introduction to Metamathematics.* Ishi Press International, New York, 2009.

This is a very important and substantial text-book of mathematical logic (the ideas presented in this chapter belong to mathematical logic). The term meta-mathematics is used to denote the study of formal systems. This is not the original edition of the book that was published by Elsevier but a cheap one and one that the reader can easily find.

- Harry R. Lewis and Christos H. Papadimitriou. *Elements of the Theory of Computation.* 2nd edition, Pearson Education, Harlow, 1998.

This book is a modern account of the classical theory of computation. It presents Turing machines and other conceptual computing devices commonly known as automata. In addition, it includes an introduction to complexity theory.

- Marvin Minsky. *Computation: Finite and Infinite Machines.* Prentice-Hall, Englewood Cliffs, NJ, 1967.

Another classical book on computability theory. The book is more suitable for people who are not so much interested in recursion theory but in machines and automata.

- Ernest Nagel and James R. Newman. *Gödel's Proof.* New York University Press, New York, 2001. Edited and with new foreword by Douglas R. Hofstadter.

If one cannot read Gödel's paper, then this book is the next best thing! The original version had a few mistakes which have been corrected in this version.

- Hartley Rogers, Jr. *Theory of Recursive Functions and Effective Computability.* The MIT Press, Cambridge, MA, 1987.

  This is one more excellent introduction to the ideas that I have presented in this chapter. Note that the late Roger's had a reputation of being an excellent teacher. Thus the book has pedagogical value.

Chapter 3

Hypercomputation[1]

In the previous chapter I presented what I call classical theory of computation. A basic "conclusion" of this theory is that no machine real or conceptual can achieve more than the Turing machine. However, this bold statement is simply wrong as we do not know enough about our world to definitely rule out forms of computation more powerful than the Turing machine.

3.1   On Problems and Their Solutions

Today's mathematics owes much to ancient Greeks because they transformed counting and simple arithmetic and geometric operations into a discipline. The Greeks studied many problems but they concluded that there are certain unsolvable problems. In particular, they could not solve the following problems using only a straightedge and a compass:

— the trisection of an angle (i.e., the division of an arbitrary angle into three equal angles);
— the construction of a cube with twice the volume of a given cube; and
— the construction of a regular heptagon (i.e., a polygon with seven sides).

For almost two millennia, mathematicians could not tell whether it is possible to solve these problems. In the 19th century, modern mathematicians showed that these problems could not be solved using the restrictions originally specified. Naturally, no one should be surprised to learn that even the ancient Greeks had invented ways to solve the first two problems exactly, using tools other than a straightedge and a

---

[1] This chapter is an extended version of my essay *Hypercomputation: fantasy or reality? A position paper.* Parallel Processing Letters, 23(1), 1350005, 2013.

compass (e.g., the mesolabio is such a tool). Of course, under the conditions that were originally specified, these problems cannot be solved. But what can we learn from this brief recount of unsolvable problems of ancient mathematics? Simply, the problems that cannot be solved under specific condition may become solvable under different conditions. The next natural question is whether there are problems that are absolutely not solvable. The answer is that there are such problems. For example, the problem of squaring a circle when working on a Euclidean space is absolutely impossible. Note that this problem was the fourth impossible problem from antiquity. The problem is impossible because when one has a circle whose radius is 1, its area is π. This number is a *transcendental* one. This means that it is not the root of any polynomial with integral coefficients. Assume that one can construct such a square. Then, its area would be equal to π. This means that the length of its side will be equal to $\sqrt{\pi}$. In mathematics, a number that corresponds to a line segment that can be constructed using only straightedge and compass is called *constructible*. However, only numbers that are *algebraic* (i.e., non-transcendental) are constructible. Thus, it is impossible to square the circle on a Euclidean space! Assume that we work on a non-Euclidean space. For example, a hyperbolic plane, that is, a "plane" where for any given line R and point A not on R, there are at least two distinct lines through A that do not intersect R. Then, it is possible to "square the circle". This happens because we have changed the meaning of square. Unfortunately, even in this weird world, there is no general construction "that begins with the corner angle σ of a square and produces the radius r of a circle with matching area".[2]

Kleene, following the pioneering work of Church and Turing, defined a hierarchy of problems, which is now known as the arithmetic hierarchy. In fact, Kleene defined a hierarchy of sets, relations, and predicates, which correspond to problems. Also, only problems that belong to the first level of the hierarchy are solvable by Turing machines and they are called *recursive* or *decidable*. Those that are in the second level are "semi-solvable". Roughly, given a semi-decidable problem, there is an algorithm that halts only when an object that solves the problem is given as input to it, while when an object that does not solve the problem is fed as input, the machine fails to halt. All other problems are completely unsolvable by Turing machines.

The statement that the Diophantine equation $x^n + y^n = z^n$ has no non-zero integer solutions for x, y, and z when $n > 2$ is known in the literature as *Fermat's last theorem*. This statement can be expressed in symbolic logic as follows:

$$\forall n[(n > 2) \rightarrow \neg(\exists x, \exists y, \exists z\, [x^n + y^n = z^n])] \tag{3.1}$$

In this logical formula, for the sake of simplicity, I have omitted to specify that x, y, and y should all be non-zero. Formula 3.1 corresponds to a "semi-solvable" problem

---

[2]William C. Jagy. *Squaring circles in the hyperbolic plane*. The Mathematical Intelligencer, 17, pp. 31–36, 1995.

[technically it is a *co-semi-decidable* problem (i.e., a Π_1^0 formula)]. This means that it is not possible to algorithmically tell whether Fermat's last theorem is true or not. Fortunately, Andrew John Wiles proved this theorem in 1995 by using tools and ideas alien to recursion theory.[3] So, there is a problem that is "semi-solvable" by a Turing machine, which means that the problem is not *decidable*, but since Fermat's last theorem has been proved, we can safely conclude that it is *decidable*! Grigori Yakovlevich Perelman's proof of Poincaré's conjecture forms yet another such oxymoron.[4,5,6] In an effort to understand this oxymoron, I posted the following question to a relevant mailing list:

Provided that it makes sense to ask, does anyone have any idea where in the arithmetical hierarchy would one put Poincaré's Conjecture? I mean is it a Π_2^0 problem, a Π_3^0 problem or what?

A member of the list responded as follows:

Now that it has been proved it is Δ_0^0 [i.e., definitely decidable]. Previously it had been known to be Π_1^0 [i.e., semi-decidable]; prior to Rubinstein's algorithm for recognizing the 3-sphere it was known to be Π_2^0 [i.e., undecidable] (for all triangulated 3-manifolds X together with a combinatorial reduction of $\Pi_1(X)$ to the trivial group, there exists a simplicial homeomorphism of X with the standard 3-sphere).

The point here is that problems that were thought to be non-decidable or semi-decidable, because the relevant mathematical theory suggested so, are in fact decidable. Therefore, the initial assessment was wrong and chances are that more such assessments are wrong.

Yet another famous problem is *Riemann's hypothesis*. This is about the non-trivial zeros of the function

$$\zeta(s) = \sum_{n=1}^{\infty} \frac{1}{n^s}$$

[3] Andrew Wiles. *Modular elliptic curves and Fermat's last theorem*. Annals of Mathematics, 142, pp. 443–551, 1995.

[4] Grisha Perelman. *The entropy formula for the Ricci flow and its geometric applications*. arXiv:math/0211159v1, 2002.

[5] Grisha Perelman. *Finite extinction time for the solutions to the Ricci flow on certain three-manifolds*. arXiv:math/0307245v1, 2003.

[6] Grisha Perelman. *Ricci flow with surgery on three-manifolds*. arXiv:math/0303109v1, 2003.

where s is a complex number. Note that this is not the ζ function but a representation of it when the real part of x is greater than one. The *functional equation*[7] of the ζ function is

$$\zeta(s) = 2^s \pi^{s-1} \sin\left(\frac{\pi s}{2}\right) \Gamma(1-s)\zeta(1-s)$$

where the gamma function, Γ, is an extension of the factorial function. Thus, Riemann's hypothesis is about the roots of the equation $\zeta(s) = 0$. This equation has a number of "trivial" solutions, which are the numbers $-2, -4, -6 \ldots$. The non-trivial solution of this equation are assumed to be of the form $1/2 + iy$. Thus, Riemann's hypothesis is the conjecture that the non-trivial Riemann ζ function zeros are of the form $1/2 + iy$. It has been shown that this problem is as hard as Poincaré's conjecture. This means that no Turing machine is able to give a definitive answer to this problem, but chances are that some person might be able to solve it.

Although the halting problem is an unsolvable problem, still there have been efforts to "approximate" this problem.[8] In particular, the authors have used the brainfuck programming language and devised some algorithms that can solve the halting problem just like the traveling salesman can be solved for a relatively small number of towns. In addition, I recently reviewed a paper for a conference where the authors proposed an algorithm capable of detecting infinite loops, thus solving the halting problem for specific cases. Thus, it is possible to partially solve the halting problem.

I firmly believe that the core of the awkward situation where problems known to be unsolvable "suddenly" become solvable is that the established trust and belief in the capabilities of the Turing machine are inflated. One could easily say that since the theory has failed to predict that certain problems are solvable, it is not a correct theory. At least this is what would happen with a physical theory (or not?). For instance, the discovery of particles that travel faster than light in the vacuum would render the theory of relativity an incorrect theory. Thus, recursion theory is an incorrect theory since it has failed to make a number of predictions. The only possible way out is to consider the idea that there might exist machines more powerful than the Turing machine that can do things Turing machines fail to accomplish. The idea that such machines are feasible, and not some imaginary Holy Grail of computer science, is known as *hypercomputation*.

3.2   Hypercomputation Explained

Hypercomputation is also the idea that we do not know the physical limits of computation. However, "hard core" computer scientists think otherwise. In a sense, it

---

[7] A functional equation is any equation that specifies a function $R(x_1, \ldots, x_n)$ with a equation $R(x_1, \ldots, x_n) = 0$.

[8] Sven Köhler, Christian Schindelhauer, and Martin Ziegler. On approximating real-world halting problems. In Maciej Liśkiewicz and Rüdiger Reischuk, editors, *Fundamentals of Computation Theory: 15th International Symposium, FCT 2005, Lübeck, Germany, August, 2005. Proceedings*, pp. 454–466, Springer, Heidelberg, 2005.

had been argued that hypercomputation is to computability theory what perpetual motion machines are to physics, that is, an unrealistic theory simply because it violates basic laws, just like perpetual motion machines violate the laws of thermodynamics. However, the basic law that hypercomputation is supposed to violate is the CTT, which is not a law, but, as was already explained, an hypothesis. In addition, it is common knowledge that an hypothesis cannot be "confirmed", because there is always the possibility that a future experiment will show that it is false. Therefore, even proponents of the CTT agree that it is, at least in principle, possible, although quite unlikely, at least for them, that one day the CTT may be falsified.

As was stated in Section 2.5, Kalmár, Péter, and Porte questioned the equivalence between recursive functions and computable functions.[9,10,11] In particular, Kalmár had argued than the class of recursive functions is a proper subclass of the functions that can actually be computed. On the other hand, Péter had claimed quite the opposite, that is, that the class of recursive functions is broader than the class of computable functions. Also, Porte had proved that there are recursive functions $f(z)$ such that, for any recursive function $g(x)$, there exist infinitely many numbers x in the range of f such that, for any argument z_0 with $f(z_0) = x$, the number of steps necessary to compute $f(z_0)$ exceeds the value of $g(x)$. Assume that g grows very fast, say

$$g(x) = 100^{100^{100^x}}$$

Then, according to Porte, the computation of $f(z_0)$ is humanly non-computable since it cannot be carried out within the life-span of a human being. And from this, Porte had concluded that the recursive function f is humanly non-computable. An immediate objection to this argument is that *humanly* computable is not the same as computable. Thus, the decimal representation of the number π is *computable*,[12] but it is not humanly computable. In spite of this, I have briefly discussed on page 164 the fact that the number π can be physically represented. So in a way here humanly computable and computable mean exactly the same thing. Still, I think that Porte's argument is valid because no one has the decimal expansion of π but we can compute whichever digit we want, provided there is enough free time. An interesting question is this: Since the decimal representation of π is computable, is it possible to answer Ludwig Josef Johann Wittgenstein's problem, that is, whether there are three consecutive 7's in the

---

[9]László Kalmár. An argument against the plausibility of Church's thesis. In Arend Heyting, editor, *Constructivity in Mathematics*, pp. 72–80, North-Holland, Amsterdam, 1959.

[10]Rózsa Péter. *Rekursivität und Konstruktivität*. In Arend Heyting, editor, *Constructivity in Mathematics*, pp. 226–233, North-Holland, Amsterdam, 1959.

[11]Jean Porte. *Quelques pseudo-paradoxes de la "calculabilité effective"*. In Actes du 2me Congrès International de Cybernetique, Namur, [Belgium], June 1956, pp. 332–334, Gauthier-Villars, Paris, 1958.

[12]Recall that the number π is computable since one can compute its nth digit, but (classically) it is not possible to have its decimal expansion in a finite amount of time.

decimal expansion of π? Not so surprisingly, the answer is no, because, according to the established view, it is not possible to have the decimal expansion of π. But if Wittgenstein's problem is not computable, why is $f(z_0)$ computable?

As was explained in the previous section, it is quite possible to solve problems that seem to be impossible under specific conditions. Thus, one could argue that although the halting problem is non-computable when computable means Turing computable, it might be computable when computable means something different. But are there such different notions of computation? In 1965, Hilary Whitehall Putnam and Mark Gold independently proposed a model of computation that is now known as *trial-and-error* machines.[13,14] These conceptual machines compute in the limit, that is, if a machine has to determine whether an element x belongs to a set X of natural numbers, it continuously prints out a sequence of responses (e.g., a sequence of 1's and 0's) and the last one is always the correct one. Trial-and-error machines can solve problems that are as hard as Riemann's hypothesis.

Martin David Davis, a student of Church and a polemic of hypercomputation, in an obvious effort to diminish the importance of trial-and-error machines, has stated that "[i]t is generally understood that in order for a computational result to be useful one must be able to at least recognize that it is indeed the result sought".[15] Unfortunately, Davis intensionally forgets that that the trial-and-error method is a general problem solving and/or knowledge acquisition method. Indeed, humans solve problems and learn new things by subconsciously employing this method. Furthermore, Gold started the field of *algorithmic learning theory* by proposing the "learning in the limit" concept, which of course is based on his work on trial-and-error machines.[16]

A conceptual computing device similar to trial-and-error machines was proposed by Kaarlo Jaakko Juhani Hintikka and Arto Mutanen.[17] This conceptual computing machine is called a *TAE-machine*. Each machine is equipped with two tapes, a working tape and a book-keeping (result-recording) tape, and a scanning head that prints on and delete from either tape. The information that is printed on the book-keeping tape can be assumed to be equations of the form $f(a) = b$, where a and b are natural numbers. These equations are used to define the function that the machine is supposed to compute. Clearly, one would be able to say that the machine computes function f if and only if all such true equations appear on the tape when the machine stops. And of course, at

[13] Hilary Putnam. *Trial and error predicates and the solution to a problem of mostowski.* Journal of Symbolic Logic, 30(1), pp. 49–57, 1965.

[14] E. Mark Gold. *em limiting recursion.* Journal of Symbolic Logic, 30(1), pp. 28–48, 1965.

[15] Martin Davis. The Church-Turing thesis: consensus and opposition. In Arnold Beckmann, Ulrich Berger, John V. Tucker, and Benedikt Löwe, editors, *CiE 2006*, volume 3988 of *Lecture Notes in Computer Science*, pp. 125–132. Springer, Berlin, 2006.

[16] E. Mark Gold. *Language identification in the limit.* Information and Control, 10, pp. 447–474, 1967.

[17] Jaako Hintikka and Arto Mutanen. *An alternative concept of computability.* In *Language, Truth and Logic in Mathematics*, pp. 175–188. Kluwer Academic Publishers, Dordrecht, the Netherlands, 1997.

the end only one equation of the form $f(a) = b$ must eventually be on the result tape for any given a from that point onwards. If no equation of this form appears on the result tape for a given a or if the equation keeps changing repeatedly, this means that $f(a)$ is not defined. TAE-machines have the capability to solve "semi-solvable" problems. Thus, they extend the notion of computation and clearly falsify the CTT. Surprisingly, there is a connection between TAE-machines and quantum computing:

> It appears that a quantum computation could in principle carry out all the alternative constructions (calculations) at the same time. If so, quantum computation could in principle facilitate (speed up) TAE-computations significantly.

The authors here refer to quantum parallelism (i.e., the ability of a quantum machine to perform simultaneously many computations at no cost).

Turing, in his doctoral dissertation,[18] considered a new kind of machine that he called *o-machines* (these are the oracle machines we discussed in Section 2.4). Here is how he described these "new" machines:

> Let us suppose that we are supplied with some unspecified means of solving number theoretic problem; a kid of oracle as it were. We will not go any further into the nature of this oracle that to say that it cannot be a machine. With the help of the oracle we could form a new kind of machine (call them o-machines), having as one of its fundamental processes that of solving a given number theoretic problem. More definitely these machines are to behave in this way. The moves of the machine are determined as usual by a table except in the case of moves from a certain internal configuration o. If the machine is in the internal configuration o and if the sequence of symbols marked with ℓ is then the well formed formula $\underline{A}$, then the machine goes into the internal configuration $\mathfrak{d}$ or $\mathfrak{n}$. The decision as to which is the case is referred to the oracle.
>
> These machines may be described by tables of the same kind as used for the description of a-machines, there being no entries, however, for the internal configuration o. We obtain description numbers from these tables in the same way as before. If we make the convention that in assigning numbers to internal configurations o, $\mathfrak{d}$, $\mathfrak{n}$ are always to be q_2, q_3, q_4, then the description numbers determine the behavior of the machines uniquely.

As we saw on page 40, an oracle machine is a Turing machine that is able to consult an external agent, called an oracle, when computing. When the machine has to decide whether an element belongs or not to some set, the oracle provides the machine with an answer to this question. Clearly, such a machine can answer many other questions.

---

[18] Alan Turing. *Systems of logic based on ordinals*. Proceedings of the London Mathematical Society, s2-45(1), pp. 161–228, 1939.

For example, it can decide whether a specific universal Turing machine will halt or not. Think of a Turing machine and the set of input values (i.e., the symbols printed on the tape) for which the machine terminates. Then, an oracle machine can determine whether an ordinary machine with a specific input value will terminate or not.

In 1999, Brian Jack Copeland and Diane Proudfoot published an article in *Scientific American* in which they discussed Turing's "forgotten ideas" in computer science.[19] In this article, the authors introduced the term *hypercomputation* and discussed the computational power of oracle machines. Although oracle machines are clearly hypermachines, still the question is whether there are physical oracles that can answer the questions the ideal oracles are supposed to answer. There are two responses to this question. According to the first one, it is possible to use random events as oracles.[20] For example, one could use some quantum phenomena as the output produced by some oracle. Of course, the question "how a random event gives an answer to a concrete question?" is left unanswered! In addition, this presupposes that somehow computation is a natural phenomenon, which is not universally accepted (I will say more on this in a while). Regardless of this, the real point of hypercomputation is that we know too little to be able to say for sure what are the limits of computation. Surprisingly, in the history of science, whenever people have expressed their deep belief that we have reached the *end of science*, something happened that made us realize that we are far from the end.

Although, TAE-machines and trial-and-error machines are more powerful than Turing machines, still for these machines, and, in fact for every other real or conceptual machine, there are limits to what they can achieve. In fact, Toby Ord and Tien D. Kieu have shown that any machine cannot solve its own halting problem.[21] Thus, even if we can build more powerful machines, always these machines will not be able to solve their own halting problem. On a broader perspective, it is quite natural to see the Turing machine to fail to solve its own halting problem. Consequently, the halting problem does not mean that one cannot build more powerful machines. Instead it means that the Turing machine cannot solve its own halting problem and nothing more! Provided there are limits to what can be achieved computationally, there is at least one problem that is ultimately non-computable. Of course that is the halting problem of the most powerful machine.

[19] B. Jack Copeland and Diane Proudfoot. *Alan Turing's forgotten ideas in computer science*, Scientific American, 280(4), pp. 98–103, April 1999.
[20] Florent Franchette. *Oracle hypermachines faced with the verification problem*. In Gordana Dodig-Crnkovic and Raffaela Giovagnoli, editors, *Computing Nature: Turing Centenary Perspective*, pp. 213–223. Springer, Berlin, 2013.
[21] Toby Ord and Tien D. Kieu. *The diagonal method and hypercomputation*. The British Journal for the Philosophy of Science, 56(1), pp. 147–156, 2005.

3.3   The Mind as a Hypercomputer

Roger Penrose has argued that the real reason why there are problems that cannot be solved by Turing machines, yet they are solvable by other means, is Gödel's theorems (see Section 2.2). In particular, Penrose concluded that Turing machines cannot reach the capabilities of the human mind since they are "realizations" of formal systems. This implies that humans are able to solve problems no Turing machine can solve. But this is not the only theory on the "computational" power of the human mind.[22] In fact, this is an argument that was first put forth by John R. Lucas. That is why it is called the Lucas–Penrose argument and it is one of the four "schools of thought" in the philosophy of hyperminds (roughly, the idea that minds can do more than machines).

Selmer Bringsjord and Michael Zenzen have defended the idea that the mind is a hypercomputer, while there are aspects of its functionality that cannot be mechanically realized though they can be simulated.[23] More specifically, *supermentalism* is about the idea that the mind has hypercomputational capabilities while it also has capabilities that are explained by "phenomena not capturable in any third-person scheme". On the other hand, Copeland[24] believes also that minds are hypermachines, but he has argued that minds are realizable by hypermachines, that is, one can create a symbol processing device that transcends the capabilities of the Turing machine though they operate under the same principles. This is exactly a version of *mechanism*, that is, the idea that our mind is a machine, something like a clock.

A fourth view lies somewhere in the middle: we will eventually be able to build minds but their architecture will be radically different from the technologies employed to build digital computers today. After all, minds are machines, not clocks but biological machines. In a sense, this view is an extension of John Rogers Searle's *biological naturalism*. Personally, I favor this idea. I was convinced by Searle's *Chinese room argument* (CRA) while I was also convinced that the CTT cannot possibly be true. In brief, the CRA goes as follows: Imagine that Renate, who cannot speak or read Chinese, is locked in a room with boxes full of Chinese ideograms. In addition, she has at her disposal a rule book that enables her to answer questions put to her in Chinese. One may think of the rule book as a computer program. Renate receives ideograms that, unknown to her, are questions; she looks up in the rule book what she is supposed to do; she picks up ideograms from the boxes, manipulates them according to the

---

[22] Roger Penrose. *The Road to Reality: A Complete Guide to the Laws of the Universe.* Alfred A. Knopf, New York, 2005.

[23] Selmer Bringsjord and Michael Zenzen. *Superminds: People Harness Hypercomputation, and More.* Kluwer Academic Publishers, Dordrecht, 2003.

[24] Brian Jack Copeland. Narrow versus wide mechanism. In Matthias Scheutz, editor, *Computationalism: New Directions*, pp. 59–86. The MIT Press, Boston, 2002.

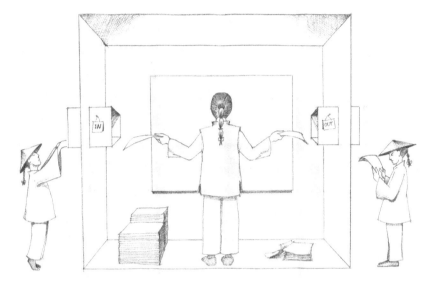

Figure 3.1: An artist's impression of the Chinese room argument. © Yiannis Kontovos.

rules in the rule book, and hands out the required ideograms, which are interpreted as answers. We may suppose that Renate is able to fool an external observer, giving the impression that she actually speaks and understands Chinese. But clearly, Renate does not understand a word of Chinese. And if Renate does not understand although she appears to do so, then no computer will actually understand Chinese just because it is equipped with a computer program much like Renate's rule book. Thus, Turing machines cannot be intelligent. Ergo, human minds are hypercomputers! Figure 3.1 shows an artist's impression of the CRA. The CRA can be formulated using the following syllogism:

(i) Programs are entirely syntactic.
(ii) Minds have semantics.
(iii) Syntax is not the same as, nor by itself sufficient for, semantics.
∴ Programs are not minds.

Computation is a symbol manipulation process. Moreover, it does not matter if we manipulate symbols on paper or electronically. And this is exactly what the first point is about. The second point is about the fact that people do use words (i.e., sequences of symbols) to communicate but these words have meanings attached to them. And that is why I cannot think in Chinese, while I have no problem thinking in Greek and in English. The meaning of the third point is that no matter how well a system imitates someone who does understand a language, the system does not understand it! Then, the conclusion follows quite naturally. It makes sense to state that

$$\frac{\text{Mind}}{\text{Brain}} \neq \frac{\text{Program}}{\text{Hardware}}$$

Based on my own experience, many people are using automatic translation tools especially when they need to know the meaning of a text in some language they do not speak. In most cases, the translations are not good (e.g., no one would trust such a tool to automatically translate subtitles of a movie) while, in some cases, they are acceptable (translation of short phrases). As a demonstration of the validity of this claim, I have used the translation tool of a well-known web search machine to translate the following text into Greek:

> The Greek government is bracing itself for violence ahead of the European Union implementing a landmark deal that, from Monday, will see Syrian refugees and migrants being deported back to Turkey en masse.

Then, I used the same tool to translate the generated text back to English:

> The Greek government prepares for violence ahead of the European Union implement a -orosimo agreement, from Monday, will see Syrian refugees and immigrants to be deported back to Turkey en masse.

The problem here, as I see it, is that the machine ignores the meaning of the words and performs the translation based on dictionaries and phrase tables. However, it has been claimed that these translation tools are static in nature, that is, their "vocabulary" is not enriched or adapted. Thus, these machines do not learn, something that is crucial for physical translator. Now suppose that somehow we solve this problem and make these tools able to learn, would anyone trust them to translate movie subtitles? The answer is again no because spoken language is quite different from written. For example, a speaker may make a gesture or a grimace to convey a special meaning to her words. Does this mean that we will never be able to have a perfect translation tool much like *Star Trek's* universal translator? This is supposed to be a device that translates spoken languages in actual conversations. The device is supposed to operate by scanning the electrical activity of the speaker's brain and using the results to create a basis for translation. Although this is pure fantasy, still this universal translator is trying to attach meaning to spoken words so as to provide a meaningful translation. An answer to the previous questions would be the following: People will be able to create perfect translators when we will be able to realize an orgasm! Jaak Panksepp, the father of *affective neuroscience*, says something similar to people who were stuck in the view that everything in the brain is computable. In particular, he used to ask them: Could you compute me an orgasm? I am sure no one could or can do it!

Davis had something to say about hyperminds. In particular, he wondered: "[h]ow finite brains are to manifest the necessarily infinite capability implied by the word 'hypercomputer' is never made clear". A direct response to this "objection" is that certain mathematical statements, whose resolution was supposed to involve infinities, have been solved without employing any infinity at all. On the other hand, mathematicians constantly reason and argue about "infinities" when they prove results about infinite *ordinals* and *cardinals* yet these infinities fit well in sheets of normal paper![25]

A third response involves a relativistic computer operating near a *Kerr black hole.* Roughly, one may say that a black hole is a dead star or better a star that has no more fuel to burn. In fact, a star that has three times the mass of our sun, will become a black hole whose "diameter" is given by the following formula:

$$R_{\text{Schwarzschild}} = \frac{2MG}{c^2} \tag{3.2}$$

where G is Newton's gravitational constant (6.673×10^{-11} Newton $\cdot$ meter$^2 \cdot$ kg^{-2}) and c is the speed of light ($299{,}792{,}458$ meters/second). For example, an object having mass 100 kg, would produce a black hole whose Schwarzschild's radius would be 148.2 zeptometer (1 zeptometer $= 10^{-21}$ meters). This radius is known in the literature as *Schwarzschild radius,* named after the German astronomer and physicist Karl Schwarzschild. A black hole is so dense that its gravity pulls so much that even light cannot escape it. Because of this, black holes are not visible. Astronomers detect black holes by observing how their gravity affects the stars and gas around it. The *event horizon* of a black hole is a sphere that marks its limits. A black hole that does not rotate is called a Schwarzschild black hole while a rotating one is called a Kerr black hole. A Kerr black hole has a second, inner event horizon, which is not seen by an external observer. However, the inner horizon hides the *singularity,* that is, the place where the space–time collapses, from the observer that has already crossed the outer event horizon.

The fabric of the universe is called *space–time.* However, an alternative definition of space–time follows:

Definition 3.3.1 Space–time is the ontological sum of all events and all things.

This view has been mathematically formalized, nevertheless, I plan not to further discuss it here so the interested reader should consult the literature for more information.[26]

---

[25]A *cardinal* number is a number that says how many elements a set has. The cardinality of the set of natural numbers (an infinite set) is denoted by $\aleph_0$ (pronounced *aleph zero*). Naturally, there are bigger *alephs.* An *ordinal* number is a number that tells the position of something in a list. Thus, the "last" element of the set of natural numbers is the infinite ordinal ω.

[26]Santiago Esteban Perez-Bergliaffa, Gustavo Esteban Romero, and Héctor Vucetich. *Toward an axiomatic pregeometry of space–time.* International Journal of Theoretical Physics, 37(8), pp. 2281–2298, 1998.

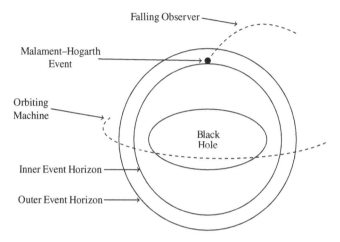

Figure 3.2:   The three-dimensional setup of a relativistic computer.

There are proposals aiming to solve non-computable problems with the use of some "infinities", but these are not infinities as most people perceive them. In particular, Gábor Etesi and István Németi[27] have proposed a realistic though not technologically feasible, at least, at the moment, method to solve the halting problem. This method involves a supertask, that is, a task that involves an infinite number of steps that finish in a finite amount of time. Etesi and Németi have shown that this is possible in a particular *space–time* that happens to be between the outer and inner event horizons of a charged or a rotating black hole. This space–time is known in the literature as Malament–Hogarth space–time. Figure 3.2 shows exactly the setup of this method. In particular, there is a machine that orbits the black hole and an observer who enters the outer event horizon. While the observer travels in space between the two event horizons, she can perform infinite operations and thus she can solve problems that involve some sort of infinity. When the observer will reach the Malament–Hogarth event, then it is sure that an infinity of things happened in a finite amount of time. Naturally, the observer has received the answer she was seeking. Of course, one can object by saying that no machine can last for ever, but that is not the point here. The problem is that one claims that finite minds cannot handle infinities, which is clearly not true!

3.4   Turing Machines and Modern Computers

Most people assume that modern digital computers are some sort of universal Turing machines. Roughly one could argue in favor of this idea simply because modern

---

[27] Gábor Etesi and István Németi. *Non-turing computations via malament-hogart-space-times.* International Journal of Theoretical Physics, 41(2), pp. 341–370, 2002.

computers can run programs, which can be viewed as ordinary Turing machines. In addition, computers have a fixed set of instructions that are used to implement any computer program. However, Turing machines cannot interact with their environment while programs can interact with users, in particular, or the environment, in general (e.g., think of a computer that waters plants). Also, a universal machine has a fixed set of commands that it executes with different input while different programs contain different commands and clearly different input. Thus there is a remote similarity between universal machines and modern computers. But why is interaction so important?

The late Arthur John Robin Gorell Milner was a very important figure in the history of computer science. Milner is known for his work on the design and implementation of ML ("metalanguage"), a computer programming language developed for implementing an automatic theorem solver, and his work on concurrency theory. This theory is about the execution of computer tasks at the same time. This might mean that they are executed simultaneously or that they are executed one after the other in an unpredictable way. In his work, Milner realized that interaction is a primitive notion. In fact, he realized that it is more primitive than the read–write operation of Turing machines. What is even more important is that most computer users perform many tasks that are not computational in nature yet they highly depend on interaction. For example, when someone chats with somebody else using some sort of chat service, there is no traditional computation involved. Similarly, when we use a web browser to visit a web page, there is no traditional computation involved. Thus there are many "computational" tasks that are not computational at all yet they are very important. Despite these clear facts, it has been suggested that web servers and other similar programs compute bizarre, huge, unwieldy functions. The problem with this approach is that one can say that walls, chairs, and even fish tanks compute also such functions. However, one should notice that a web server may crash or stop working due to reasons beyond our control. For example, when a web administrator is shutting down the server for maintenance such termination happens. Also, a web server may crash because someone has hacked it or because there was a long power failure. Of course, one might argue that these events act like oracles to the computation the web server is performing. What is left is to see what is the result of these computations!

When a kid is using an abacus, then most people would agree that the kid is doing some arithmetic operation. Now, if a bonobo (*Pan paniscus*) is playing with an abacus, I think most people will agree that the bonobo is not doing an arithmetic operation. The reason for this distinction lies in the idea that we perceive the actions of the kid as some sort of computation while the same does not hold true for the bonobo. This is exactly the reason why I advocate the idea that computation is not a physical phenomenon. Only a conscious being with some mathematical maturity can set up a physical process so as to perform some sort of computation. In different words, I advocate the that computing is not discovered in nature but people either use naturally occurring phenomena (e.g., the movement of the *Physarum*) or build computing devices or systems in order to perform computations. One could say that an interactive system consists of simple parts that are actually some sort of Turing machine. However, as I have pointed out, a Turing machine is not able to interact with its environment. In particular, exchanging information that travels through a communication channel. Clearly, this operation is not one that can be realized by storage read/write operations. Of course, one can construct a simulation of what happens during a communication process. However, here the point is that the simulation of a quantum computer on conventional hardware does not imply that the simulation will be able to achieve quantum parallelism inside non-quantum hardware! Think that, this is exactly the reason why Richard Phillips Feynman proposed quantum computers. I will say more on this in Section 5.4.

In Section 2.4, I showed that the Gödel number of a Turing machine is a very big number. In order to print such numbers on the tape of a Turing machine, one may need decades or even centuries! Recall that for the Turing machine that computes the sum of two natural numbers, we will need $2^{2490862226078016000000} \times 3^{6027271559398656000} \times 5^{195283598524516454400} \times 7^{1181345225642136576000} \times 11^{956889632770130626560000}$ cells to write its Gödel number. A typical Turing machine may have a few such expressions, which means that its Gödel number is an incredibly big number. Practically, this means that no one can actually construct a universal Turing machine! Selim G. Akl went a step further and questioned the existence of universal machines.[28,29] Naturally, this idea should not surprise anyone mainly because we know that not all conceptual computing devices have a universal counterpart (later we will see that there is no universal fuzzy Turing machine). Akl's argument is based on the idea that a machine can be characterized as universal only when it can perform an infinite number of operations per step. In different words, only a machine be able to perform supertasks that can be characterized as a universal machine. The heart of Akl's argument is very simple. Imagine that you have n robots that are roaming on the surface of planet Mars. At specific moments, each robot sends back to Earth its coordinates $c_i(t) = (x_i(t), y_i(t))$. These coordinates are used to compute the distance d_i to a specific location $L(t)$ using a function F_i. A Turing machine cannot compute all the F_i simply because by the time $c_0(t)$ is placed on the tape, we are at time $t + 1$ at least. This means that the universal machine is far too slow to perform any computation at all. In fact, it is an idealization and as such it cannot actually exist.

---

[28] Selim G. Akl. *Three counterexamples to dispel the myth of the universal computer.* Parallel Processing Letters, 16, pp. 381–403, 2006.
[29] Selim G. Akl. *Even accelerating machines are not universal.* International Journal of Unconventional Computing, 3, pp. 105–121, 2007.

3.5   Quantum Computers and Hypercomputation

Quantum computing is a method of computation that exploits the properties of matter at the quantum level. This method of computation is particularly interesting since it can be used to solve difficult problems. For instance, it has been argued that quantum computers can solve some problems in a few months while ordinary computers can solve the same problem in few millions years (see Section 5.9). However, it was argued that quantum computers can solve non-computable problems. The peculiarities of quantum computing as well as its ability to quickly solve difficult problems will be discussed in Chapter 5. Here I will try to see if quantum computers can be used to solve non-computable problems.

To the best of my knowledge, Tien D. Kieu was the first researcher who proposed that quantum computers can be used to solve non-computable problems![30] In particular, Kieu proposed a method by which one can solve any Diophantine equation. In Chapter 2, we explained why it is impossible to devise a method in order to solved any Diophantine equation. Clearly, this is an oxymoron: one claims that has a solution to a problem that cannot be solved. However, as I have explained in Section 3.1, there are unsolvable problems that become solvable once we relax or alter certain restrictions imposed.

Kieu's solution relies on adiabatic quantum computing. What is really interesting, at least to this author, is the fact that the first commercial quantum computer was an adiabatic quantum computer. This computer was built by D-Wave, a Canadian technology company. Recently, D-Wave built a machine that exploits the *quantum annealing* metaheuristic for solving optimization problems.[31] In particular, quantum annealing is a very similar approach to quantum computation that differs from adiabatic quantum computing. First, the evolution is not required to be adiabatic and second the final Hamiltonian is restricted to a certain form (i.e., is has to be diagonal in the computation basis), with a ground state representing the solution to a difficult optimization problem.

There are some people who do not believe that D-Wave has actually managed to build a quantum computer that actually works. However, even today, there are people who do believe that Earth is flat and of course this does not mean they are right. Certainly, this is not a knockout argument but when technology giants and space exploration organizations buy such expensive machines, it follows that these computers must be able to do what they manufacturers promise they can do. As regards Kieu's method, there are many objections which I will not discuss them here. However, I found one objection that was put forth by Davis. The argument goes as follows:

---

[30] Tien D. Kieu. *Computing the non-computable.* Contemporary Physics, 44(1), pp. 51–71, 2003.

[31] A.B. Finnila, M.A. Gomez, C. Sebenik, C. Stenson, and J.D. Doll. *Quantum annealing: A new method for minimizing multidimensional functions.* Chemical Physics Letters, 219(5–6), pp. 343–348, 1994.

Now, evidently there are equations that have positive integer solutions, but for which the least such solution is enormous, for example so large, that to write the numbers in decimal notation would require a space larger than the diameter of our galaxy! In what sense could such numbers be read off a piece of equipment occupying a small part of our small planet? And how can we suppose that it would be feasible to substitute numbers of such magnitude into an equation and to carry out the arithmetic needed to determine whether they satisfy the equation?

A naïve answer to this questions is that if there are universal machines that can read these extremely huge numbers, then obviously there are machines that can read the integer solutions of Diophantine equations! Now, assume that this argument is valid. Then, clearly, Porte's argument is also valid and the CTT is invalid!

Third, it has been argued that adiabatic quantum computers are able to solve computationally hard problems.[32] This may imply that even complexity theory might be somehow flawed, which makes sense since complexity theory is based on the properties and the capabilities of the Turing machine.

3.6   Closing Remarks

In this chapter, I have tried to introduce hypercomputation and to briefly address a number of objections against hypercomputation. My aim was to show that hypercomputation is feasible and meaningful. Of course, this does not mean that one can go to a computer store and buy a hypercomputer today, though there are efforts to build such machines. Nevertheless, the important point is that the hypercomputational proposals and the arguments in favor of hypercomputation have revealed that the CTT poses an arbitrary limit to what can be actually computed. As we will see in the next chapter, we know so little about our cosmos and the way it "operates" that it is almost hubris to claim that we know what can and what cannot be computed.

Annotated Bibliography

- Selmer Bringsjord and Michael Zenzen. *Superminds: People Harness Hypercomputation, and More.* Kluwer Academic Publishers, Dordrecht, 2003.

This is a book that describes in detail Bringsjord's thesis about minds and their capabilities. He assumes that since souls exists there are capabilities that cannot be mechanized. Naturally, the book is based on his work and ideas.

---

[32] Neil G Dickson. *Elimination of perturbative crossings in adiabatic quantum optimization.* New Journal of Physics, 13(7), p. 073011, 2011.

- Mark Burgin. *Super-Recursive Algorithms*. Springer, New York, 2005.

  Inductive Turing machines are conceptual computing devices with hypercomputational capabilities that have been introduced by Mark Burgin and they are described in detail in this monograph. In addition, the book contains brief presentations of many approaches to hypercomputation. Also, the book introduces the notion of *sub-recursive* processes and their applications.

- John Earman. *Bangs, Crunches, Whimpers, and Shrieks*. Oxford University Press, New York, 1995.

  This book is about "phenomena" whose theoretical basis is the general theory of relativity (GTR). In particular, the book discusses singularities, cosmic censorship, supertasks, and time travel. Although many people are familiar with these "phenomena", this book tries to explain whether they are feasible and what are their consequences. The book assumes some familiarity with the mathematical formalism of the GTR.

- Robert Geroch. *General Relativity from A to B*. The University of Chicago Press, Chicago, 1981.

  A little book that introduces the basic ideas of the GTR. Since many ideas that the GTR has introduced are somehow counterintuitive, the book tries to introduce them by introducing ideas that gradually led to them.

- Gustavo E. Romero and Gabriela S. Vila. *Introduction to Black Hole Astrophysics*, volume 876 of *Lecture Notes in Physics*. Springer, Heidelberg, 2014.

  This is a very interesting introduction to the theory of black holes. It even contains a discussion of the prospects of detecting gravitational waves (the book was published before the announcement of the discovery of gravitational waves).

- John R. Searle. *Mind: A Brief Introduction*. Oxford University Press, Oxford, 2004.

  A book about the philosophy of the mind written by a pioneer of the field. This is a book I would recommend to anyone willing to learn a thing or two about the mind and its philosophy. Naturally, the author "promotes" his own ideas, nevertheless, it gives a balanced overview of most ideas in the field.

- Apostolos Syropoulos. *Hypercomputation: Computing beyond the Church–Turing Barrier*. Springer New York Inc., Secaucus, NJ, USA, 2008.

  This is a book that fully covers the field of hypercomputation. This is a book I wrote so I will not say more about it.

Chapter 4

Natural Computing

A number of researchers and thinkers assume that computing is a natural phenomenon and as such it happens spontaneously in the physical world. One can successfully argue that computation exists just because some intelligent being is able to interpret a sequence of events as computation. This means that computation is not a physical phenomenon and, consequently, does not happen in nature. However, one can "configure" a physical system and then set it in "motion" in order to perform some computational activity that will deliver some result. In what follows, I will explain how one can "configure" DNA molecules, slime mould, cells, and groups of insects or animals, in order to "perform" a computing task.

4.1   DNA Computing

In order to understand how information is encoded in DNA molecules and how these molecules "compute", we need to have a basic understanding of the structure of DNA molecules and their properties.

4.1.1   A Non-technical and Brief Overview of DNA

Most people know that DNA is a molecule that somehow is related to heredity. Also, people know that children inherit the color of their eyes or the color of their hair from the "genes" of their parents. However, scientists now know that a gene is a region of a DNA molecule that forms the molecular unit of heredity.

First of all, "DNA" stands for "Deoxyribo-Nucleic Acid", which means that DNA is some sort of acid. DNA molecules are found in cell nuclei and are condensed into *chromosomes*. The DNA molecule was first observed by the Swiss biochemist

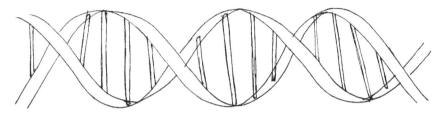

Figure 4.1: A DNA double helix.

Frederich Miescher in the late 1800s. Our bodies contain trillions of cells and DNA molecules are the operation centers of each and every cell. DNA molecules are like the controlling device of a Turing machine. A DNA molecule is very long and it consists of two strands that coil around each other to make a *double helix* or double spiral (see Figure 4.1). Each one of the two strands is made up of *nucleotides* that form hydrogen bonds with nucleotides of the complementary strand; these bonds are the basis of the secondary structure of DNA, the famous double helix. The nucleotides are relatively complex molecules that are made of three parts: a sugar, a phosphate (i.e., a compound that contains one phosphorus and four oxygen molecules), and a nitrogenous base. There are four different nitrogenous bases in all known DNA molecules: adenine (A), guanine (G), cytosine (C), and thymine (T). Consequently, there are four different types of nucleotides. Each base can form a bond with only one base. In particular, base A can form a bond with base T and base G with base C. Thus, if we have a double helix and we choose a specific nucleotide on the left strand, then if it has an A base, the corresponding nucleotide on the right strand will be nucleotide with a T base (see Figure 4.2). This pairing mechanism is called the *Watson–Crick complementarity*. James Dewey Watson is an American zoologist and molecular biologist who codiscovered the structure of DNA with the British molecular biologist Francis Harry Compton Crick in 1953. For this discovery, Watson, Crick, and Maurice Hugh Frederick Wilkins were awarded the Nobel Prize for Physiology or Medicine in 1962.

DNA is used to synthesize proteins, that is, DNA is used to specify the composition and structure of protein molecules. A DNA molecule contains many *genes* along its length. Genes do not have fixed length and one gene might be longer than another one. Now genes are like programs that tell the cell in which particular order to assemble *amino acids*. The order of amino acids in a protein is determined by the order of nucleotides in the corresponding part of a DNA molecule. There are 20 amino acids and each one is specified by three nucleotides. For example, "TTT" specifies phenylalanine and "AAA" specifies lysine. Interestingly, only a small part of the long DNA molecule in a chromosome contains instructions to make specific proteins. For example, in humans, this small part is 1–2%, while the rest non-coding region does things we do not currently understand and are the hotspot of ongoing research.

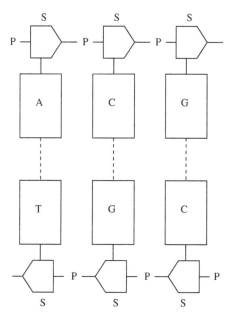

Figure 4.2: Part of a double strand with three nucleotides on each side showing their sugar (S), phosphate (P) and base.

A restriction enzyme is a protein produced by bacteria and archaea[1] and cuts DNA at or near specific nucleotide sequences along the molecule by making incisions through the sugar–phosphate backbone of DNA. Using a restriction enzyme, one can *cut* part of a DNA strand and later using DNA ligase one can *paste* it to another DNA strand. This way one can recombine DNA in order to clone genes, etc.

4.1.2 Computing with DNA Molecules

In 1959, Feynman gave a talk describing the possibility of miniaturizing the computer[2] so as to have wires whose diameter would be 10 or 100 atoms. In a sense, this talk inspired Leonard Max Adleman to create a device that could perform "computations" using DNA molecules. In particular, he used a test tube filled with a solution of DNA molecules to solve the seven-point Hamiltonian path problem.[3]

---

[1]Microorganisms that usually live at high temperatures or produced methane and together with bacteria and eukaryota form the three *domains of life*.
[2]Richard P. Feynman. *There's plenty of room at the bottom.* Engineering and Science, 23(5), pp. 22–36, 1960. Engineering & Science is a publication of the Caltech Office of Public Relations.
[3]Leonard M. Adleman. *Molecular computation of solutions to combinatorial problems.* Science, 266(5187), pp. 1021–1023, 1994.

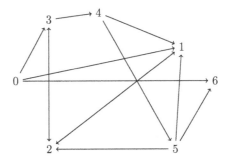

Figure 4.3: A graph with a Hamiltonian path for $v_{in} = 0$ and $v_{out} = 6$.

A graph is a collection of points (*vertices*) of a plane that are connected by lines (*edges*). In a way, a graph is mathematical idealization of a set of connected sites. Sometimes, a graph is directed. This means that most edges are one-way routes from one vertex to another. In this case, the line segments between vertices become arrows that specify the directionality of routes. A double arrow between vertices a and b means that one is allowed to go from a to b and back. Assume, we have a directed graph with two designated vertices v_{in} and v_{out}. Then, the graph has a Hamiltonian path if and only if there exists a sequence of arrows that begins at v_{in}, ends at v_{out}, and passes from all the other vertices exactly one time. The graph depicted in Figure 4.3 has a Hamiltonian path for $v_{in} = 0$ and $v_{out} = 6$ given by $0 \rightarrow 1$, $1 \rightarrow 2$, $2 \rightarrow 3$, $3 \rightarrow 4$, $4 \rightarrow 5$, and $5 \rightarrow 6$. Note that if edge $2 \rightarrow 3$ was not part of the graph, then the resulting graph with same designated vertices would not have a Hamiltonian path. Also, if $v_{in} = 3$ and $v_{out} = 5$, there is no Hamiltonian path (why?).

In general, the problem of deciding whether an arbitrary directed graph with designated vertices has a Hamiltonian path is a difficult problem (recall the discussion in Section 2.6). Thus, all algorithmic solutions to the general problem require a huge amount of computer time in order to say whether the graph has a Hamiltonian path or not. Since this problem is a difficult one, one cannot expect to see a solution that will deliver an answer in polynomial time. However, the following non-deterministic algorithm solves the directed Hamiltonian path problem:

(i) Generate paths in the graph randomly.
(ii) Remove those paths that do not begin with v_{in} and end with v_{out}.
(iii) Remove all paths that have more or less vertices than the total number of vertices of the graph.
(iv) Remove all paths that do not include at least one of the vertices of the graph.
(v) If no path remains, the answer is "No"; otherwise, the answer is "Yes".

Let us now see how this algorithm can be implemented using DNA strands. The first step of the algorithm is realized by associating each vertex i of the graph with a random

DNA sequence O_i that consists of 20 nucleotides. For example, here is how vertices 2, 3, and 4 are encoded:

$$O_2 = TATCGGATCGGTATATCCGA$$
$$O_3 = GCTATTCGAGCTTAAAGCTA$$
$$O_4 = GGCTAGGTACCAGCATGCTT$$

Each vertex O_i can be thought of consisting of two strands having 10 nucleotides. These two strands will be written as $s_i^{(1)}$ and $s_i^{(2)}$. Obviously, $O_j = s_j^{(1)} s_j^{(2)}$. Now, given two vertices i and j, where $i \neq 0$ and $j \neq 6$, the edge $i \rightarrow j$ will be encoded by $s_i^{(2)} s_j^{(1)}$. For example,

$$O_{2 \rightarrow 3} = GTATATCCGAGCTATTCGAG$$

Edges $0 \rightarrow j$ are encoded using the general "formula" $s_j^{(2)} O_0$. Similarly, edges $i \rightarrow 6$ are encoded using the general "formula" $O_6 s_i^{(2)}$. Also, given a "vertex" O_i, the Watson–Crick complementary to it is denoted by $\overline{O}_i$. For example,

if $O_2 = TATCGGATCGGTATATCCGA$, then $\overline{O}_i = ATAGCCTAGCCATATAGGCT$

For $i = 2, 3, 4, 5$, Adleman used 0.66 μg of $\overline{O}_i$ [1 μg is one millionth (1×10^{-6}) of a gram] and 0.66 μg of $O_{i \rightarrow j}$ in a single *ligation reaction*. Roughly, ligation refers to a laboratory procedure where DNA fragments are joined together to create recombinant DNA molecules. Therefore, the ligation reaction creates DNA molecules that encode random paths through the graph. The second step of the algorithm was implemented by amplifying the output of the first step. The amplification was done by a *polymerase chain reaction*, which is a technology that is able to generate thousands to millions of copies of a particular DNA sequence. The polymerase chain reaction used O_0 and $\overline{O}_6$ as *primers*, that is, short nucleotide sequences that are used as starting points for DNA synthesis. The net result of this procedure was that only molecules that encoded paths from 0 to 6 were amplified. In the third step, Adleman used a method to separate a mixed population of DNA in a matrix of *agarose*. This is a polysaccharide polymer material generally extracted from seaweed. In step four, he used a *biotin–avidin magnetic beads system*, which is a biomagnetic separation system, to "purify" the output of step three. In the last step, the result of step four was amplified by a polymerase chain reaction and run on an agarose gel. The whole process took 7 days of laboratory work to complete. In particular, the last step of the process was accomplished in 1 day.

Although this particular problem was relatively easy since even a human could solve it quite quickly, still it showed how one can use DNA strands to compute. However, DNA strands can be used to solve really difficult problems. For example, it was shown that DNA strands can be used to solve the 3-SAT problem with 20 variables (3-SAT is particularly difficult problem that is described in Section 5.7).[4] Both experiments showed that one can use test tubes with DNA strands to solve problems, yet it was not clear if one could build some sort of DNA computer.

4.1.3   DNA Computers

A *finite automaton* can be seen as a Turing machine whose scanning head can read only cells while it can move in only one direction. Initially, the scanning head is positioned on the leftmost cell while a number of symbols are printed on consecutive cells starting with the leftmost cell. Also, the machine enters a default initial state. Each machine is associated with a number of *transition rules*. A transition rule has the general form $q_i \xrightarrow{s} q_j$, where q_i and q_j are states and s some symbol. The meaning of this rule is that if the automaton is in state q_i, it will enter state q_j only if the next symbol is s. When the machine starts, it reads the first symbol and if there is a transition rule that includes this symbol and the current state, then the scanning head moves to the right and the machine enters a new state. If the machine enters the final state, then it accepts the input and terminates. The machine may suspend without completion when no transition rule applies. The alphabet of the machine consists of the letters that the scanning head can recognize. The following figure shows a finite automaton with two states whose alphabet is $\{a, b\}$.

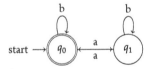

The symbols in the circles are the states, the symbol in the double circle is the accepting state, and the symbols over the arcs are the symbols that the automaton consumes. Thus, this is a compact way to write the various transition rules. This automaton determines if an input sequence of symbols over its alphabet contains an even number of a's. For example, if the input is the sequence "*abba*", then the following table shows what has to be done in order to have this sequence accepted by this automaton.

Current state	Unread characters	Transition rule
q_0	*abba*	$q_0 \xrightarrow{a} q_1$
q_1	*bba*	$q_1 \xrightarrow{b} q_1$
q_1	*ba*	$q_1 \xrightarrow{b} q_1$
q_1	*a*	$q_1 \xrightarrow{a} q_0$
q_0		Input accepted!

[4]Ravinderjit S. Braich, Nickolas Chelyapov, Cliff Johnson, Paul W. K. Rothemund, and Leonard Adleman. *Solution of a 20-variable 3-SAT problem on a DNA computer.* Science, 296, pp. 499–502, 2002.

A team of scientists from the Weizmann Institute of Science, Israel, has managed to devise a DNA-based finite automaton that computes via "repeated cycles of self-assembly and processing".[5] In particular, they managed to implement the automaton presented above using double-stranded DNA molecules that can grow at both ends and which realized both the software and the input/output. The hardware of the automaton consists of DNA restriction and ligation enzymes using ATP, an energy-carrying molecule found in the cells of all living things, as fuel.

Ordinary digital computers are built using digital logical gates and quantum computers are "built" using quantum logical gates; therefore it follows logically that a DNA computer should be "built" using some sort of DNA logical gates. In order to build such gates, one must decide on how to encode "true" and "false" with 13–25 nucleotides. Typically, one can assign truth values if a given section of DNA is present or absent or if it has a forward or reverse orientation. Then, a gate handling DNA data may recombine these data in order to yield the desired result. Milan M. Stojanovic, Tiffany Elizabeth Mitchell, and Darko Stefanovic managed to construct "DNA"-based logic gates.[6] In fact, they have not used DNA but DNA enzymes that are also known as deoxyribozymes. These enzymes function much like other ordinary enzymes by catalyzing specific chemical reactions. A deoxyribozyme is typically an *oligonucleotide* [ὀλίγος (*oligo*) in Greek means few or small] consisting of 13–25 nucleotides. Assuming that an oligonucleotide consists of 17 nucleotides, then one says that this oligonucleotide has a length 17 mer. The name "mer" is derived from the root of the Greek word μέρος (*meros*), which means part. Figure 4.4 depicts the mechanism that underlies the construction of deoxyribozyme-based gates. Here, two oligonucleotides I_A and I_B are the inputs for these logic gates, and a d product oligonucleotide O_F as an output. These gates have been used by Stojanovic and Stefanovic to create MAYA, a DNA-based computer that can play tic-tac-toe.[7] Later on, Joanne Macdonald and her colleagues developed an improved version of MAYA.[8] While MAYA used an array of 23 logic gates, MAYA-II used over 100 logic gates and represented the first "medium-scale integrated molecular circuit".

The aims of *synthetic biology* are the design and construction of new biological parts, devices, and systems and the redesign of existing, natural biological systems for useful purposes. For example, the creation of networks of cells that will process input

[5] Yaakov Benenson, Rivka Adar, Tamar Paz-Elizur, Zvi Livneh, and Ehud Shapiro. *DNA molecule provides a computing machine with both data and fuel*. Proceedings of the National Academy of Sciences, 100(5), pp. 2191–2196, 2003.

[6] Milan N. Stojanovic, Tiffany Elizabeth Mitchell, and Darko Stefanovic. *Deoxyribozyme-based logic gates*. Journal of the American Chemical Society, 124(14), pp. 3555–3561, 2002.

[7] Milan N. Stojanovic and Darko Stefanovic. *A deoxyribozyme-based molecular automaton*. Nature Biotechnology, 21(9), pp. 1069–1074, 2003.

[8] Joanne Macdonald, Yang Li, Marko Sutovic, Harvey Lederman, Kiran Pendri, Wanhong Lu, Benjamin L. Andrews, Darko Stefanovic, and Milan N. Stojanovic. *Medium scale integration of molecular logic gates in an automaton*. Nano Letters, 6(11), pp. 2598–2603, 2006.

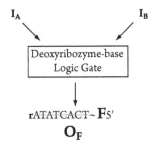

5′ CATTGGTGTTAACTT   5′ CATTGGACATAACTT

I_A I_B

Deoxyribozyme-base
Logic Gate

rATATCACT~ F5′

O_F

Figure 4.4: Basic idea for the construction of deoxyribozyme-based logic gates: input oligonu-cleotides I_A and I_B may yield the output part O_F; this depends on the interactions with deoxyribozyme-based logic gates.

signals for actuation is a central goal of synthetic biology. There have been some efforts to construct artificial logic gates and memory devices, but the problem is that one needs both devices in order to perform complex operations. For instance, memory is necessary when it makes sense to remember previous states of a system. There have been efforts to devise strategies for the construction of circuits in single cells and the same time to have DNA-encoded memory storage.[9] A major advantage of using a DNA-based memory is that it allows long-term storage, since it propagates when cells divide while it is stable even after cell death. This strategy allowed the creation of all 16 two-input Boolean logic functions in living *Escherichia coli* cells without the need to have multiple logic gates. In addition, it was demonstrated that memory can "survive" for at least 90 cell generations. This approach allowed the creation of two-bit digital-to-analog converters. Hopefully, ideas like this one will allow researchers to construct complex cellular state machines, which might be useful for therapeutic and diagnostic applications.

Typically, when people talk about computers, they have on their minds systems that are static whereas when then they talk about robots, they have on their minds artificial systems able to move by themselves. In both cases, the systems are computers, but robots are autonomous or semi-autonomous systems (e.g., think about the rovers on planet Mars). Since there are computing devices based on DNA, is it possible to build DNA-based robots? Of course, any animal is a DNA-based robot, but obviously we are interested in *artificial* and not *natural* devices.

---

[9]For example, see Piro Siuti, John Yazbek, and Timothy K. Lu. *Synthetic circuits integrating logic and memory in living cells.* Nature Biotechnology, 31(5), pp. 448–452, 2013.

DNA origami is technique by which it is possible to create arbitrary shapes using DNA strands. Typically, one uses a long single-stranded DNA, called the scaffold, which is bent into the shape we like by using glue strands, known as staples. The DNA origami technique was developed by Paul Wilhelm Karl Rothemund who managed to bend a viral genome whose length was 7249 mer to a smiley face.[10] Researchers have used cadnano (i.e., an open source tool that simplifies the process or designing DNA origami nanostructures) to create a nanorobot in the form of a hexagonal tube with dimensions of 35 nm × 35 nm × 45 nm. These nanorobots carry a cargo and some external stimulus can trigger the release of the cargo. For example, if these nanorobots could carry drugs or nanoparticles, then they could be used to harm or destroy cancerous cells. Of course, these nanorobots could recognize these cells from their surface proteins. In fact, these researchers have released such nanorobots in a mixture of healthy and cancerous human blood cells, half of the cancer cells were destroyed within 3 days whereas no healthy cells were harmed.[11]

There are many other applications using DNA-based nanorobots. However, it is not my intention to present every possible nanorobot of this kind. The interested reader should consult the bibliography.

4.2   Cellular Computing

DNA is not the only part of living organisms that inspired researchers to devise either real or conceptual models of computation. In this section, we are going to explore cellular computing, which includes membrane computing, amorphous computing, and cellular automata. The inspiration for the cellular computing paradigm is the cell, its properties and the way it lives and functions.

4.2.1   Membrane Computing

Membrane computing was introduced by the Romanian researcher Gheorghe Păun and it was the result of his attempt to formulate a model of computation based on the structure and functioning of a living cell. In particular, cells have a number of organelles that are surrounded by a porous membrane that allows certain *particles* to enter and leave the compartment. Imagine that one builds a hierarchical membrane structure, that is, a membrane that surrounds objects and/or membrane structures. Each such membrane structure may contain objects and/or other smaller membrane structures. It is quite possible that objects that are included in a membrane structure are identical as,

---

[10] Paul W. K. Rothemund. *Folding DNA to create nanoscale shapes and patterns*. Nature, 440(7), pp. 297–302, 2006.
[11] Shawn M. Douglas, Ido Bachelet, and George M. Church. *A logic-gated nanorobot for targeted transport of molecular payloads*. Science, 335(6070), pp. 831–834, 2012.

for example, the three €1 coins that I have in my wallet right now. In mathematics, a collection of possible identical items is called a *multiset* and I will say more about them in a moment. The objects enclosed in a membrane can be changed by a set of *multiset-rewrite* rules. These rules imitate the behavior of the various organelles that input chemical substances (e.g., nutrients) and output other chemical substances (e.g., excrement). The rules are characterized as *multiset* since an organelle may "consume" a number of identical objects and similarly, it may "export" identical objects. Such a device is called a *P system*. Thus, a P system is a closed system divided into compartments that may contain other compartments, where each compartment contains possible indistinguishable objects and there are rules that describe how specific objects can be replaced with others inside or outside a specific compartment. A special compartment called the *output* compartment holds the result of the computation. At the end of computation, that is, when no multiset-rewrite rule is applicable, the result of the computation equals the number of elements that reside inside the output compartment. Mathematically speaking, the result of the computation equals the *cardinality* of the multiset (i.e., the number of elements of the multiset) contained in the output compartment. Typically, the cardinality of a set or multiset B is denoted by $|B|$. Inside a P system, actions do not have their own speed, but they just start and finish at the same time and always follow a specific *clock*. Thus, at each tick of this clock, all operations finish and new ones start. A far more general arrangement of membranes is established when one builds a network of them with communication channels between them. In this case, one talks about *tissue-like* membrane systems.

Multisets

In Section 2.2, I briefly described sets as a collection of pairwise different elements. This simply means that a set contains elements such that no two elements are the same. A multiset is a mathematical structure that "violates" this restriction by allowing repeated elements to be part of it.[12,13] For example, the structure $\{4, 4, 4, 3, 3, 2, 2\}$ is a multiset. There are many cases that can be described by multisets. In general, there is always some "universe" that supplies elements that are used in the construction of multisets. In the case of $\{a, b, b\}$, the "universe" is the English alphabet. Clearly, a string (i.e., a sequence of symbols) is possibly a multiset since it may contain repeated elements (e.g., "lulu" is a multiset). Note that the order of letters in a word representing a multiset is irrelevant. Thus, both lulu and ulul represent the same multiset. The processes in a computer system (the programs running in a computer system, for example) form

---

[12]Apostolos Syropoulos. Mathematics of multisets. In Cristian S. Calude, Gheorghe Păun, Grzegorz Rozenberg, and Arto Salomaa, editors, *Multiset Processing*, volume 2235 in Lecture Notes in Computer Science, pp. 347–358, Springer, Berlin, 2001.
[13]Apostolos Syropoulos. *Categorical models of multisets*. Romanian Journal of Information Science and Technology, 6(3–4), pp. 267–402, 2003.

a multiset. In addition, multisets occur in many mathematical structures, but since explaining these structures is quite involved, I will not discuss them.

The cardinality of a set is the number of its elements. So, the cardinality of the multiset $\{4, 4, 4, 3, 3, 2, 2\}$ is 7 since it contains exactly seven elements. The union of two sets is a new set that includes the common and non-common elements of both sets. The same applies to multisets with one exception: if the multisets A and B have in common some element x and A contains n copies of x and B contains m copies of x, their union contains $\max\{n, m\}$ copies of x. In the case of intersection of two sets, the result is a new set that contains only the common elements while when dealing with multisets, the result is actually a union that contains $\min\{n, m\}$ copies of element x. There is a third operation between multisets that is meaningless for sets. This operation is the sum of two multisets. If multiset A contains n copies of x and B contains m copies of x, then their sum will contain $n + m$ copies of x.

Multiset Rewriting Rules

Let's assume that there is some "universe" O (i.e., a set from which multisets draw their elements) and we build multisets from it. Then, a multiset rewriting rule $x \rightarrow y$ transforms multiset x into y, where both x and y are strings representing multisets. For example, consider the following multiset rewriting rule:

$$aabccc \rightarrow bdddd$$

This rule transforms two copies of a, one copy of b, and three copies of c into four copies of d, while b remains intact (e.g., one can think of b as a *catalyst*). One can apply this rule to the multiset *aaabccccccdd* but not to *abccccccdd* since the former contains as substring the string *aabccc* while the latter does not.

Each P system has a membrane structure that can be seen as a bubbles-inside-bubbles structure, that is, a bubble that contains bubbles which, in turn, contain other bubbles, etc. Figure 4.5 shows a structure that resembles the membrane structure of a P system. Each bubble, or compartment, is associated with a set of multiset rewriting rules whereas it is populated by a possibly repeated number of objects. The rules have the general form $u \rightarrow v$, where u is a string consisting of symbols drawn from the "universe" O and v is a pair consisting of string and a "target designation". This designation is one of the words *here*, *out*, and *in*. The word *here* means that the string part should replace u in the current bubble; the word *out* means that the string will be placed in the bubble that surrounds the current one; and the word *in* means that the string will be sent to any enclosed bubble. In case there is no such bubble, the rule is simply non-applicable. It is possible to replace *in* with in_j where j is a number designating a specific compartment (or bubble in our terminology). This means that when such a rule is applicable, then its application results in the transportation of a specific multiset of objects into a specific compartment. Even more generally, one can

Figure 4.5:   A bubbles-inside-bubbles structure that resembles the membrane structure of a P system.

specify where each of the produced objects should go. Each operation takes place at the tick of a global clock (i.e., the system operates in discrete rather than continuous time). When a system is set up, then for each rule $u \rightarrow v$ associated with compartment h, the following happens:

(i)   Objects present in u in the specified multiplicities are removed from h.
(ii)   Objects present in v in the specified multiplicities are produced.
(iii)   The produced objects are placed either in h or in the specified target designations.

One may consider P systems that "interact" with their environment by exporting objects to the environment while importing other objects from the environment, something very familiar for all living organisms. In this case, we assume that the environment is an endless source of objects. In addition, the rules are now associated with the membrane that surrounds the compartments and not the compartments. This is necessary in order to have rules that import or export objects to the environment.

An interesting question is this: What happens when two or more rules that are associated with a specific compartment are applicable? If you have guessed that there is some order by which rules are applied, then you have guessed wrong. Since in any living organism, many things happen at the same time, in any P system, all rules are applied in parallel. Of course, there is no good way to elaborate on this, but one can see it as some sort of race where each rule is applied until it is not applicable any more.

Each P system has a designated compartment, called the *output* compartment. When no rule is applicable, a P system has ceased to operate and the result of the computation is equal to the number of objects found in the output compartment. In certain cases, one may consider systems that should halt the very moment some compartment is associated with rules that are not applicable any more. In a sense, this means that if one "organ" fails, then the whole "body" fails.

There are a number of extensions to the standard models presented so far. One extension introduces the notion of active membranes. This simply means that a membrane can be dissolved or split after the application of a rule. Also, it is possible to introduce rules that create membranes after the successful application of the rule. In particular, the rule $u \rightarrow v\delta$ replaces the multiset u with the multiset v and then the surrounding membrane dissolves. However, it is not possible to dissolve the membrane that delimits the system itself. The rule $[a]_h \rightarrow [b]_h[c]_h$ is a simple example of one that is used to divide a compartment. Here, a, b, and c are objects while h is the name of a membrane. The rule means that membrane h should split and all a's residing in the first half should be replaced by b's while all a's residing in the second half should be replaced by c's. A rule of the form $a \rightarrow [b]_h$ replaces each occurrence of a with a new membrane that contains a single b. In addition, the rule $[a \rightarrow [b]_h]_g$ will replace each occurrence of a with a singleton compartments containing a b inside membrane g.

The first interesting simulation of P systems was presented in 2003.[14] All previous simulations were implemented by ignoring the parallelism that is supposed to make membrane computing quite interesting. In the 2003 simulation, each compartment was realized by a single computer and the whole system was realized by a network of interconnected computers. In a sense, even the Internet can be viewed as an enormous P system. This simulation was interesting because a good number of people working in the area had used it as a basis to build their own simulations and/or realizations of P systems. In addition, later on, I proposed a very simple computer architecture to realize P systems using these processors.[15] Each processor is used to realize a compartment and a network of these processors realizes a P system.

Since P systems make use of parallelism, they should be able to solve difficult problems just like DNA computers do. However, P systems have not been implemented and they basically are a theoretical model of computation. The literature on P systems is full of ideas but nothing concrete. However, I will say more on P systems when I discuss vagueness and its use in computation.

---

[14] Apostolos Syropoulos, Eleftherios G. Mamatas, Peter C. Allilomes, and Konstantinos T. Sotiriades. A distributed simulation of transition P systems. In Carlos Martín-Vide, Giancarlo Mauri, Gheorghe Păun, Grzegorz Rozenberg, and Arto Salomaa, editors, *Membrane Computing*, volume 2933 of *Lecture Notes in Computer Science*, pp. 357–368. Springer, Berlin, 2004.

[15] Apostolos Syropoulos. *Π Machines: Virtual machines realizing graph structured transition P systems*. ACM SIGPLAN Notices, 42(12), pp. 15–22, 2007.

4.2.2   Amorphous Computing

Mammalian cells have been used as containers in which Boolean logic gates have been synthesized.[16] These gates could be used to create circuits that would be used to construct some sort of cell-based computer. In addition, bioengineered bacteria have been used to build logical gates.[17] The purpose of this project was to build some sort of computer with all these gates, which of course is a step forward. Nevertheless, I think it would be far more interesting to have either tiny computers having the size of a cell or even bioengineered cells that act as computers so as to build some sort of *amorphous* computer [the word amorphous is derived from the ancient Greek word ἄμορφος (ámorphos) that means "shapeless"]. Thus, an amorphous computer should be made of many cell-sized computers that form a network. In a way, these *computational particles* remind me of the nanites of *Stargate Atlantis*.[18] In this fictional world, the nanites were tiny machines that could enter a person's body and do harm or good. Sometime in the plot of the show, these machines collaborated and took human form, becoming the Asurans. Thus, each fictitious Asuran was a collections of nanites. In fact, the people, who introduced the idea of amorphous computing,[19] proposed some sort of smart paint consisting of computational particles that could "sense and report on traffic and wind loads and monitor structural integrity of the bridge. A smart-paint coating on a wall could sense vibrations, monitor the premises for intruders, or cancel noise".

W. Richard Stark proposed[20] a model of amorphous computing where each computational particle is a special automaton that processes multisets instead of single symbols. Initially, cells "know" their neighborhood and their next state depends on this. Later on, they develop links with other cells, which may lead to a global behavior of the collective. It is important to note that we can only program individual cells, everything else is the result of cell interaction.

---

[16]Takafumi Miyamoto, Robert DeRose, Allison Suarez, Tasuku Ueno, Melinda Chen, Tai-ping Sun, Michael J. Wolfgang, Chandrani Mukherjee, David J. Meyers, and Takanari Inoue. *Rapid and orthogonal logic gating with a gibberellin-induced dimerization system*. Nature Chemical Biology, 4, pp. 465–470, 2012.

[17]Martyn Amos, Ilka Maria Axmann, Nils Blüthgen, Fernando de la Cruz, Alfonso Jaramillo, Alfonso Rodriguez-Paton, and Friedrich Simmel. *Bacterial computing with engineered populations*. Philosophical Transactions of the Royal Society of London A: Mathematical, Physical and Engineering Sciences, 373(2046), Paper ID 20140218, 2015.

[18]Stargate Atlantis was a Canadian–American science fiction television series created by Brad Wright and Robert C. Cooper.

[19]Harold Abelson, Don Allen, Daniel Coore, Chris Hanson, George Homsy, Thomas F. Knight, Radhika Nagpal, Erik Rauch, Gerald Jay Sussman, and Ron Weiss. *Amorphous computing*. Communications of the ACM, 43(5), pp. 74–82, 2000.

[20]W. Richard Stark. *Amorphous computing: Examples, mathematics and theory*. Natural Computing, 12(3), pp. 377–392, 2013.

4.2.3   Cellular Automata

Cellular automata are considered as very important modeling and simulation tools in science and technology. They are discrete systems like most of the conceptual computing devices that we have seen so far. The theory of cellular automata is based on the work of Zuse, Stanisław Marcin Ulam, and John von Neumann. In the 1970s, Stephen Wolfram tried to revive cellular automata and, to some degree, their current "success" is due to his work.

When a video camera aims to a monitor that displays the camera's live video image, video feedback takes place. Then one can see that the monitor shows an "endless" repetition of what the camera is shooting. In particular, the monitor shows what the camera is shooting and then the camera shoots this, etc. In simple words, the output of the camera is its input at the same time. In general, systems that exhibit this kind of behavior are called *feedback machines*. Typically, a cellular automaton is a feedback machine that consists of an array of cells. These arrays are either one-dimensional, in which case cells are lined up like a chain, or two-dimensional, in which case cells form a grid. More specifically, they are finite state machines that change the state of their cells step by step. Each cell may enter a finite number of states and Figure 4.6 shows a one-dimensional, two-state automaton. Each cell is either white or black and we can assume that a white cell is an "alive" one while a black cell is a "dead" one. Figure 4.6 shows the evolution of a cellular automaton. The first generation is on the top of the figure and the last one at the bottom of the figure.

In order to run a cellular automaton, we need to know the initial state of the automaton and the set of evolution rules. The line on the top of Figure 4.6 is the initial state. Thus, the next state depends on its current state and the current state of its

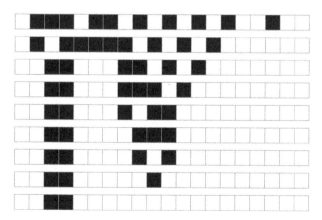

Figure 4.6: Evolution of one-dimensional cellular automaton. Here, each row represents a generation while time's direction is from top to bottom.

neighbors. Assume that a cell stays alive if it has only one alive neighbor, while when both of its neighbors are alive, the cell dies because there are not enough resources to keep it alive. Now, if a dead cell has two alive neighbors, then the cell is resurrected. The first cell of the automaton has no neighbor left, so it seems the rules are not applicable. However, the left neighbor of this cell is the last cell. Similarly, the right neighbor of the last cell is the first cell. This fairly simple "game" can be described by a set of rewriting rules. An evolution rule has the general form $S_l S_c S_r \rightarrow S_c$, where S_c is the state of a cell we are interested in and S_l, S_r the states of its left and right neighbors, respectively. In the following set of evolution rules, "0" means dead and "1" means "alive":

$$000 \rightarrow 0$$

$$001 \rightarrow 0 \quad \text{One neighbor does not give birth}$$

$$010 \rightarrow 0 \quad \text{Dies without enough neighbors}$$

$$011 \rightarrow 1 \quad \text{Needs one neighbor to survive}$$

$$100 \rightarrow 0 \quad \text{One neighbor does not give birth}$$

$$101 \rightarrow 1 \quad \text{Two neighbors give birth}$$

$$110 \rightarrow 1 \quad \text{Needs one neighbor to survive}$$

$$111 \rightarrow 0 \quad \text{Starved to death.}$$

We can create a new "game" if we change what each rule yields. Thus, if we change these rules to yield 0, 1, 0, 1, 1, 0, 1, and 0, correspondingly, then we get a new automaton whose evolution is shown in Figure 4.7. Initially, we start with only one black cell that lies in the middle of automaton. The resulting "image" shows 1026 generations together and it corresponds to the Sierpiński triangle, named after its inventor Wacław Franciszek Sierpiński. The Sierpiński triangle is a *fractal*, that is, an image that exhibits a repeating pattern that displays at every scale. Figure 4.5 on p. 82 is another fractal.

For a two-dimensional cellular automaton, its evolution rules might have the following general form:

$$S_c S_s S_w S_n S_e \rightarrow S_c$$

where the letters "s", "w", "n", and "e" stand for *south, west, north,* and *east*, respectively. It is equally possible to consider all nine neighbors. Two-dimensional cellular automata became particularly popular when John Horton Conway invented a cellular automaton called the *Game of Life*. This is actually a simulation game because it resembles the evolution of a society of living organism. The evolution rules of the Game of Life are based on the following principles:

(i) There should be no way to tell beforehand whether the population can grow without limit.

(ii) It should be possible to set up a system that *apparently* grows with no limit.

Figure 4.7: Evolution of a one-dimensional cellular automaton "producing" the Sierpiński triangle (1026 generations are shown, first generation is shown on the top).

(iii) After some initial growth, a population should fade away, settle into a stable state and remain unchanged thereafter, or it should enter an oscillating phase in which it repeats an infinite cycle of two or more periods.

These rules make sure that the behavior of the population will be interesting and unpredictable. The evolution rules follow:

(i) Every cell that has two or three alive neighbors survives for the next generation.

(ii) A cell that has four or more alive neighbors dies. Also, if a cell has only one neighbor or no neighbors, it dies from isolation.

(iii) A dead cell that has three or more alive neighbors is resurrected.

So far, I presented a system that can be used to make beautiful drawings and/or to play interesting games, nevertheless, nothing has been said about the computational capabilities of cellular automata. Now, Von Neumann applied transition rules a two-dimensional grid where each cell has 29 states and proved the existence of a setup of about 200,000 cells that would self-reproduce. This particular cellular automaton was able to simulate a Turing machine, thus showing that cellular automata are powerful as Turing machines. In addition, the Game of Life can be used to simulate any Turing machine, therefore, the Game of Life is some sort of universal computer!

4.3   *Physarum* Machines

Physarum polycephalum is a slime mold. These organisms exist in at least three distinct life forms. In the first one, *Phsyarum* lives as a slimy yellow mass of protoplasm (i.e., the usually colorless and jelly-like living part of cells) with no specific form. In this form of life, the *Physarum* lives in the dark, it hides under the bark of dead trees, feeds on organic matter and microorganisms and becomes around 30 cm in diameter. But what is really interesting is that it can sense food and crawl towards it like a huge amoeba. For this last property, *Physarum* was considered to be some sort of animal, although even today their place in biosystematics is still disputed. In this life form, *Physarum* is basically a relatively large single cell with thousands of nuclei. These cells are formed when individual cells (amoebae) having one or more whip-like organelles called *flagella* flock together and fuse. The resulting cell contains many *diploid* nuclei. A *haploid* cell contains one complete set of chromosomes (e.g., a spermatozoon is a haploid cell). A diploid cell contains two sets of chromosomes. Thus, a *Physarum* contains the nuclei of many diploid cells. This cellular organization is known as *plasmodium*.

In a second form of life, the *Physarum* consists of a colony of black fruiting bodies that are 1–2 mm tall and have a stalk and a head. This form is responsible for the "polycephalum" part of its name. The word "polycephalum" is a Latinized Greek word that means multiheaded. In a third form of life, the *Physarum* consists of microscopic myxoamoebae that are typically 12–15 μm in diameter. These amoebae hatch from spores that are specialized cells born in the heads of the fruiting bodies.

As was pointed out, *Physarum* crawls towards food. But what happens when it is exposed to two different sources of food? The answer was given by Toshiyuki Nakagaki, Hiroyasu Yamada, and Agota Toth in a one-page paper that was published in 2000.[21] These authors had noticed that when *Physarum* is placed between two points where food is placed, then it will grow out pseudopodia (i.e., temporary projections) so as to connect with the two food sources. In addition, they showed that *Physarum* has the ability to find the minimum-length path between two points in a labyrinth. In particular, they took a growing tip from a large plasmodium and put it in a 25 × 35 cm culture trough and divided it into small pieces. Then, each of these pieces was put in a maze. These pieces managed to grow and find the food placed at the start and the end of the maze.

I have learned about *Physarum* computing while I was skimming through a book catalog that included a book by Andrew Adamatzky. Later on, I found out that he had published many research papers and two books on *Physarum* computing, so in a sense, he is responsible for the popularization of this computing *paradigm*.[22] Adamatzky argues that in a sense, a *Physarum* "computer" is a form of a *chemical* computer. These

---

[21] Toshiyuki Nakagaki, Hiroyasu Yamada, and Agota Toth. *Intelligence: Maze-solving by an amoeboid organism*. Nature, 407, p. 470, 2000.

[22] Thomas S. Kuhn defines as paradigm any achievement that is at the same time sufficiently "unprecedented to attract an enduring group of adherents away from competing modes of scientific activity" and "open-ended to leave all sorts of problems for the redefined group of practitioners to resolve" (see *The Structure of Scientific Revolutions*, 3rd edition. The University of Chicago Press, Chicago, 1996).

computers are using various chemical effects such as the *Marangoni* effect. Situations where a fluid flows from areas of lower surface tension to areas of higher surface tension are manifestations of the Marangoni effect. Surface tension is the property of the surface of a liquid that allows it to resist an external force. A typical example of the Marangoni effect are the so-called wine tears that are produced when the water in a glass of wine moves away from the lower tension alcohol, forming tears on the sides of the glass that slide down. Recently, it was shown that the Marangoni effect can be used to solve maze problems (i.e., finding the shortest route between two points or, more generally, all possible routes).[23] The problem was solved by filling all channels of the maze with a solution of caustic potash and by putting a solution of hydrochloric acid at the exit of the maze. Moments after the addition of the hydrochloric acid solution, a small amount (around 0.3 mg) of phenol (carbolic acid) red dye powder was placed in the liquid. The dye particles moved towards regions having lower pH, thus solving the maze problem!

The first problem solved by a *Physarum* "computer" was a maze problem and obviously chemical computers have been successfully used to solve maze problems too. Thus, this shows the validity of Adamatzky's claim that *Physarum* "computers" are chemical computers. Of course, *Physarum* "computers" involve the use of a living organism, nevertheless, the basic idea involves some sort of chemical stimulus.

Given a set of points of a plane, which are called *sites*, a *Voronoi* diagram is a collection of regions that divide the plane. These diagrams are named after Georgy Feodosevich Voronoy (Георгій Феодосійович Вороний). Each region contains one and only one site while all points in some region are closer to the site of the region than to any other site. An example of a typical use of these diagrams is the Post Office Problem: Given a set of locations where post offices are placed, how do we determine the post office closest to a given house? If we have the Voronoi diagram of the post office locations, then in order to find which post office is closest to a given house, one just has to find to which region the house belongs. More generally, Voronoi diagrams have found many applications in astronomy, anthropology, archeology, meteorology, etc. It has been demonstrated that *Physarum* can be used to approximate a planar Voronoi diagram. In particular, a Voronoi diagram is approximated by a plasmodium by injecting other plasmodia on each site or set of sites. These plasmodia are placed on a nutrient substrate and pseudopodia grow circularly from each site and stop when they collide with each other. The result is an approximation of a Voronoi diagram.

The Kolmogorov–Uspensky machine[24] is a very general model of computation that transcends the capabilities of the Turing machine. The reason is that there is at least one problem that these machines can solve while no Turing machine can solve

---

[23] Kohta Suzuno, Daishin Ueyama, Michal Branicki, Rita Tóth, Artur Braun, and István Lagzi. *Maze solving using fatty acid chemistry*. Langmuir, 30(31), pp. 9251–9255, 2014.

[24] See Apostolos Syropoulos. *Theory of Fuzzy Computation*, pp. 26–33. Springer, New York, 2014.

it. Roughly, one can view a Kolmogorov–Uspensky machine is some sort of graph that is transformed during computation. Now, according to Adamatzky, a *Physarum* "computer" is actually a physical realization of the Kolmogorov–Uspensky machine. What remains unanswered is whether a *Physarum* "computer" can actually solve the problem that Turing machines cannot solve. If this would be the case, then *Physarum* machines would be more powerful than any existing computer. In different words, it is an open problem to determine the computational power of *Physarum* machines.

A problem that seems suitable for *P. polycephalum* when being plasmodium is road planning. In particular, given that cities are represented by oat flakes and plasmodium of *P. polycephalum* introduced into one of them, will the plasmodium develop a propoplasmic network connecting cities that are similar to the road network? It seems that *Physarum* machines can satisfactorily approximate the motorway network of the United Kingdom by linking the ten most densely populated urban areas in the UK. However, they have "failed" in a couple of cases. In fact, they did not fail, but they managed to find better routes, something quite impressive.

The exposition in Chapter 2 should have made it clear that computation is about symbol manipulation. However, *Physarum* machines are not processing any symbols and so one may say that these are not genuine computing devices. I think I am not a purist, thus, I think as long as we can solve mathematical problems with some *device*, this *device* is probably a specialized computer. After all, the computing-as-symbol-manipulation paradigm is just an abstraction.

4.4   Swarm Intelligence

A few years ago, I received an e-mail about a new journal that was launched by Springer. The title of the journal, *Swarm Intelligence*,[25] did not make any sense to me. I tried to see what this was about, but I did not find anything particularly interesting at that time. However, later on, when I managed to understand what *Swarm Intelligence* was about, I realized that I was familiar with the subject! In fact, I had read a couple of articles about ant colonies and their "intelligence". In a sense, one can say that swarm intelligence is about intelligence being social. An extreme example of this social intelligence is the brain of a typical human. The brain is composed by approximately 86,000,000,000 *neurons* (i.e., brain cells) and although no single cell is intelligent, the totality of neurons, which make up our brain, is obviously intelligent. Of course, we are not interested here in brain cells but in bee hives and ant colonies.

One could argue that *emergence*, which is roughly the idea that some properties of a system are irreducible, plays a central rôle in swarm intelligence. An ant or a bee has some intelligence, but the insect alone cannot achieve what a particular totality can

---

[25]A swarm is a very large number of insects moving together.

achieve. But what exactly can this totality achieve? First of all, it is necessary to say a few things about ants and their behavior. Most of ant communication is based on the use of *pheromones*, that is, chemicals produced by the ants. In particular, *trail pheromones* are used by certain ant species for marking paths on the ground. Thus, when an ant goes from the nest to some food source and back to nest, it drops pheromones on the ground forming a pheromone trail.

Although difficult problems cannot in principle be solved so as to deliver an answer quickly, there are approximate methods which can deliver results quite quickly. These methods, which are not *general* solutions to problems, are known as *heuristics*. A *metaheuristic* is a set of ideas and concepts that can be used to define heuristic methods applicable to a wide set of different problems. Thus, a metaheuristic can be seen as a very general heuristic method that can be used in the construction of a particular problem-specific heuristic. For example, *evolutionary computation* is a metaheuristic that is based on the ideas of evolution and survival of the fittest. In this method, one encodes potential solutions as data structures that have the characteristics of genes. Starting with a first generation of such data structures and by allowing them to "mutate", "fuse", etc., one can create a number of generations and in the end, one hopes to get the best solution to the initial problem. The *Ant Colony Optimization* (ACO) metaheuristic is based on the idea that a colony of artificial ants cooperate in order to find good solutions to some sort of difficult problems. In ACO, cooperation plays a very important role. ACO has been used to propose solutions to a wide range of problems such as the vehicle routing problem. This problem is about the transportation of items between storehouses and customers by using a fleet of vehicles. For example, mail delivery, school bus routing, and solid waste collection are instances of this problem.

In order to solve a problem by a machine, we need to somehow encode it. Thus, the next logical question is how do we encode a problem using ACO? As an example, let us discuss a well-known problem: *the traveling salesman* problem. This problem is about a salesman who starts from some town and has to visit a number of towns. The salesman has to visit each town only once before returning to the starting point while the trip must be the shortest possible. In a sense, this problem is similar to the Hamiltonian path problem. The problem is represented by a graph where each town is a vertex and the edges the road connections between towns. The graph has n vertices while there are m ants to solve the problem. These ants are randomly placed on vertices. Initially, each ant can choose to go to one of $n - 1$ towns and while moving they drop pheromones. The ants use the pheromone concentrations in the edge that connects the current town and the remaining towns in order to make a probabilistic selection. After the ants had moved to the second town, they can choose from $n - 2$ towns and they use the same "technique" to choose their next stop. This procedure continues until all m ants have visited n towns. Then the ants need to return to their starting point to generate a solution of the problem.

A typical multi-variable optimization problem is to find the maximum and/or minimum values of functions of several variables over prescribed domains. Unfortunately, in most cases, such problems cannot be solved exactly in a short time. Thus, classical methods fail. The *bees algorithm*[26] is a new approach to the solution of *optimization* problems. This algorithm is inspired by the food foraging behavior of honey bees. Initially, scout bees search for promising patches of flowers. Naturally, they have to visit many patches in order to determine the most promising ones. When the scouts return to the hive, those of them who have found a promising patch of flowers deposit their nectar and perform the *waggle dance* so as to show others where the patches are. The bees algorithm is inspired by this behavior.

In order to have a meaningful algorithm, one has to set a number of parameters. In particular, it necessary to know the number of scout bees (n), the number of sites selected out of n visited sites (m), the number of best sites out of m selected sites (e), the number of bees required for best e sites, and the initial size of flower patches. Now, given an optimization problem, one creates an initial population of random solutions and then places n scout bees in the search space. After evaluating the fitness of the population, one has to perform the following steps as many times as necessary:

— select sites for search;
— assign bees to each site (the more promising sites get more bees) and evaluate fitness;
— select the fittest bee from each patch;
— the remaining bees are free to go wherever they want, but their fitness is also evaluated.

This is the simplest form of the algorithm, but it gives an idea of how it can be applied to solve optimization problems.

Particle swarm optimization (PSO) is one more metaheuristic that is based on the social foraging behavior of flocks of birds or fish schools and has been used to solve optimization problems. Individuals in the swarm are following the fitter members of the swarm. The swarm always prefers to move to areas it has visited before and that have been proved to be rich feeding grounds. The goal of an algorithm derived from the PSO is to have all individuals locate the optimal values in space of values. Initially, we position all individuals to random positions and give them small initial velocities. Next, the individuals change their position and after each step, there is a position evaluation. In time, the individuals converge around the best position or positions. Typically, the number of individuals should be 20–40, while for most problems, 10 individuals are enough for good results. Some difficult problems might require 100 or even 200

[26]D. T. Pham and M. Castellani. *The Bees algorithm: Modeling foraging behavior to solve continuous optimization problems.* Proceedings of the Institution of Mechanical Engineers, Part C: Journal of Mechanical Engineering Science, 223, pp. 2919–2938, 2009.

individuals. Also, the speed of individuals should be determined by the boundaries of the search area. In addition, the change of speed might be limited for certain types of problems.

From the discussion so far, it should be obvious that swarm intelligence is not a novel model of computation but a methodology for the construction of clever algorithms that can be used to solve certain kinds of problems. In addition, swarm intelligence vividly demonstrates that nature is an almost unlimited source of inspiration.

4.5   Chaos Computing

In the Mediterranean region, snow is something one does not see everyday during winter. As a matter of fact, snowing is considered as a major event! Now, imagine what happens when the Meteorological Service predicts that in some areas, there will be some snowfall, but instead another sunny day passes by! Some people think that the Meteorological Service is kidding people, but the fact is that weather forecasting is not easy. It is known that we cannot predict how will be the weather in say 10 or 20 days from now. What is not widely known is why this happens. Moreover, it is not known if there is room for improvement.

Edward Norton Lorenz was a mathematician and meteorologist at the Massachusetts Institute of Technology. Lorenz wanted to use computers to predict the weather. He created a simple model, but soon he realized that when we slightly change the input parameters, we get completely different results. For example, he noticed that when his computer simulation was fed with decimal numbers with three decimal digits (e.g., numbers like 0.306) instead of decimal number with six decimal digits (e.g., numbers like 0.306127), the results were not the same as one would expect. Although his simulation involved 12 ordinary differential equations, one can observe the same effect using a much simpler mathematical expression. For example, one can use the quadratic expression $p + rp(1 - p)$ with initial value $p_0 = 0.1$ and $r = 3$. Next, one computes the expression $p' = 0.1 + 3 \times 0.1 \times (1 - 0.1)$ and uses p' to recompute the expression $p' + rp'(1 - p')$ and so on. If at some point, the iteration stops and p is truncated to three decimal digits and the operation resumes with this value and goes to the end without any other interruption, the result will be quite different from what we will get if no interruption happened. Table 4.1 shows two iterations: one where an interruption is accompanied by a truncation of the output and one where nothing happens and the process finishes normally. Lorenz published his findings in 1963.[27] What happens here is an *effect* that is known in the literature as the *sensitive dependence*

---

[27] Edward N. Lorenz. *Deterministic nonperiodic flow.* Journal of the Atmospheric Sciences, 20, pp. 130–141, 1963.

Table 4.1: Iteration of a quadratic expression with interruption (value is truncated) and with no interruption.

Evaluations	Interrupted	Uninterrupted
0	0.0397	0.0397
1	0.15407173	0.15407173
2	0.545072626044421	0.545072626044421
3	1.2889780011888	1.2889780011888
4	0.171519142109176	0.171519142109176
5	0.597820120107099	0.597820120107099
6	1.3191137924138	1.3191137924138
7	0.0562715776462566	0.0562715776462566
8	0.21558683923263	0.21558683923263
9	0.722914301179573	0.722914301179573
10	**1.324**	**1.32384194416844**
30	0.0478558352394752	1.07662917142894
50	0.231494428753942	0.076224636147602
70	0.986591070904675	0.943055131268702
100	0.15834900709827	1.1099460083857

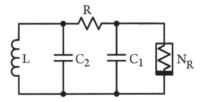

Figure 4.8: The basic design of Chua's circuit.

on initial conditions effect. Lorenz is also known for another effect: the butterfly effect. This was documented in his talk at the 139th meeting of the American Association for the Advancement of Science on December 29, 1972. His talk was titled "Predictability: Does the Flap of a Butterfly's Wings in Brazil Set Off a Tornado in Texas?" In this talk, he essentially asserted that small causes can have large effect. Because of this, he concluded that it will be impossible to answer the question posed by the title of his talk in a few years. Of course, we cannot answer this question with certainty today.

The butterfly effect and the sensitive dependence on initial conditions effect are manifestations of *chaos theory*, which is a theory that studies complex systems. In general, a system is chaotic when its evolution depends greatly on initial conditions and when the system is not in general predictable. Chaos theory has found many applications in physics, economics, biology, electronics, etc. In electronics, there is a simple circuit that is called *Chua's circuit*, named after its inventor Leon Ong Chua.

This is an electronic circuit that exhibits chaotic behavior.[28] Figure 4.8 depicts the basic design of Chua's circuit. The component with the label N_R is called Chua's diode, which is a negative resistance. In a typical circuit with a resistor following Ohm's law, the current decreases or increases when voltage decreases or increases, respectively, while in the case of a negative resistance, the current increases when voltage decreases and vice versa.

In 1998, it was proposed that chaotic systems might be utilized to develop computing devices.[29] In particular, it was proposed that a chaotic computer would consist of a network of chaotic elements. It was envisioned that these devices could operate in discrete space and time while its state variable could be continuous. Consider such a chaotic element whose state is represented by a value x. The realization of the basic logic gates (i.e., AND, OR, NOT, and XOR) involves the following steps.[30]

(i) Inputs

$$x \rightarrow x_0 + X + Y \quad \text{for the AND, OR, and XOR operations}$$
$$x \rightarrow x_0 + X \quad \text{for the NOT operation}$$

where x_0 is the initial state of the system. Also, $X = 0$ when $I = 0$ and $X = \delta$, where δ is a positive constant, when $I = 1$.

(ii) Using a chaotic function $f(x)$ to perform chaotic update, that is, $x \rightarrow f(x)$.

(iii) Threshold mechanism to obtain output Z:

$$Z = 0 \quad \text{if } f(x) \leq x_* \quad \text{and} \quad Z = f(X) - x_* \quad \text{if } f(x) > x_*$$

where x_* is a critical value. When $Z = \delta$, we assume that the gate yields 1 while when $Z = 0$, it yields 0. By convention, 0 stands for false and 1 for true.

What is left to specify in order to have a reliable definition of a gate are the conditions that are given in Table 4.2. Note that typically $f(x) = 4ax(1 - x)$, that is, the *logistic map*, where $a = 1$. The constant $\delta = 1/4$ and $x_0 = 0$ and $x_* = 3/4$ for the AND operation; $x_0 = 1/8$ and $x_* = 11/16$ for the OR operation; $x_0 = 1/4$ and $x_* = 3/4$ for the XOR operation; and $x_0 = 1/2$ and $x_* = 3/4$ for the NOT operation. These gates have been implemented as electronic circuits while there is a project to implement a computer processor with chaotic gates.

---

[28] Takashi Matsumoto. *A chaotic attractor from chua's circuit*. IEEE Transactions on Circuits and Systems, 31(12), pp. 1055–1058, 1984.

[29] Sudeshna Sinha and William L. Ditto. *Dynamics based computation*. Physical Review Letters, 81(10), pp. 2156–2159, 1998.

[30] William L. Ditto, K. Murali, and Sudeshna Sinha. *Chaos computing: Ideas and implementations*. Philosophical Transactions of the Royal Society A, 366, pp. 653–664, 2008.

Table 4.2: The necessary and sufficient conditions to be satisfied simultaneously by a chaotic element so as to implement the basic logical operations.

Input set (I_1, I_2)	Output for AND operation	Necessary and sufficient condition
$(0,0)$	0	$f(x_0) \leq x_*$
$(0,1)/(1,0)$	0	$f(x_0 + \delta) \leq x_*$
$(1,1)$	1	$f(x_0 + 2\delta) - x_* = \delta$

Input set (I_1, I_2)	Output for OR operation	Necessary and sufficient condition
$(0,0)$	0	$f(x_0) \leq x_*$
$(0,1)/(1,0)$	1	$f(x_0 + \delta) - x_* = \delta$
$(1,1)$	1	$f(x_0 + 2\delta) - x_* = \delta$

Input set (I_1, I_2)	Output for XOR operation	Necessary and sufficient condition
$(0,0)$	0	$f(x_0) \leq x_*$
$(0,1)/(1,0)$	1	$f(x_0 + \delta) - x_* = \delta$
$(1,1)$	0	$f(x_0 + 2\delta) - x_* = \delta$

Input set (I)	Output for NOT operation	Necessary and sufficient condition
0	1	$f(x_0) - x_* = \delta$
1	0	$f(x_0 + \delta) \leq x_*$

4.6 Analog Computing

Analog computers are machines that use analogies to perform basic arithmetic operations. For example, a machine could use voltage to perform addition. Thus, to add 3 and 2, one should add 3 V and 2 V to get the answer 5 instantaneously. Of course, it is possible to perform far more complex operations, but the principle is the same. In the 1940s, Claude Elwood Shannon introduced his *general-purpose analog computer* (GPAC), however, a more versatile computer than the GPAC is the *extended analog computer* (EAC), which was introduced by Lee Albert Rubel.[31] He introduced the EAC to support his idea that the brain is an analog computer.

The Extended Analog Computer[32]:   Rubel assumed that the EAC is a conceptual computing device, nevertheless, the device was realized later on as we will see below. The EAC consists of a number of "initial settings", $s_1, s_2, \ldots, s_m$, that are arbitrary real numbers. In addition, the machine has a finite number of independent variables, whose

---

[31] Lee Albert Rubel. *The extended analog computer*. Advances in Applied Mathematics, 14(1), pp. 39–50, 1993.

[32] This section assumes some familiarity with notions from calculus. Readers not familiar with them should consult section 5.2 for an overview of these notions.

number is not fixed, while the machine output consists of real-analytic functions of these variables. The machine is composed of a hierarchy of levels. Thus, the output of level $N - 1$ is used as input to level N. Each level consists of nodes and one can view the machine as a graph. The nodes at level zero work algebraically with polynomials and practically produce real numbers. At level one, work is done with differentially algebraic functions that have real numbers as inputs, which are generated at level zero. The inputs and outputs are functions of a finite number of independent variables x_1, x_2,.... Computation is carried out by nodes, which are of the following types:

Constant: These nodes produce *arbitrary* real constants, which are not necessarily computable by a Turing machine.

Independent variable: Nodes with no input that produce any of the variables x_i.

Adders: These nodes have as input any two functions $u_1(x_1,...,x_k)$ and $u_2(x_1,...,x_k)$ and yield their sum $u_1(x_1,...,x_k) + u_2(x_1,...,x_k)$ as output.

Multipliers: These nodes have as input any two functions $u_1(x_1,...,x_k)$ and $u_2(x_1,...,x_k)$ and yield their product $u_1(x_1,...,x_k) \cdot u_2(x_1,...,x_k)$ as output.

Substituters: When the functions

$$u_1(x_1,...,x_k),...,u_l(x_1,...,x_k)$$

and $v(x_1,...,x_l)$ are inputs, this node produces as output the function

$$v(u_1(x_1,...,x_k),...,u_l(x_1,...,x_k))$$

Inverters: Assume that at level $n - 1$, the machine has produced the functions

$$f_1(x_1,...,x_n,x_{n+1},...,x_{n+l}),...,f_l(x_1,...,x_n,x_{n+1},...,x_{n+l})$$

Given the variables $x_1,...,x_n,x_{n+1},...,x_{n+l}$ as input, the inverters solve the following equations:

$$f_1(x_1,...,x_n,x_{n+1},...,x_{n+l}) = 0$$
$$\vdots$$
$$f_l(x_1,...,x_n,x_{n+1},...,x_{n+l}) = 0$$

for $x_{n+1},...,x_{n+l}$ as well-defined real-analytic functions of $x_1,...,x_n$.

Differentiators: For each function $f(x_1,...,x_n)$, these nodes produce at level n any (mixed) partial derivative of $f(x_1,...,x_n)$:

$$\frac{\partial^{a_1+\cdots+a_n} f}{\partial x_1^{a_1} \cdots \partial x_n^{a_n}}$$

Analytic continuation: The nodes start with a function f such that $A = \text{dom}(f)$ [where $\text{dom}(f)$ is the domain of f (i.e., all the possible values of its argument)], produced at level n, and a set A^* produced by that time, with $A \cap A^* \neq \varnothing$, where $\varnothing$ a symbol for the empty set. Given two sets A and B, the set $A \cap B$ contains only all the elements that belong to both A and B. It may be that f has a unique analytic continuation f^* (i.e., a way of extending the domain over which f is defined as an analytic function) from $A \cap A^*$ to all of A^*. This node produces, at level n, the function that is f on A and f^* on A^* if it is well defined.

Quintessential: This is a "boundary-value-problem" node that solves a finite system of partial differential equations (PDE), which may include some ordinary differential equations (ODE), on a set A. The system of PDEs is subject to certain prescribed boundary values and bounds. Each PDE is of the form

$$F(x_1, \ldots, x_k : u, u_1, \ldots, u_l) = 0$$

where F is a function computed at a previous level and the u_i are partial derivatives of u. An example of a typical boundary-value requirement is $u = u_0$ on a piece γ_0 of the boundary of A, where we use only functions u_0 that have been defined by level $n - 1$. The set A has to be defined by level $n - 1 + \frac{1}{2}$. Note that the machine is capable of producing certain sets in Euclidean space at "half-levels" such as $2\frac{1}{2}$. If at level n, the machine has produced the function $f(x_1, \ldots, x_k)$, with $\Lambda = \mathrm{dom}(f)$, at level $n + \frac{1}{2}$, it can produce both:

$$\Lambda_1 = \{(x_1, \ldots, x_k) \in \Lambda | f(x_1, \ldots, x_k) > 0\}$$

and

$$\Lambda_1' = \{(x_1, \ldots, x_k) \in \Lambda | f(x_1, \ldots, x_k) \geq 0\}$$

If the sets $\Lambda_1, \ldots, \Lambda_l$ are produced at level $n + \frac{1}{2}$, then the machine can produce at the same level both their union and intersection. After this parenthesis, let us finish the presentation of quintessential nodes. The bounds, for example on a function u occurring in the boundary-value problem, should be defined by level n.

As it stands, the EAC can produce any real-analytic function. However, Rubel was not comfortable with this idea. He believed that any real or conceptual device can be called a computer only if there are some numbers or functions that it cannot compute. So, he decided to restrict the capabilities of the EAC to make it a *real* computing device. More specifically, assume that a function g is produced at level $n - 1$ and a set A is produced by level $n - 1 + \frac{1}{2}$; also suppose that $B \subset A$ is also produced by level $n - 1 + \frac{1}{2}$. Then, we allow the function ϕ, with $B = \mathrm{dom}(\phi)$, if for every $x_0 \in B$,

$$\lim_{\substack{x \in A \\ x \to x_0}} g(x) = \phi(x_0)$$

Similar requirements are put on the derivatives of ϕ. This process is "implemented" by *restricted limit* nodes.

Figure 4.9:   EAC to the left of a laptop.
Source: Reprinted from Physica D, Vol. 237, Jonathan W. Mills, The nature of the Extended Analog Computer, 1235–1256, Copyright © 2008, with permission from Elsevier.

Jonathan Wayne Mills devised an implementation of the EAC (see Figure 4.9).[33] This means that the mathematical model is not in a one by one correspondence with the implementation as, for example, the implementation contains components that do not perform a computation. The EAC implementation is a set of devices that compute specific functions by analogy. After all, this is an analog machine! In order to compute with this machine, one has to configure it, not to program it, and then wait for its evolution. At the end, one has to inspect the machine in order to get the result of the computation. The machine can be configured by sending a series of commands that consist of data inputs and outputs. The machine starts computing the moment it is turned on. Computation stops when either the machine is turned off or when a stable configuration has been reached. Note that the machine has no provision for program memory where a program could be stored. The reason of course is that the machine computes without following some algorithm. Since the machine contains nodes, it was suggested that cellular automata can model this implementation of the EAC. However, one can show that each cell is actually a miniature machine that operates in discrete time while the EAC operates in continuous time.

Memcomputing: The von Neumann computer architecture, named after John von Neumann, is a computer architecture that was first used in the construction of ENIAC

---

[33]Jonathan W. Mills. *The nature of the extended analog computer*. Physica D: Nonlinear Phenomena, 237(9), pp. 1235–1256, 2008.

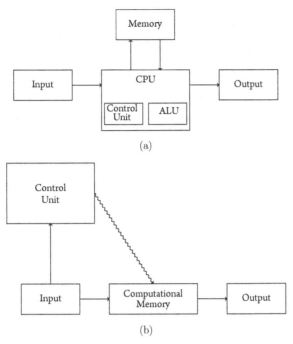

Figure 4.10: (a) The von Neumann computer architecture. (b) The memcomputing computer architecture. Comparison of the two computer architectures. Straight arrows indicate flow of data, while the zigzag arrow is used to indicate that a signal is sent. Note that in the von Neumann architecture, input goes straight to the CPU while in memcomputers, it might go either to the computational memory or the control unit.

and it is still in wide use today. Computers built with this architecture consist of a *control unit*, an *arithmetic logic unit* (ALU), and a memory unit. Nowadays, the control unit and the ALU are part of the central processing unit (CPU) or just processor [see Figure 4.10(a)]. The control unit is responsible for moving data and code into and out of the memory while executing the instructions of the program. Intermediate values generated during program execution are stored in *registers*. Finally, the ALU carries out calculations (e.g., additions, subtractions, etc., as well as comparisons and other logical operations). One basic problem of this computer architecture is that instructions are carried out sequentially (i.e., one after other) and this demands a lot of time to transfer data to and from the memory. This is known in the literature as the *von Neumann bottleneck* and is the reason why people are looking for better alternatives to this computer architecture.

One way to overcome the von Neumann bottleneck is to build parallel machines, that is, machines that carry out many instructions simultaneously. For example, a modern CPU consists of a specific number of *cores* (i.e., actual CPUs) that are attached to one another. Naturally, all these cores must be coordinated so as to perform a particular computational task. This means that the Neumann bottleneck reappears in a rather different form. Memcomputing is a promising new computer architecture that was introduced by Massimiliano Di Ventra and Yuriy V. Pershin.[34] This architecture is based on a very simple idea: The memory as well as the CPU should be physically the same. Of course, this idea is not entirely novel since our brains consist of neurons that "compute" and "store" information at the same time. Figure 4.10(b) depicts the basic characteristics of the memcomputing computer architecture. Naturally, the next logical question is what these machines can achieve.

Recently, Fabio Lorenzo Traversa, Di Ventra and their colleagues[35] examined the computational power of memcomputer and they concluded that they can solve difficult problems. In particular, they have built a machine that can solve instances of the *subset sum problem* that can be phrased as follows: Consider a finite set G of integers (i.e., $G \subset \mathbb{Z}$) having n elements, is there a non-empty subset K of G (i.e., $K \subset G$) whose elements sum up to s? The machine they built in order to solve this problem is a *universal memcomputer*[36] that consists of a control unit, a network of memprocessors, which play the rôle of computational memory, and a readout unit. The control unit consists of devices that generate electronic signals and each memprocessor is an electronic device that is built from standard electronic components. The readout unit consists of a frequency shift device (i.e., a device that takes the individual frequency components of its input signal and shifts them by the same number of hertz) and two multimeters (i.e., test tools used to measure two or more electrical values, such as voltage, current, and resistance). The memprocessors are connected with two wires. The control unit feeds the memprocessors with a signal that has the form of a sine wave. The collective state of all memprocessors is given by the real and the imaginary part of the following function:

$$g(t) = 2^{-n}(1 + e^{i\omega_1 t})(1 + e^{i\omega_2 t}) \cdots (1 + e^{i\omega_n t})$$

$$= 2^{-n} \prod_{j=1}^{n}(1 + e^{i\omega_j t}) \tag{4.1}$$

The Greek capital letter $\prod$ (pi) denotes the product operator. Assume that $x_1, x_2, \ldots, x_n$ are all the elements of a set of numbers. Then, their product is written as

$$\prod_{i=1}^{n} x_i.$$

---

[34] Massimiliano Di Ventra and Yuriy V. Pershin. *The parallel approach*. Nature Physics, 9, pp. 200–202, 2013.

[35] Fabio Lorenzo Traversa, Chiara Ramella, Fabrizio Bonani, and Massimiliano Di Ventra. *Memcomputing NP-complete problems in polynomial time using polynomial resources and collective states*. Science Advances, 1(6), e1500031, 2015.

[36] Fabio Lorenzo Traversa and Massimiliano Di Ventra. *Universal memcomputing machines*. IEEE Transactions on Neural Networks and Learning Systems, 26(11), pp. 2702–2715, 2015.

Also, it holds that $e^{ix} = \cos x + i \sin x$, a formula that is used to transform the expression $e^{i\omega_j t}$ into a sum. In Equation (4.1), n is the number of memprocessors. Assume that a_j is an element of G and $\omega_j = 2\pi a_j f_0$, where f_0 is some fundamental frequency. Then, the elements of G are encoded as frequencies and the readout device extracts the answer from the collective state (4.1).

Although this machine solves an instance of a difficult problem, still, the people who invented the machines and, consequently, the solution, claim that their work does not solve the $\mathcal{P} \overset{?}{=} \mathcal{NP}$ problem. This view is based on the fact that memcomputers are not Turing machines, which, of course, is true. But what matters is whether we can quickly solve a problem and not if we can quickly solve a problem by using a Turing machine. For instance, if one will build a machine that can solve the halting problem, then we will know it is solvable. So, if memcomputers can quickly solve difficult problems, this implies that we cannot ignore this in our quest to definitely answer the $\mathcal{P} = \mathcal{NP}$ question.

4.7   Artificial Neural Networks

The human brain is collection of a huge number of interconnected neurons. These brain cells are unique for many reasons. First of all, their shape is unlike the shape of any other cell. Second, neurons are quite long cells and sometimes, they are the longest cells of our bodies. Typically, a neuron can be 1 m long while the diameter of any other "normal" cell is 20 μm.

Each neuron sends messages to other neurons. These messages are transmitted either electrically or chemically. Messages travel inside neurons as electrical signals whereas chemical mechanisms are used when messages go from neuron to another. In particular, electrical transmission starts as electrical discharge at the cell body and then travels down the axon to the various synaptic connections (see Figure 4.11). The synapse is the joint that allows a neuron to pass a signal to another neuron. The myelin sheath that is shown in Figure 4.11 is a sort of plasma membrane wrapped around the nerve axon. Myelin is an electrical insulator.

Artificial neural networks (ANNs) are tools that are used to solve problems related to learning and optimization among others. The theory of ANNs is based on ideas related to the nature of the brain. An ANN is a directed graph having the following properties:

(i)   A state variable n_i is associated with each vertex i.

(ii)   A real-valued weight w_{ik} is associated with each edge between two vertices i and k.

(iii)   A real-valued bias ϑ_i is associated with each vertex i.

(iv)   For each vertex i, there is a transfer function f_i that yields the state of the vertex; its return value depends on its bias, on the weight of the incident edges, and the states of the vertices directly connected by these edges. Thus, $f_i(n_k, w_{ik}, \vartheta_i)$ determines the state of edge i.

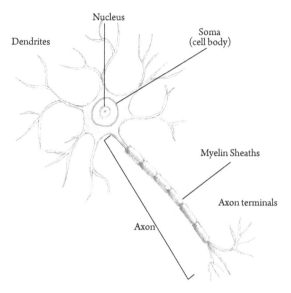

Figure 4.11: Neuron anatomy.

It is customary to use the term neuron for a vertex, edges are called synapses, and the bias is known as the activation threshold. Any neuron that has no edges such that the neuron is the destination is called an input neuron. Similarly, any neuron that has no edges such that the neuron is the origin is called an output neuron. A feed-forward network is a neural where the synapses between neurons do not form a cycle. A recurrent neural network (RNN) is any neural network where synapses between neurons form a directed cycle.

When compared to conventional computing devices (e.g., modern personal computers), ANNs are entirely different "devices". First of all, an ANN is a distributive system in the sense that all neurons equally participate in the computation process and there is no central processor. Each neuron gets some input and in the simplest case just adds up its input. In a more complex situation, each neuron is actually another ANN that performs more complicated operations. Thus, ANNs do not execute series of commands, but neurons respond simultaneously to the pattern of inputs presented to it. In its simplest form, each neuron stores a binary digit. For some neuron i, when the state $n_i = 0$, the neuron rests while $n_i = 1$, the neuron is active. For neural networks, time flows in discrete steps $t = 0, 1, 2, \ldots$. For a neuron i, its new state is determined by the following equation:

$$h_i(t) = \sum_j w_{ij} n_j(t) \tag{4.2}$$

Here, w_{ij} is an element of a matrix that represents the *synaptic efficacies* between neurons j and i. In the simplest case, the next state of i is computed by formula that follows:

$$n_i(t + 1) = \theta(h_i(t) - \vartheta_i) \qquad (4.3)$$

where $\theta(x) = 1$ when $x > 1$ and $\theta(x) = 0$ when $x < 1$.

Data are stored in associative memory of ANNs. When data are stored to memory and recalled from memory by association with other information, this memory is an associative one. This means that information can be recalled from the memory when there is a partial knowledge of its content whereas the memory location is not needed. Contrast this with modern computers where data are stored in memory cells, each of them having its own memory address. In the later case, data recall is an operation that demands precise knowledge of how data are stored in the memory. On the other hand, the human memory is not organized in this way. For example, it is of no use to know that someone told us something 11 days ago, while trying to remember that incredible joke. What would really matter would be a characteristic word or phrase so to remember the joke. Naturally, there are other associations such as the place where something happened or an event at which something happened that can prove equally useful.

Mathematically, an associative memory is defined as follows. First, we suppose that p binary patterns, each containing N bits of information, are stored in the memory. Moreover, suppose that we denote these patterns with v_i^{μ}, where $i = 1, ..., N$ and $\mu = 1, ..., p$. Thus, v_3^4 is the 4th bit of the 3rd pattern. Assume that a new pattern n_i is presented and the pattern v_i^{λ} closely resembles this one, which implies that v_i^{λ} and n_i should differ in as few places as possible. This, in turn, means that

$$H_{\mu} = \sum_{i=1}^{N}(n_i - v_i^{\mu})^2$$

is minimal for $\mu = \lambda$. The quantity H_{μ} is called the *Hamming distance*.

Question: Can we store patterns in a neural network of N neurons in such a way that the network evolves from the initial configuration n_i, corresponding to the presented pattern, into the desired configuration v_i^{λ} under its own dynamics?

In order to solve this problem, we start by using the following substitutions:

$$s_i = 2n_i - 1, \quad \sigma_i = 2v_i - 1$$

Thus, the new variables take the values $+1$ and -1 instead of 0 and 1. The *square deviation* is written as follows:

$$(n_i - v_i^{\mu})^2 = \frac{1}{4}(s_i - \sigma_i^{\mu})^2 = \frac{1}{4}(s_i^2 - 2s_i\sigma_i^{\mu} + (\sigma_i^{\mu})^2) = \frac{1}{2}(1 - s_i\sigma_i^{\mu})$$

Note that $s_i^2 = 1$ and $(\sigma_i^\mu)^2 = 1$. Instead of looking for the minimum value of H_μ, we should look for the *maximal* value of the function

$$A_\mu(s_i) = \sum_{i=1}^{N} \sigma_i^\mu s_i, \quad \mu = 1,\ldots,p \tag{4.4}$$

Under this transformation, the state of each neuron i at time t is equal to $s_i(t)$:

$$s_i(t+1) = \text{sgn}\big(h_i(t)\big) = \text{sgn}\left(\sum_{j=1}^{N} w_{ij}s_j(t)\right) \tag{4.5}$$

where

$$\text{sgn}(x) = \begin{cases} -1 & \text{if } x < 0 \\ 0 & \text{if } x = 0 \\ 1 & \text{if } x > 0 \end{cases}$$

It is quite possible to introduce neural networks where the value of $s_i(t+1)$ is not definite, but instead its value depends on a probability function. Thus, depending on the value of this function, $s_i(t+1)$ takes one of the values $+1$ or -1.

$$\Pr[s_i(t+1)] = f[h_i(t)] \tag{4.6}$$

A standard choice for f is the following function:

$$f(h) = (1 + e^{-2\beta h})^{-1}$$

Here, β is a parameter that must satisfy the following requirement:

$$\lim_{\beta \to \infty} f(h) = \theta(h)$$

where θ is the unit step function [see Equation (4.3)].

Hava T. Siegelmann introduced *recurrent artificial neural networks* (RANNs). These systems are similar to ANNs. Assume that such a system consists of n neurons and that they are presented with m binary digits, which are "stored" in a vector u, where u_j denotes the jth component. Then, the following formula computes the next state of a neuron:

$$n_i(t+1) = \sigma\left(\sum_{j=1}^{n} a_{ij}x_j(t) + \sum_{j=1}^{} mb_{ij}u_j(t) + c_i\right) \tag{4.7}$$

where σ is usually defined as

$$\sigma(x) = \begin{cases} 0 & \text{if } x < 0, \\ x & \text{if } 0 \le x \le 1, \\ 1 & \text{if } x > 1, \end{cases} \quad \text{or as} \quad \sigma(x) = \frac{1}{1 + e^{-x}}$$

Also, the numbers a_{ij}, b_{ij}, and c_i are the *weights* of the network. These weights are arbitrary real numbers. Siegelmann argues that these numbers are similar to the various constants found in most equation in physics, that is, one can think that a_{ij} are just like the constant h. In the case the weights are rational numbers, then the resulting systems are as powerful as Turing machines. However, when weights are real numbers, then the resulting networks are more powerful than Turing machines! Although Siegelmann has given a quite specific description of the class of problems solvable by these networks, I think it suffices to say that it can solve problems that are as hard as the halting problem.

Annotated Bibliography

- Andrew Adamatzky. *Physarum Machines: Computers from Slime Mould*, Volume 74 of World Scientific Series on Nonlinear Science, Series A. World Scientific, Singapore, 2010.

  A book that thoroughly presents *Physarum* computing. Of course, the book does not focus on the author's own work but presents all relevant results. In addition, it contains information about the biology of the organism and how one can grow *Physarum*.

- Chris R. Calladine, Horace R. Drew, Ben F. Luisi, and Andrew A. Travers. *Understanding DNA: The Molecule & How It Works*, 3rd edition. Elsevier, Amsterdam, 2004.

  This is a good introduction to the various aspects of the DNA molecule. The first chapter of the book is an "easily digestible" presentation of the molecule and its characteristics and I have used it for my own short presentation.

- Harish Chandran, Nikhil Gopalkrishnan, and John Reif. DNA Nanorobotics. In Constantinos Mavroidis and Antoine Ferreira, editors, *Nanorobotics*, pp. 355–382. Springer New York, 2013.

  This book chapter presents the field of DNA nanorobotics, that is, nanorobots built of DNA. I think it is a very good presentation. To the best of my knowledge, there is no book-length presentation of the field.

- Marco Dorigo and Thomas Stützle. *Ant Colony Optimization*. The MIT Press, Cambridge, MA, 2004.

  This book has been written by the people who invented the ACO metaheuristic. They present the general ideas and many applications of AKO.

- Martin Gardner. *Wheels, Life and other Mathematical Amusements*. W. H. Freeman, New York, 1983.

The last three chapters of this book contain a very good introduction to the game of life. In fact, each chapter is an article that the author had published in the *Scientific American* magazine.

• James Kennedy and Russell C. Eberhart. *Swarm Intelligence*. Morgan Kaufmann Publishers, San Francisco, CA, 2001.

The authors of this book have started the field of swarm intelligence and present the general ideas as well as particle swarm optimization with examples.

• Berndt Müller, Michael T. Strickland, and Joachim Reinhardt. *Neural Networks: An Introduction*. 2nd edition. Springer, Berlin, 1995.

This is the book that I have consulted in order to write the section on neural networks. I think it is a good introduction to the relevant ideas and concepts. However, there are many good online introductions to the subject such as Daniel Shiffman's *The Nature of Code* or David Kriesel's *A Brief Introduction to Neural Networks*.

• Heinz-Otto Peitgen, Hartmut Jürgens, and Dietmar Saupe. *Chaos and Fractals: New Frontiers of Science*. Springer, New York, 2004.

A classic introduction to the theory of chaos and fractals. This book comes with programming examples. Unfortunately, the code is bit dated, but I think it is not difficult to rewrite most examples using a modern programming language.

• Gheorghe Păun, Grzegorz Rozenberg, and Arto Salomaa. *DNA Computing: New Computing Paradigms*. Springer, Berlin, 1998.

This is an interesting book that introduces DNA computing. The only problem I see is that they focus more on the mathematical side of DNA computing and less on the practical aspects. Of course, this is justified since the authors are mathematicians and computer scientists.

• Gheorghe Păun, Grzegorz Rozenberg, and Arto Salomaa, editors. *The Oxford Handbook of Membrane Computing*, Oxford Handbooks in Mathematics, Oxford, 2009. Oxford University Press.

In this volume, the various authors tried to give an idea of what is going on in the field of membrane computing. The first chapter is quite interesting. The others not so much.

• Helmut Sauer. *Developmental Biology of Physarum*, Volume 11 of Developmental and Cell Biology Series. Cambridge University Press, Cambridge, 1982.

This is a book for people willing to know more about the strange *P. polycephalum*. I could not find a printed or an electronic copy of this book that is reasonably priced

(I had a very low budget). Fortunately, the book was available in Google Books, so I had the chance to read part of it online.

- Hava T. Siegelmann. *Neural Networks and Analog Computation: Beyond the Turing Limit*. Birkhäuser, Boston, 1999.

In this book, the author presents her own work regarding recurrent artificial neural networks. Although this is a research monograph, it is self-contained to a certain degree.

- Stephen Wolfram. *A New Kind of Science*. Wolfram Media, Champaign, IL, 2002.

This book is about cellular automata. The author assumes that almost everything in this universe, including the universe, is a cellular automaton, but see the discussion in Section 3.4. The book is freely available online and it is an excellent source of information about cellular automata.

Chapter 5

Quantum Computing

Ordinary computers process signals that represent binary digits. Specialized circuits realize logical gates that are used to process these signals. Quantum computers harness and exploit properties of matter at the quantum level to represent bits and to process them. Thus quantum computing is an alternative method to compute and one that looks quite promising.

5.1   Probability Theory

We are all familiar with words that have a colloquial or everyday meaning and at the same time a quite specialized one. For example, in ordinary speech and writing, the word *affect* is most often used as a verb meaning "to act on or to cause a change" while in psychology affect is the experience of feeling or emotion. The word *probability* is another such word. Typically, probabilities are associated with future events and express the likelihood degree that something is going to happen. For example, one may say that

— it is quite probable that Bayern Munich will win the Champions League this season, or
— there is a 20% probability that it will rain tomorrow, or
— the probability of throwing two dice and obtaining two sixes is 1/36.

In the first sentence, there is no number specified, yet the expression "quite probable" is a linguistic expression denoting some number. Furthermore, all these sentences make sense and most of us may have used similar sentences in our everyday chitchats, but one must remark that none of them uses the term *probability* in the sense used in the mathematical theory of probability.

In the mathematical theory, probabilities are relative *measures* of sets. This means that one compares the number of elements contained in different subsets of a specific set. When these sets are finite, one can obtain these measures by simply counting, while when the sets involved are infinite, then one has to use some measurement method (e.g., integration which is explained in Section 5.2). Clearly, the measuring process does not involve chance or randomness. So probabilities and randomness are quite different notions. Also, it should be clear that the statement "there is a 20% probability that it will rain tomorrow" has nothing to do with probabilities! Not so surprisingly, most people will object to this and will say that this statement definitely involves probabilities. The answer is that "probability" is a statistical measurement of probabilities, that is, one performs some statistical analysis and based on her data deduces that tomorrow it is not so likely to see rain in her town.

Quantum computing is making use of the laws of quantum mechanics, and the current interpretation of quantum mechanics is based on "probabilities" (but see the discussion on the indeterminacy of quantum mechanics in Section 5.3). Now, quantum mechanics was formalized in 1926 while probability theory was formalized in 1930. Thus, quantum mechanics is interpreted using statistical measurements of probabilities and no *pure* probabilities. In order to make the distinction absolutely clear, I will give a simple example:

Assume you have a cube where each of its six faces is marked with a different number from 1 to 6. Then, one can ask about the probability that the face up has the number 5 marked on it. To answer this question, you have to measure (or count in this particular case) all the faces of the cube and then the faces that are marked with 5. Thus, the probability we are looking for is:

$$\frac{\text{The number of faces marked with 5}}{\text{The total number of faces of the dice}} = \frac{1}{6} \tag{5.1}$$

Similarly, the probability that an even number is marked on the face of a dice is:

$$\frac{\text{The number of faces marked with 2, 4, and 6}}{\text{The total number of faces of the dice}} = \frac{3}{6} \tag{5.2}$$

Now, let's proceed with a simple experiment.

Suppose that we have a dice and ask Maxine to throw it a large number of times while we keep record of the throws and the outcome of each throw. Also, we should make a graphical representation of the distribution of our data. Then, we can ask Maxine to pick a number from one to six. The *probability*, $\Pr[\ldots]$ that a side of the dice is equal to Maxine's number M is:

$$\Pr[M] = \frac{N(M)}{N} \approx \frac{1}{6} \tag{5.3}$$

where $N(M)$ is the total number of throws whose outcome was M and N is the total number of throws. This fraction is a statistical measurement and not a measure of any set. In addition, if N is not large enough, then it makes sense to ask what is the most probable outcome. To find the answer, one has to find the maximum of $N(1), N(2), \ldots, N(6)$. Now, let's compute the *average* outcome of throw:

$$\langle M \rangle = \frac{\sum M \times N(M)}{N} = \sum MP(M) \qquad (5.4)$$

The Greek capital letter $\sum$ (sigma) denotes the summation operator. Assume that $x_1, x_2, \ldots, x_n$ are all the elements of a set of numbers. Then, their sum is written as

$$\sum_{i=1}^{n} x_i \qquad (5.5)$$

Here i is the *index of summation* and it is quite common to also use the letters j, k, etc., for the same purpose; the numbers below and atop the summation operator are lower and upper summation limits; and the expression $\sum_{i=1}^{n} x_i$ denotes the sum of all variables x_i for integer values of i from 1 to n. In quantum mechanics, the quantity $\langle M \rangle$ is usually one that we are interested in and it is usually called the *expectation value*. The next question is about the *squares* of outcomes of throws:

$$\langle M^2 \rangle = \sum M^2 P(M) \qquad (5.6)$$

The *standard deviation* expresses the concentration of data around the average value. Obviously, the smaller the standard deviation is, the more concentrated the data are. The standard deviation is given by the formula $\sigma_M = \sqrt{\langle M^2 \rangle + \langle M \rangle^2}$.

We now know that probabilities in quantum mechanics are not some measure of sets but a statistical result, which is required for our quick exploration of quantum mechanics. However, this is not enough: we need to *remind* ourselves a few things from calculus.

5.2   A Summary of Calculus

Recall that a function is a correspondence between two sets, which in many cases are the same. In general, the set whose elements are mapped to the elements of another set is called the *domain* of the function while the other set is called the *codomain* or *range* of the function. Calculus is about the functions *differentiation* and *integration*. Let us see what these operations are about.

When one differentiates a function, the result is the computation of the *derivative* of this particular function. The derivative of a function that has a simple variable is a measure of the rate at which the value of the function changes with respect to the change of the variable. For example, every time we get into a car, we observe differentiation first hand. We can define a simple function, $s(t)$, that gives the position of the car as a function of time. Thus $s(100)$ gives the position of the car after 100 seconds. Here is an easy recipe to define such a function. Create a table with two columns. In the first column, you should write times and in the second columns positions (e.g., how many meters has the car moved since it started). It is better to write down the positions in specific time intervals (e.g., every 15 seconds). Then you should plot the data and then you should connect the individual points. Although the last step is a bit arbitrary, it will give you an idea of the position function. From this diagram, one can compute the speed of the car. Here is how:

(i) Identify two points on the curve.

(ii) Say that the coordinates of the first one are (x_1, y_1) and of the second one (x_2, y_2).

(iii) Use the following equation to calculate the slope:

$$\text{slope} = \frac{y_2 - y_1}{x_2 - x_1} = \frac{\Delta y}{\Delta x}$$

When the two points are very close so that Δx is almost equal to zero, the fraction gives the instantaneous speed at this given moment. Mathematically, the instantaneous speed is the value of the derivative at this particular time. This simply means that

$$v(t) = \frac{ds(t)}{dt}$$

is the function that gives us the velocity of the car and d/dt is the *differentiation operator*. Similarly, the acceleration of the car is given by

$$a(t) = \frac{dv(t)}{dt} = \frac{d^2 s(t)}{dt^2}$$

Thus, the acceleration of a moving object is the first derivative of its velocity or the second derivative of its position function. Suppose we have a function $f(x)$. Then, there are specific rules that should be used in order to get the derivative of $f(x)$. For example if $f(x) = x^n$, then

$$\frac{df(x)}{dx} = n x^{n-1}$$

When people make deposits to a bank, the interest they will get depends on the interest rate and on the total time their money will be kept in the bank account. Also, when a gun fires a projectile, its range depends upon the weight of the projectile, the angle of elevation of the gun, the resistance of the air, and many other conditions. These two examples are cases of functions of several variables. A function of several variables is typically written as $f(x_1, x_2, \ldots, x_n)$. Suppose that $g(x, y)$ is a function of two variables, then

$$\frac{\partial g}{\partial x} \quad \text{and} \quad \frac{\partial g}{\partial y}$$

are the partial derivatives of g with respect to x and y, respectively. In order to compute the derivatives, one assumes that all other variables are constants and performs ordinary derivation of the function with respect to the variable that appears on the "denominator" of the operator. Also,

$$\frac{\partial^2 g}{\partial x^2} = \frac{\partial}{\partial x}\frac{\partial g}{\partial x} \quad \text{and} \quad \frac{\partial^2 g}{\partial y^2} = \frac{\partial}{\partial y}\frac{\partial g}{\partial y}$$

are the second partial derivative of g with respect to x and y, respectively. Finally,

$$\frac{\partial^2 g}{\partial x\partial y} = \frac{\partial}{\partial x}\frac{\partial g}{\partial y} \quad \text{and} \quad \frac{\partial^2 g}{\partial y\partial x} = \frac{\partial}{\partial y}\frac{\partial g}{\partial x}$$

are the second partial derivatives of g first with respect to y and second with respect to x and first with respect to x and second with respect to y, respectively.

Suppose we have a rectangle whose horizontal sides have length equal to x and whose vertical sides have length equal to y. Clearly, the area of this rectangle is $z = x \cdot y$. The partial derivative of z with respect to x, $\frac{\partial z}{\partial x}$, expresses the rate of change of z with respect to x. Similar things can be said about $\frac{\partial z}{\partial y}$.

Assume that $f(x)$ is a function of one variable. Also, suppose that we plot the function on a coordinate system and then we choose two points on the horizontal axis that belong to its domain [say, $(a, 0)$ and $(b, 0)$, such that $a < b$]. Let us draw two lines perpendicular to the horizontal axis that cross these two points. The question is: Can we compute the area of the region that is delimited by the horizontal axis, the two perpendicular lines, and the plot of $f(x)$? This is a very old problem and one approach to its solution is this: Starting from the perpendicular that crosses $(a, 0)$, create a narrow rectangle whose lower coordinates are at $(a, 0)$ and $(a + \Delta x, 0)$, where Δx is a very small number. The next narrow rectangle will have coordinates at $(a + \Delta x, 0)$ and $(a + 2\Delta x, 0)$, etc. Thus, the area will be the sum of all these rectangles. Suppose that the width of the rectangle Δx is very small, then the area of the rectangle is the *definite integral* of the function $f(x)$ between a and b or in symbols:

$$f(a)\Delta x + f(a + \Delta x)\Delta x + f(a + 2\Delta x)\Delta x + \cdots + f(a + n\Delta x)\Delta x$$

where $a + n\Delta x = b$. When n becomes very big and Δx almost equal to zero, then we write

$$\lim_{n\to\infty}\sum_a^b f(x)\Delta x = \int_a^b f(x)\mathrm{d}x$$

Here $\mathrm{d}x$ is called an infinitesimal and denotes something that is so small that one cannot measure it. The first part can be read as: the limit as n becomes extremely large (theoretically equal to infinity) so that the line segment that starts at $(a, 0)$ and ends at $(b, 0)$ is divided in *infinitesimals* (i.e., line segments that are almost equal to zero).

A *differential equation* contains one or more terms involving (partial) derivatives. For example,

$$\frac{dy}{dx} = 2x$$

is a very simple differential equation. The solution of a differential equation is a function that satisfies it (can you guess what is the solution of this equation?).

5.3 A Quick Exploration of Quantum Mechanics

The pillars of modern physics are quantum mechanics and general relativity. One could say that general relativity is the physics of the macrocosm while quantum mechanics is the physics of the microcosm. In different words, one could say that quantum mechanics is the physics of molecules, atoms, and elementary particles while general relativity is the physics of planets, stars, and galaxies.[1] However, it is really weird that the two theories do not "mix".

Quantum mechanics started by Max Karl Ernst Ludwig Planck who proposed that electromagnetic energy is emitted and absorbed in the form of "packages", or *quanta* (plural of quantum), in order to solve a particularly difficult problem. Planck suggested that the energy of each quantum solely depends on the frequency of the radiation, and is described by the following formula:

$$E = h\nu \tag{5.7}$$

where E denotes the energy, h is Planck's constant, and ν is the frequency of the radiation. The value of h is (approximately) $6.62606957 \times 10^{-34}$ Joule · second. In what follows, I will present the basic ideas and results of quantum mechanics.

Let me start with a simple thought experiment. Assume that we have a particle of mass m that can move only along a straight line. Moreover, a force, $F(x, t)$, is exerted on this particle as it moves. Then, a basic problem of classical mechanics is to determine the position $x(t)$ of the particle at any moment. By knowing its position, it is possible to figure out the velocity, the momentum, or any other variable of interest. In order to determine the position of the particle, we apply Newton's second law: $F = ma$, where a is the acceleration. The meaning of this equation is that the acceleration of an object as produced by the overall force acting on this object is directly proportional to the magnitude of the force, in the same direction as the force, and inversely proportional to the mass of the object. Of course, Newton's second law is not enough to determine the position — we need to know the initial position and velocity (i.e., when $t = t_0$).

---

[1] Strictly speaking this is not correct. General relativity introduces the idea of gravity that acts through a gravitational field, similar to a magnetic field. Such a field affects space and time in various ways.

In classical mechanics, the total energy of a moving particle, that is, its kinetic plus its potential energy, is given by the following equation:

$$E = H(x, t) = \frac{p_x^2}{2m} + V(x) \tag{5.8}$$

where m is the mass of a particle moving on a straight line in a potential $V(x)$ and having momentum p_x. The quantity $H(x, t)$ is called the *Hamiltonian* of the system. The equation that follows is analogous to Equation (5.8) in the quantum setting.

$$\underbrace{i\hbar \frac{\partial \Psi(x, t)}{\partial t}}_{\substack{\text{total} \\ \text{energy}}} = \underbrace{-\frac{\hbar^2}{2m} \frac{\partial^2 \Psi(x, t)}{\partial x^2}}_{\substack{\text{kinetic} \\ \text{energy}}} + \underbrace{V\Psi(x, t)}_{\substack{\text{potential} \\ \text{energy}}} \tag{5.9}$$

Here $\hbar$ is the reduced Planck's constant and it is equal to h divided by 2π and π is the ratio of the circumference of a circle to its diameter. This equation is the *Schrödinger equation*, which was formulated by Erwin Rudolf Josef Alexander Schrödinger. In quantum mechanics, the solution of the problem above is given by the particle's *wavefunction*, that is, function $\Psi(x, t)$. In general, the wavefunction provides the *quantum state* of a particle or a system. Clearly, the wavefunction is completely determined by the Schrödinger equation provided some suitable initial conditions are given. Once we have found the wavefunction of some setup, how can we use the wavefunction to determine the position of a particle?

According to Bohr's *statistical interpretation* of the wavefunction, which was named after Niels Henrik David Bohr, $|\Psi(x, t)|^2$ gives the (statistical) *probability* of finding the particle at point x at time t. If we plot $|\Psi(x, t)|^2$ and choose two points a and b that belong to the horizontal axis and then compute the area under the curve delimited by these points, then this area is equal to the probability of finding the particle between a and b, at time t. This is expressed mathematically as follows:

$$\int_a^b |\Psi(x, t)|^2 dx = \begin{Bmatrix} \text{probability of finding the particle} \\ \text{between } a \text{ and } b, \text{ at time } t \end{Bmatrix} \tag{5.10}$$

Bohr's interpretation introduces some sort of *indeterminacy* into quantum mechanics, since it is usually impossible to predict with certainty the position of a particle. However, if we can determine more precisely a particle's position, then we are able to determine its momentum with less precision. In different words, the position and momentum of a particle cannot be simultaneously measured with any arbitrarily precision. This fact is known in the literature as *uncertainty principle* and is expressed mathematically as follows:

$$\sigma_x \sigma_p \geq \frac{\hbar}{2} \tag{5.11}$$

where σ_x is the standard deviation in x (position) and σ_p is the standard deviation in p (momentum). The reason for this indeterminacy is that quantum mechanics offers *statistical* information about the possible positions of a particle. Assume that one measures the position of a particle and she finds it to be in the *vicinity* of a point C. Then, it makes perfect sense to wonder about the position of the particle before the measurement. Currently, there are two plausible answers to this question: (a) the particle was at C (*realistic* position) and (b) the particle was not really anywhere (*orthodox* position). If the realistic position is the right one, then quantum mechanics is an incomplete theory because the theory could not predict this. Therefore, some additional information (known as *hidden variables*) is needed in order to have a fully functional theory. In the second case, the idea behind this weird answer is that the measurement is responsible for finding the particle at this particular position. For example, it may force the particle to appear at point C just after the experiment. This view is known in the literature as the *Copenhagen interpretation*.

Solving the Schrödinger equation for any potential $V(x, t)$ is quite difficult. However, if V is independent of time (i.e., it is not a function of time), then one can employ the method of *separation of variables* to solve it. In particular, we expect solutions to be simple products:

$$\Psi(x, t) = \psi(x)\varphi(t) \tag{5.12}$$

Note here that ψ (not the capital Ψ!) is a function of x and φ is a function of t. If we replace $\Psi(x, t)$ with $\psi(x)\varphi(t)$ and do a few mathematical operations, we will get the following time independent form of the equation:

$$-\frac{\hbar^2}{2m}\frac{d^2\psi}{dx^2} + V\psi = E\psi \tag{5.13}$$

In quantum mechanics, the position x and the momentum p are *operators*, that is, instructions that do something to the function that follows them. For example, the instruction for the position operator x is to just multiply it by x. The Hamiltonian of a quantum system is also an operator:

$$\hat{H} = -\frac{\hbar^2}{2m}\frac{\partial^2}{\partial x^2} + V(x) \tag{5.14}$$

where $(\hbar/i)(\partial/\partial x)$ is the momentum operator. This simply means that the time-independent Schrödinger equation can be written as

$$\hat{H}\psi = E\psi \tag{5.15}$$

In physics, all quantities are expressed in some units and there are two kinds of quantities: scalar and vector quantities. A scalar quantity is one that is completely determined by its *magnitude* (a numerical value). For example, the mass of a body, as well as the temperature of a room are completely determined by numbers that represent the mass in kilograms and the temperature in degrees. On the other hand, vector quantities are specified by a usually finite ordered list of elements [e.g., $(1,2,3)$] that determine their magnitude and their direction. For example, the displacement of a particle is a vector quantity since one needs to know both the magnitude (how far the particle has traveled) and the direction of displacement. When one divides or multiplies a vector quantity by a scalar, the result is a new vector quantity that has the same direction and its magnitude is the result of dividing or multiplying the magnitude of the vector by the magnitude of the scalar. Thus, the velocity by which some displacement takes place is a vector quantity. Henceforward, I will use the term *vector* to mean a vector quantity.

Vectors are depicted by arrows and the length of each arrow is the magnitude of the vector while the direction of the arrow is the direction of the vector. When working on a plane, it is possible to define a pair of perpendicular vectors whose magnitude is equal to 1. These vectors are called unit vectors and each plane vector can be written in terms of these two vectors, which are called a *basis*. In particular, given some plane vector $|A\rangle$ and some unit vectors $|i\rangle$ and $|j\rangle$, then $|A\rangle$ can be written as follows:

$$|A\rangle = a_1|i\rangle + a_2|j\rangle \tag{5.16}$$

The numbers a_1 and a_2 are the coordinates of the vector and unit vectors $|i\rangle$ and $|j\rangle$ are a basis. The magnitude of $|A\rangle$ can be computed by its coordinates:

$$\|A\|^2 = a_1^2 + a_2^2 \tag{5.17}$$

where $\|A\|$ is the magnitude of $|A\rangle$. The direction, θ, can be computed by the following formula:

$$\theta = \arctan\left(\frac{a_2}{a_1}\right) \tag{5.18}$$

Vectors live in mathematical universes called vector spaces. In particular, Hilbert spaces are vector spaces where the coordinates of each vector are complex numbers. In addition, these vector spaces can be either finite-dimensional or infinite-dimensional. In the latter case, vectors can be functions where each value of the function is part of an infinite ordered list of elements [i.e., $(f(0), f(1), f(2),...,)$]. Thus wave functions live in Hilbert spaces. Also, the states of a quantum system are characterized by vectors of some Hilbert space. The inner product of two functions $f(x)$ and $g(x)$ is defined as follows:

$$\langle f \mid g \rangle = \int_a^b f(x)^* g(x)\mathrm{d}x \tag{5.19}$$

where f^* is the conjugate of f and $[a, b]$ is an *interval* and both f and g are *square-integrable* functions on this interval:

$$\int_a^b |f(x)|^2\mathrm{d}x < \infty \tag{5.20}$$

In a finite-dimensional Hilbert space of dimension n (which is also called a Hermitian space), vectors can be represented as column matrices:

$$|a\rangle = \begin{pmatrix} a_1 \\ a_2 \\ \vdots \\ a_n \end{pmatrix} \tag{5.21}$$

where a_i are complex numbers. The inner product $\langle a|b\rangle$ is

$$\langle a|b\rangle = \sum_{i=1}^{n} a_i^* b_i \tag{5.22}$$

In fact, this is the matrix product of the row matrix

$$\langle a| = (a_1^*, a_2^*, ..., a_n^*) \tag{5.23}$$

with the column matrix $|b\rangle$, which is a special case of matrix multiplication. However, we do not need to know how to multiply matrices. A matrix is collection of data arranged in tabular form. Each matrix is characterized by a pair of numbers that are used to specify the number of rows and the number of columns. Thus a 2×2 matrix is the following one:

$$\frac{1}{\sqrt{2}}\begin{pmatrix} 1 & 1 \\ 1 & -1 \end{pmatrix} = \begin{pmatrix} \frac{1}{\sqrt{2}} & \frac{1}{\sqrt{2}} \\ \frac{1}{\sqrt{2}} & -\frac{1}{\sqrt{2}} \end{pmatrix} \tag{5.24}$$

This matrix is a 2×2 Hadamard matrix and is denoted by H_2 but in what follows, I will simplify this to just H.

Observables are represented by operators and correspond to physical quantities, such as energy, spin, or position, that can be measured. The expectation value of an observable $Q(x, p)$ is expressed as follows:

$$\langle Q \rangle = \int \psi^* \hat{Q}\psi \, \mathrm{d}x = \langle \psi|\hat{Q}\psi\rangle \tag{5.25}$$

Note $\hat{Q}$ is an operator that represents the observable Q. In finite-dimensional Hilbert space of dimension n, observables are represented by matrices, thus in $\langle \Phi|\hat{Q}\Phi\rangle$ the expression $\hat{Q}|\Phi\rangle$ is the product of a matrix by a column matrix. The following formula explains how to multiply an $n \times n$ matrix $\mathbf{A}$ by column an $n \times 1$ matrix (i.e., a column) $\mathbf{B}$:

$$\mathbf{A} \times \mathbf{B} = \begin{pmatrix} a_{11} & a_{12} & \cdots & a_{1n} \\ a_{21} & a_{22} & \cdots & a_{2n} \\ \vdots & \vdots & \ddots & \vdots \\ a_{n1} & a_{n2} & \cdots & a_{nn} \end{pmatrix} \times \begin{pmatrix} b_1 \\ b_2 \\ \vdots \\ b_n \end{pmatrix} = \begin{pmatrix} a_{11}b_1 + a_{12}b_2 + \cdots + a_{1n}b_n \\ a_{21}b_1 + a_{22}b_2 + \cdots + a_{2n}b_n \\ \vdots \\ a_{n1}b_1 + a_{n2}b_2 + \cdots + a_{nn}b_n \end{pmatrix} \tag{5.26}$$

From this, it is easy to deduce how to multiply an $n \times k$ matrix by a $k \times m$ matrix. In addition, one can add two matrices but one has to make sure that both matrices have exactly the same number of rows and columns. To add two matrices, one simply adds the corresponding elements. Thus, if $\mathbf{C} = \mathbf{A} + \mathbf{B}$, then $c_{ij} = a_{ij} + b_{ij}$. Furthermore, one can multiply a matrix by a scalar (e.g., a number) by multiplying each elements of the matrix by the scalar.

Operators representing observables have the following property:

$$\langle f|\hat{Q}f\rangle = \langle \hat{Q}f|f\rangle \quad \text{for all } f(x) \tag{5.27}$$

Operators having this property are called *Hermitian*. Thus observables are represented by Hermitian operators.

In finite-dimensional Hilbert space, this equation takes the following form:

$$\langle \mathbf{A}^\dagger \alpha|\beta\rangle = \langle \alpha|\mathbf{A}\beta\rangle \tag{5.28}$$

Here $\mathbf{A}^\dagger$ is the *hermitian conjugate* of $\mathbf{A}$:

$$\begin{pmatrix} a_{11}^* & a_{21}^* & \cdots & a_{n1}^* \\ a_{12}^* & a_{22}^* & \cdots & a_{n2}^* \\ \vdots & \vdots & \ddots & \vdots \\ a_{1n}^* & a_{2n}^* & \cdots & a_{nn}^* \end{pmatrix} \tag{5.29}$$

The transpose of a square matrix $(n \times n)$ is obtained by writing all of its rows as columns and all of its columns as rows. Thus the *transpose* of a matrix $\mathbf{A}$ is the matrix $\mathbf{A}^\mathsf{T}$:

$$\mathbf{A}^\mathsf{T} = \begin{pmatrix} a_{11} & a_{21} & \cdots & a_{n1} \\ a_{12} & a_{22} & \cdots & a_{n2} \\ \vdots & \vdots & \ddots & \vdots \\ a_{1n} & a_{2n} & \cdots & a_{nn} \end{pmatrix} \tag{5.30}$$

Assume that one prepares a set of identically prepared systems all in the same state Ψ. Then, when one measures an observable Q on these systems, one does not get the same result each time. This is known as the *indeterminacy* of quantum mechanics. One may wonder whether it is possible to prepare a state such that every measurement of Q would with certainty give the same result q? Clearly, such a state would be *determinate* state for Q. For each determinate state Ψ, an equation like the following is valid:

$$\hat{Q}\Phi = q\Phi \tag{5.31}$$

This equation is called the *eigenvalue* equation for the operator $\hat{Q}$, while Φ is an *eigenfunction* of $\hat{Q}$, and q is the corresponding *eigenvalue*. Note that q is a number. Also, remember that the time-independent Schrödinger equation is

$$\hat{H}\psi = E\psi \tag{5.32}$$

This simply means that the determinate states of the total energy are eigenfunctions of the Hamiltonian.

To every quantum system (e.g., an electron, a photon, a molecule, and even larger systems such as balls or even stars), we can associate a Hilbert space. Depending on the number of levels of the system (e.g., energy levels, position, etc.), the corresponding Hilbert space has the same number of unit vectors. Certainly, it is possible to have an infinite number of unit vectors but in quantum computing, we use Hilbert spaces with a finite number of unit vectors. Elementary particles have a property that is called spin. For educational purposes, the spin can be considered as the intrinsic angular momentum of an elementary particle. Depending on the way a particle spins around its axis, it creates a magnetic field similar to the magnetic field of the Earth. However, one should not forget that the spin is a quantum mechanical concept without any analogue in classical physics. An electron can have a spin "up" designated by $|\uparrow\rangle$ and a spin "down" designated by $|\downarrow\rangle$. Thus, it is a quantum system with two levels and it can be represented by a Hilbert space of dimension 2, which is written as $\mathcal{H}_2$. Vectors of this space would have the form $c_1|\uparrow\rangle + c_2|\downarrow\rangle$, where $|c_1|^2 + |c_2|^2 = 1$. The numbers $|c_1|^2$ and $|c_2|^2$ are called probability *amplitudes* and express the probability that the electron is in state $|\uparrow\rangle$ or in state $|\downarrow\rangle$, respectively. So it is quite possible that an electron has some "up" and some "down" spin at the same time! This property is called *superposition*.

Suppose we have a system of two electrons. Then, we can describe the system by the Hilbert space $\mathcal{H}_4 = \mathcal{H}_2 \otimes \mathcal{H}_2$. The operator $\otimes$ is called *tensor product* and it is a way to combine two Hilbert spaces and create a new one but it is also a way to create new vectors. When combining two Hilbert spaces, the unit vector are $|\downarrow\rangle \otimes |\downarrow\rangle$, $|\downarrow\rangle \otimes |\uparrow\rangle$, $|\uparrow\rangle \otimes |\downarrow\rangle$, and $|\uparrow\rangle \otimes |\uparrow\rangle$. In order to simplify notation, one can write the vector $|a\rangle \otimes |b\rangle$ as $|ab\rangle$. Also, one should bear on mind that in general $|ab\rangle \neq |ba\rangle$. The tensor product is defined as follows:

$$|a\rangle \otimes |b\rangle = \begin{pmatrix} a_1 \\ a_2 \end{pmatrix} \otimes \begin{pmatrix} b_1 \\ b_2 \end{pmatrix} = \begin{pmatrix} a_1 b_1 \\ a_1 b_2 \\ a_2 b_1 \\ a_2 b_2 \end{pmatrix} \tag{5.33}$$

Thus, it is easy to compute the tensor product of two vectors. In addition, the rule is applicable when multiplying other vectors — the first coordinate of the first vector is multiplied by all coordinates of the second and each multiplication is a coordinate in the new vector, the same applies for the second coordinate of the first vector, etc.

A state z of $\mathcal{H}_4$, or more generally of $\mathcal{H}_n$, that can be written as $z = x \otimes y$ is called *decomposable*; otherwise, it is called *entangled*. When the state is decomposable, then any measurement of x will not allow one to get information for y but this is not true for entangled states. If two quantum systems x and y are entangled, when we measure x, automatically we get to know the value of y. However, there are further consequences for entangled states. In 1935 Einstein, Boris Yakovlevich Podolsky, and Nathan Rosen[2] analyzed the idea of entangled states and found out that according to

---

[2] Albert Einstein, Boris Yakovlevich Podolsky, and Nathan Rosen. *Can quantum-mechanical description of physical reality be considered complete?* Physical Review, 47(10), pp. 777–780, 1935.

the principles of quantum mechanics, when, for example, two particles collide and each moves away from the other, surprisingly, we can measure the momentum of the first particle and then immediately we know the momentum of the second particle. But what is intriguing is that even if the two particles are very far from each other, one ancillary (or auxiliary) particle gets the information instantly. Thus, information travels faster than light, something impossible according to Einstein's theory of general relativity! This "paradox" is known in the literature as the EPR paradox.

One very interesting consequence of the EPR paradox is the "teleportation" of information, which was discovered by Bennett and his colleagues.[3] Although it is widely accepted that instantaneous information transfer is not possible, still it is possible to use entanglement to transfer a quantum state from one place to another. In particular, the research team that discovered quantum teleportation has proved that given a photon or any other quantum scale particle (e.g., an atom), it is possible to transfer its *properties* (e.g., the polarization of a photon) but not the particle itself to another photon even if the two are light years apart from each other. Because of the *no cloning* theorem, according to which the creation of identical copies of an arbitrary unknown quantum state is forbidden by quantum mechanics, the state of the original particle must be destroyed. The teleportation procedure involves an entangled ancillary pair of particles that are given to observers A and B and another particle whose state will be teleported. Observer A takes particle 2, observer B takes particle 3, and the particle that will teleported is particle 1. Observer A wants to teleport the initial state of particle 1:

$$|\phi_1\rangle = \alpha|\downarrow_1\rangle + \beta|\uparrow_1\rangle \tag{5.34}$$

while the entangled pair is in state

$$|\phi_{23}\rangle = \frac{1}{\sqrt{2}}\left(|\downarrow_2\rangle \otimes |\uparrow_3\rangle - |\uparrow_2\rangle \otimes |\downarrow_3\rangle\right) \tag{5.35}$$

To couple particle 1 with the entangled pair, observer A performs a complete measurement of particles 1 and 2 (technically she performs a Bell-state measurement but the details of this measurement are beyond the scope of this brief introduction). Observer A has to send the result of her measurement as classical information to observer B. When observer B receives this information, she can perform some sort of transformation on particle 3 so that its state is the state of the original particle.

Superposition and entanglement are exactly the laws of quantum mechanics that one harnesses and exploits in order to process information at the quantum level. However, we need to know how these two laws are used in the computational process.

---

[3] Charles Henry Bennett, Gilles Brassard, Claude Crépeau, Richard Jozsa, Asher Peres, and William K. Wootters. *Teleporting an unknown quantum state via dual classical and Einstein-Podolsky-Rosen channels.* Physical Review Letters, 79(13), pp. 1895–1899, 1980.

5.4   What Is Quantum Computer?

In 1980, Paul Benioff published a paper[4] where he described how a quantum mechanical system could be used to model a Turing machine. Benioff showed that a quantum mechanical system can be set up so to reliably perform computations. Unfortunately, this effort did not advanced computer science and technology in any significant way. Fortunately, the effort to use quantum mechanics to compute did not stop with Benioff's work. Indeed, two years later, the famous American theoretical physicist and Nobel price laureate Richard Phillips Feynman published a paper[5] where he pondered about the possibility of simulating a physical system with a computer. And by "physical system" he meant a quantum mechanical system.

Initially, Feynman examined whether it is possible to simulate and not to imitate time. Currently, the accepted thesis is that time is continuous and not discrete (see Section 7.2 for a detailed discussion). However, on a computer system with its limited accuracy, it makes sense to assume that time is discrete. Typically, computer simulations of classical physical systems are quite reliable because classical physics is *local* (i.e., an object is only directly influenced by its immediate surroundings), *causal*, and *reversible*.[6] However, quantum mechanics is not local as the EPR paradox has demonstrated. Nevertheless, time cannot be simulated but it can be imitated because the "simulation" involves a transition from one state to another. Next, he examined whether it is possible to simulate probabilities. Note that Feynman used the term probability to mean exactly what ordinary people call probability. Feynman concluded that probabilities can be simulated by two different methods — the computation of probabilities by an ordinary system or the use of a probabilistic computer. The main problem of the first method is that computers have limited accuracy and so it is quite possible that some event will be ignored because the associated probability is less than the system's number accuracy. Also, simulation is not feasible as it requires so many physical values that the problem becomes a difficult one. The second approach can be used to produce some statistical result after running the computer a number of times. The problem is that nature is unpredictable and when one has a large number of parameters it makes no sense to employ a probabilistic computer in the hope that on a run we will predict the real probabilities. One possible solution to Feynman's problem

[4] Paul Benioff. *The computer as a physical system: A microscopic quantum mechanical hamiltonian model of computers as represented by Turing machines.* Journal of Statistica Physics, 22(5), pp. 563–591, 1980.
[5] Richard P. Feynman. *Simulating physics with computers.* International Journal of Theoretical Physics, 21(6/7), pp. 467–488, 1982.
[6] This statement is not generally correct. For instance, thermodynamical systems are not reversible because entropy always grows while at the celestial level, planets are affected by stars. It is my understanding, that Feynman had on his mind simple systems where temperature does not play any role and where objects are affected by the gravity of Earth only.

would be to use a quantum computer, which has been called *quantum simulator* by Feynman. Since probabilities and time cannot be simulated, can a quantum system be simulated by a probabilistic computer?

The answer to this question is that the probabilistic computer cannot represent the results of quantum mechanics. For example, there are quantum systems whose components are associated with *negative* probabilities and this is something no ordinary computer can deal with. The next logical step was to describe how a quantum computer would look like. Indeed, Feynman described in detail the computer that would simulate nature in his plenary talk presented at the CLEO/IQEC Meeting in 1984.[7] After explaining that classical computers use bits, registers, and logical gates, he proposed that quantum computers should use quantum bits, quantum registers, and quantum gates.

A bit is either the digit 0 or the digit 1. Thus a sequence of these digits is a string of bits. In particular, a sequence of eight bits is called a *byte*. A *qubit* is a quantum system (typically a polarized photon, a nuclear spin, etc.) in which the two digits are represented by two quantum states: $|0\rangle$ and $|1\rangle$. These states are represented by the following matrices:

$$|0\rangle = \begin{pmatrix} 1 \\ 0 \end{pmatrix} \quad \text{and} \quad |1\rangle = \begin{pmatrix} 0 \\ 1 \end{pmatrix} \tag{5.36}$$

Also, these two states are "basic" states (i.e., they are a basis of a Hilbert space) and any other state of the qubit can be written as a superposition $\alpha|0\rangle + \beta|1\rangle$, where α and β are complex numbers that are called normalization factors and they must obey the normalization condition $|\alpha|^2 + |\beta|^2 = 1$. For example, consider a photon which can be polarized in the x direction or in the y direction and assume that these states are represented by the vectors $|\uparrow\rangle$ and $|\rightarrow\rangle$, respectively, then one can use $|\uparrow\rangle$ for $|0\rangle$ and $|\rightarrow\rangle$ for $|1\rangle$.

A *quantum register* of size n is a collection of n qubits. It is quite convenient to assume that information is stored in quantum registers in binary form. Thus, the numbers 7 and 3 are written as 111 and 011 in the binary system and so a quantum register is in state $|111\rangle$ or in state $|011\rangle$, respectively. As expected, $|111\rangle$ is a vector that belongs to $\mathcal{H}_8$:

$$|111\rangle = |1\rangle \otimes |1\rangle \otimes |1\rangle$$

$$= \begin{pmatrix} 0 \\ 1 \end{pmatrix} \otimes \begin{pmatrix} 0 \\ 1 \end{pmatrix} \otimes \begin{pmatrix} 0 \\ 1 \end{pmatrix}$$

---

[7]Richard P. Feynman. *Quantum mechanical computers*. Foundations of Physics, 16(6), pp. 507–531, 1986.

$$|111\rangle = \begin{pmatrix} 0 \\ 0 \\ 0 \\ 1 \end{pmatrix} \otimes \begin{pmatrix} 0 \\ 1 \end{pmatrix}$$

$$= \begin{pmatrix} 0 \cdot 0 \\ 0 \cdot 1 \\ 0 \cdot 0 \\ 0 \cdot 1 \\ 0 \cdot 0 \\ 0 \cdot 1 \\ 1 \cdot 0 \\ 1 \cdot 1 \end{pmatrix} = \begin{pmatrix} 0 \\ 0 \\ 0 \\ 0 \\ 0 \\ 0 \\ 0 \\ 1 \end{pmatrix}$$

Try the same for $|011\rangle$. Note that when one has n qubits, it is possible to encode the numbers from 0 to $2^n - 1$. By using superposition, it is possible to store two or even more numbers using three qubits. Instead of setting the first qubit to either $|0\rangle$ or $|1\rangle$, it is possible to prepare a superposition $\frac{1}{\sqrt{2}}(|0\rangle + |1\rangle)$ and get

$$\frac{1}{\sqrt{2}}(|0\rangle + |1\rangle) \otimes |1\rangle \otimes |1\rangle = \frac{1}{\sqrt{2}}(|011\rangle + |111\rangle) \tag{5.37}$$

Furthermore, if all qubits are prepared in superposition, then one can encode all integers from 0 to 7:

$$\frac{1}{\sqrt{2}}(|0\rangle + |1\rangle) \otimes \frac{1}{\sqrt{2}}(|0\rangle + |1\rangle) \otimes \frac{1}{\sqrt{2}}(|0\rangle + |1\rangle) \tag{5.38}$$

which can be written as follows:

$$\frac{1}{\sqrt{2}}(|000\rangle + |001\rangle + |010\rangle + |011\rangle + |100\rangle + |101\rangle + |110\rangle + |111\rangle) \tag{5.39}$$

Although I have explained what superposition is and a usage example was given, still it is not clear how a superposition is prepared. The answer is that one should use a *quantum gate*, that is, a device that performs an operation on selected qubits in a specific period of time. Mathematically, a quantum gate is represented by a *unitary* matrix. Remember that a matrix is a table of numbers. Now, a unitary matrix is one whose elements are complex numbers and when one gets its transpose and then the conjugate of each number in the matrix and, finally, multiplies this matrix by the original one, the result should be a matrix having all elements equal to 0 except those that lay on the diagonal (the one from the left to right); those elements are all equal to 1. However, it is necessary that when one multiplies the original matrix by the transposed and "conjugated" one, the result should be again this peculiar matrix (called the identity matrix). The following "equation" shows exactly what a unitary matrix is:

$$\begin{pmatrix} a & b \\ c & d \end{pmatrix}\begin{pmatrix} a^* & c^* \\ b^* & d^* \end{pmatrix} = \begin{pmatrix} 1 & 0 \\ 0 & 1 \end{pmatrix} = \begin{pmatrix} a^* & c^* \\ b^* & d^* \end{pmatrix}\begin{pmatrix} a & b \\ c & d \end{pmatrix} \tag{5.40}$$

The simplest quantum gate is the *quantum NOT gate*. This gate operates on single qubits and if the qubit is $|0\rangle$, it yields qubit $|1\rangle$ and vice versa. If 1 symbolizes the value "true" and 0 the value "false", then NOT gate turns "true" into "false" and "false" into "true". And this is exactly the reason why it is called a NOT gate. The quantum NOT gate is represented by the following matrix:

$$X = \begin{pmatrix} 0 & 1 \\ 1 & 0 \end{pmatrix} \tag{5.41}$$

In fact, the NOT gate is represented by one of the *Pauli matrices*; the other two matrices are:

$$Y = \begin{pmatrix} 0 & -i \\ i & 0 \end{pmatrix} \quad \text{and} \quad Z = \begin{pmatrix} 1 & 0 \\ 0 & -1 \end{pmatrix} \tag{5.42}$$

It is easy to verify that $X|0\rangle = |1\rangle$ and $X|1\rangle = |0\rangle$:

$$X|0\rangle = \begin{pmatrix} 0 & 1 \\ 1 & 0 \end{pmatrix}\begin{pmatrix} 1 \\ 0 \end{pmatrix} = \begin{pmatrix} 0\cdot 1 + 1\cdot 0 \\ 1\cdot 1 + 0\cdot 0 \end{pmatrix} = \begin{pmatrix} 0 \\ 1 \end{pmatrix} = |1\rangle \tag{5.43}$$

The verification of $X|1\rangle = |0\rangle$ is left as an exercise to the reader. The Hadamard matrix

$$H = \frac{1}{\sqrt{2}}\begin{pmatrix} 1 & 1 \\ 1 & -1 \end{pmatrix} \tag{5.44}$$

is a representation of the Hadamard gate. This gate has the following properties:

$$H|0\rangle = \frac{1}{\sqrt{2}}|0\rangle + \frac{1}{\sqrt{2}}|1\rangle$$

$$H|1\rangle = \frac{1}{\sqrt{2}}|0\rangle - \frac{1}{\sqrt{2}}|1\rangle$$

From this definition, it should be obvious that the Hadamard gate prepares a superposition. However, applying the Hadamard gate twice to a qubit does not produce what one would expect:

$$H\big(H|0\rangle\big) = H\left(\frac{1}{\sqrt{2}}|0\rangle + \frac{1}{\sqrt{2}}|1\rangle\right)$$

$$= \frac{1}{\sqrt{2}}H|0\rangle + \frac{1}{\sqrt{2}}H|1\rangle$$

$$= \frac{1}{\sqrt{2}}\frac{1}{\sqrt{2}}(|0\rangle + |1\rangle) + \frac{1}{\sqrt{2}}\frac{1}{\sqrt{2}}(|0\rangle - |1\rangle)$$

$$= \frac{1}{2}|0\rangle + \frac{1}{2}|1\rangle + \frac{1}{2}|0\rangle - \frac{1}{2}|1\rangle$$

$$= |0\rangle$$

The reader is invited to verify that $H\big(H|1\rangle\big) = |1\rangle$. Of course, the reason why applying twice the Hadamard gate does not produce something really complex is the fact that a qubit can be in one of two states and a superposition is a case where a qubit is in both states to some degree. Naturally, it would not make any sense to expect to see a qubit to be in one state with some degree and at the same time to be in this same state with some other degree!

In order to use a quantum gate, one must prepare the qubits. Then the unitary transformation is applied to these qubits and the result of the computation is obtained by performing a measurement and a calculation of the probability amplitudes. Consider the function f that maps 1 to 0 and 0 to 1. A quantum gate U_f computing f would evolve vectors of $\mathcal{H}_2$ to vectors of $\mathcal{H}_2$. In particular, U_f would evolve $|a\rangle|b\rangle$ into $|a\rangle|b \veebar f(a)\rangle$, where $\veebar$ is the "exclusive or" or just XOR operator (see Section 1.3). Recall that when a and b are the same, then $a \veebar b = 0$; otherwise $a \veebar b = 1$. Since all quantum gates must be reversible, U_f processes two qubits but leaves the first one intact but computes the XOR of the second qubit with the result of evaluating f on the value of the first qubit, that is:

$$U_f\big(|a\rangle|b\rangle\big) = |a\rangle|b \veebar f(x)\rangle \tag{5.45}$$

Figure 5.1 shows how U_f performs the specific evolution.

We are now ready to describe quantum parallelism by means of a simple example. We are given a function f whose argument is a binary digit and yields another binary digit. Also, the function is either constant (i.e., it yields the same number regardless of its argument) or balanced (i.e., it yields as many 0s as 1s over its domain) and we want to determine whether it is constant or balanced. Then, the only possible constant

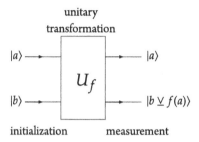

unitary
transformation

$|a\rangle$ ——————— $|a\rangle$

U_f

$|b\rangle$ ——————— $|b \vee f(a)\rangle$

initialization measurement

Figure 5.1: Evolution mechanism of quantum gates.

functions are $f(x) = 0$ and $f(x) = 1$. On the other hand, the only balanced functions are the following ones:

$$f(x) = \begin{cases} 0, & \text{if } x = 0 \\ 1, & \text{if } x = 1 \end{cases} \quad f(x) = \begin{cases} 1, & \text{if } x = 0 \\ 0, & \text{if } x = 1 \end{cases} \tag{5.46}$$

An ordinary machine has to test the function for each possible argument in order to determine whether it is balanced or constant. Technically, the machine has to compute two function values. Interestingly, a quantum computer can determine the same thing in just one step! Here is how this can be implemented.[8]

Initially, what we need to do is to prepare two $|0\rangle$ qubits. Then we send them through a NOT gate and then through a Hadamard gate:

$$(H \otimes H)(X \otimes X)(|0\rangle|0\rangle) = (H \otimes H)(|1\rangle|1\rangle)$$

$$= \frac{1}{2}(|0\rangle - |1\rangle)(|0\rangle - |1\rangle)$$

$$= \frac{1}{2}(|0\rangle|0\rangle - |1\rangle|0\rangle - |0\rangle|1\rangle + |1\rangle|1\rangle)$$

Now we send the two qubits through U_f (see also Figure 5.2):

$$\frac{1}{2}U_f(|0\rangle|0\rangle - |1\rangle|0\rangle - |0\rangle|1\rangle + |1\rangle|1\rangle) = \frac{1}{2}(|0\rangle|0 \vee f(0)\rangle - |1\rangle|0 \vee f(1)\rangle$$

$$- |0\rangle|1 \vee f(0)\rangle + |1\rangle|1 \vee f(1)\rangle)$$

$$= \frac{1}{2}\left(|0\rangle|f(0)\rangle - |1\rangle|f(1)\rangle - |0\rangle|\bar{f}(0)\rangle + |1\rangle|\bar{f}(0)\rangle\right)$$

where $f(x) = 0 \vee f(x)$ and $\bar{f}(x) = 1 \vee f(x)$. Observe how U_f acts on a "sum" of qubits and delivers the result in just one step. This specific evolution is the quantum parallelism

---

[8]This implementation was first proposed by Deutsch, nevertheless, the description below follows the exposition in Michael E. Cuffaro's paper titled, "Many worlds, the cluster-state quantum computer, and the problem of the preferred basis", Studies in History and Philosophy of Modern Physics, 43, pp. 35–42, 2012.

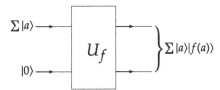

Figure 5.2: Quantum parallel computation. The operator Σ is used to compactly write the "sum" of various qubits.

process and it was proposed by Deutsch. In order to explain this *phenomenon*, he employed the *many worlds* interpretation of quantum mechanics. This interpretation of quantum mechanics was an attempt to solve the problem of quantum measurement — the equations of quantum mechanics cease to be valid when we intervene to make a measurement in a system. Hugh Everett III proposed the many worlds interpretation as a means to solve this problem. The many worlds interpretation is nicely summarized by Jim Baggot as follows:

> The different possible outcomes of a quantum measurement or the different possible final states of a quantum transition are all assumed to be realized, but in different equally real worlds which either split from one another or exist in parallel.

In a sense, the many world interpretation beats a resemblance of the use of *forces* in physics — one introduces a new "concept" to explain something we do not really understand. I think the following quote from the third chapter of Frederick Engels's *Dialectics of Nature* best describes this idea:

> As conceded on all hands (from Hegel to Helmholtz), the notion of force is derived from the activity of the human organism within its environment. We speak of muscular force, of the lifting force of the arm, of the leaping power of the legs, of the digestive force of the stomach and intestinal canal, of the sensory force of the nerves, of the secretory force of the glands, etc. In other words, in order to save having to give the real cause of a change brought about by a function of our organism, we fabricate a fictitious cause, a so-called force corresponding to the change. Then we carry this convenient method over to the external world also, and so invent as many forces as there are diverse phenomena.

It is rather important to say that there are models of quantum computing that by definition are free from the need to explain quantum parallelism with some absurd idea.

In the case of quantum parallelism, each term in the initial superposition corresponds to different universes or worlds (the two words mean exactly the same here).

These terms describe the state of each universe. Somehow these universes communicate through the superposition and submit their result through the quantum logic gate. This means that each particular value is computed in a different universe. The many worlds interpretation is quite problematic for various reasons which will be discussed in Chapter 7. Let us continue with our example:

Assume that the function is constant. Then, $f(0) = f(1)$ and $\bar{f}(0) = \bar{f}(1)$, which means that the state can be rewritten as follows:

$$\frac{1}{2}\Big(|0\rangle - |1\rangle\Big)\big((|f(0)\rangle - |\bar{f}(0)\rangle\big) \tag{5.47}$$

Similarly, if the function is balanced, then $f(0) \neq f(1)$, $f(1) = \bar{f}(0)$, and $\bar{f}(1) = f(0)$, which means that the state can be rewritten as follows:

$$\frac{1}{2}\Big(|0\rangle + |1\rangle\Big)\big((|f(0)\rangle - |\bar{f}(0)\rangle\big) \tag{5.48}$$

Now let us send the first qubit of each state through a Hadamard gate and we get

$$|1\rangle\frac{1}{\sqrt{2}}(|f(0)\rangle - |\bar{f}(0)\rangle) \quad \text{and} \quad |0\rangle\frac{1}{\sqrt{2}}\big(||f(0)\rangle - |\bar{f}(0)\rangle\big) \tag{5.49}$$

The last thing to do is to measure the first qubit and depending on the result of the measurement, we can deduce if the function is constant or balanced. This procedure is a simple *quantum algorithm* that can be described compactly as follows:

$$(H \otimes I)U_f(H \otimes H)(X \otimes X)\big(|0\rangle|0\rangle\big) \tag{5.50}$$

Although the TOFFOLI gate can be used in quantum circuits, still it is not a gate that is considered as a universal one. The CNOT logic gate together with other gates form a universal set of gates. The CNOT gate is defined as follows:

$$|00\rangle \xrightarrow{\text{CNOT}} |00\rangle$$

$$|01\rangle \xrightarrow{\text{CNOT}} |01\rangle$$

$$|10\rangle \xrightarrow{\text{CNOT}} |11\rangle$$

$$|11\rangle \xrightarrow{\text{CNOT}} |10\rangle$$

In other words, the CNOT gate flips the second qubit (the target qubit) if and only if the first qubit (the control qubit) is $|1\rangle$. One set includes the Hadamard gate, the "phase gate" $S = \left(\begin{smallmatrix} 1 & 0 \\ 0 & i \end{smallmatrix}\right)$, and the "$\pi/8$ gate" $T = \left(\begin{smallmatrix} 1 & 0 \\ 0 & e^{\pi i/4} \end{smallmatrix}\right)$, where the constant e is the base of the natural logarithm and $e = 2.71828182845904\ldots$.

Roughly, when using ordinary computers, the result of the computation is obtained by measuring the output from digital gates. In the case of quantum computers, we need to measure qubits in order to get the result of a computation. The problem is that when one attempts a measurement, information is lost and here is the reason why. Suppose that a qubit is in a state $|\psi\rangle$, which is in a superposition of the two states $|0\rangle$ and $|1\rangle$. After a measurement, $|\psi\rangle$ will collapse to either $|0\rangle$ or $|1\rangle$. For example, if the particle in state $|\psi\rangle$ is a photon, then the output of the measurement will be that the photon is polarized either in the x direction or in the y direction. But can we predict what will be the output of a measurement? We know that $|\psi\rangle = a|0\rangle + b|1\rangle$ and that $|a|^2$ and $|b|^2$ are the probabilities of obtaining a $|0\rangle$ or a $|1\rangle$, respectively, upon measurement. Currently, it is not known why states collapse upon measurement, or why superpositions are possible, but these are phenomena that have been experimentally verified and observed.

One basic problem of quantum computing is *decoherence*, which refers to the problem of maintaining a superposition of a large number of states whose evolution must be controlled in such a way that all the properties of a superposition are preserved. In other words, it is not easy to maintain a large number of qubits in superposition for a *long* time. Basically, there are at least two ways to avoid decoherence:

(i) Any register that evolves must be extremely well protected from the outside environment or else decoherence effects will emerge. These may destroy the superposition.

(ii) When the system is affected by some external disturbance, it is necessary to have some form of error correction codes in order to set the computer in the same state as where it was before the external disturbance happened.

What is really astonishing is that despite a number of serious obstacles, it is still possible to implement error correction for quantum computers. A reasonable approach is to use three particles (e.g., three spins) to represent each qubit. Thus $|0\rangle \rightarrow |000\rangle$ and $|1\rangle \rightarrow |111\rangle$. Now if the spin-flip rate is low (i.e., the number of particles that spontaneously change their spin is low), it is possible to identify errors by checking if all three spins are the same. For example, if the spins are in the state $\alpha|000\rangle + \beta|111\rangle$ and the first spin has flipped erroneously, the spins are in the state $\alpha|100\rangle + \beta|011\rangle$. It is possible to detect this error by checking whether the first spin is the same as the other two. Most importantly, this operation does not require a measurement. When an error is detected in the first spin, it corrected by flipping the first spin. Obviously, this process should be repeated for the second and the third spin.

Recently, a team of researchers performed experiments that may help us better understand the very nature of decoherence.[9] More specifically, this team performed

---

[9] This research is documented in Y. Glickman, Sh. Kotler, N. Akerman, and R. Ozeri, *Emergence of a measurement basis in atom-photon scattering*, Science, 339, pp. 1187–1191, 2013.

experiments in which they fired photons at atoms and then studied the results using a detector. When the photons hit the atoms, they were deflected (or scattered in quantum mechanical parlance). When a photon hit an atom whose spin was not in the same direction as its path, then the photon and the atom became entangled. However, when the spin of the photon and the atom were not in the same direction, then entanglement did not occur. One can use this remark to prevent decoherence. More specifically, when the photon and the atom did not become entangled, decoherence did not happen because there never was a superposition state. In addition, one might conclude that decoherence can be controlled by taking advantage of an atom's spin state.

The cluster-state model of quantum computation is about coherent quantum information processing, which is accomplished by a sequence of single-qubit measurements. In addition, topological quantum computation is an approach to quantum computing that considers decoherence as unwanted noise and strives at remaining deaf to this noise!

5.5   Cluster-State Quantum Computing

Cluster-state quantum computing[10] or *one-way* quantum computing shows the importance of both measurement and entanglement in an impressive way. Cluster-state computation simulates quantum circuits using, among others, *one-bit* teleportation, which makes up a class of teleportation methods that use one ancillary qubit, which resides on the sender's side. The various approaches are based on simple ideas that are described below:

Given an unknown qubit state $|\psi\rangle$ and the qubit state $|0\rangle$, one can swap them using only two CNOT logic gates, as shown below:

$$
\begin{array}{c}
|0\rangle \,\text{---}\oplus\text{---}\bullet\text{---}\, |\psi\rangle \\
|\psi\rangle \,\text{---}\bullet\text{---}\oplus\text{---}\, |0\rangle
\end{array}
\qquad (5.51)
$$

This is a typical quantum circuit and it is necessary to say a few things about it. First of all, time proceeds from left to right. Lines represent wires, which do not necessarily correspond to a physical wire. A "wire" may correspond to the passage of a physical particle such as a photon moving from one location to another. Measurements are represented by the "meter" symbol, while for each quantum gate, there is a specific symbol. The "•" symbol is used to indicate that the "control" qubit passes unaltered while the "⊕" indicates that the qubit that reaches this point will undergo a XOR

---

[10] Michael A. Nielsen. *Cluster-state quantum computation.* arXiv:quant-ph/0504097, 2005.

operation with the other qubit (remember that $|\psi\rangle = |0 \veebar \psi\rangle$ and $|0\rangle = |\psi \veebar \psi\rangle$). Note that circuit (5.51) is a visual representation of the following equation:

$$\text{CNOT}^{\text{T}}\text{CNOT}|\psi 0\rangle = |0\psi\rangle \tag{5.52}$$

where CNOT^{T} is the transpose of CNOT.

It is known that $X = HZH$, where X and Z are Pauli matrices. Also, given two matrices A and B that correspond to some one-qubit quantum gates, then the gate defined by their direct sum

$$A \oplus B = \begin{pmatrix} A & 0 \\ 0 & B \end{pmatrix} = \begin{pmatrix} A_{11} & A_{12} & 0 & 0 \\ A_{21} & A_{22} & 0 & 0 \\ 0 & 0 & B_{11} & B_{12} \\ 0 & 0 & B_{21} & B_{22} \end{pmatrix} \tag{5.53}$$

is a "controlled" gate that works as follows: If the first qubit is in state $|0\rangle$, then operation A is applied to the second qubit; otherwise, if the first qubit is in state $|0\rangle$, then operation B is applied to the second qubit. The CNOT gate is represented by $\left(\begin{smallmatrix} \mathbb{1} & 0 \\ 0 & X \end{smallmatrix}\right)$, where $\mathbb{1} = \left(\begin{smallmatrix} 1 & 0 \\ 0 & 1 \end{smallmatrix}\right)$ is the identity operator, that is, an operator that does not change a qubit at all. In a nutshell, the following "equation" is true:

The following "equation" depicts an interesting fact:

Here the last part of the "equation" is a controlled phase shift gate, $\phi(\delta)$, which is defined by $|0\rangle \rightarrow |0\rangle$ and $|1\rangle \rightarrow e^{i\delta}|1\rangle$, recall that $e^{i\delta} = \cos\delta + i\sin\delta$. This last equality is known as Euler's formula. Now, in this particular case, $|xy\rangle \rightarrow (-1)^{xy}|x,y\rangle$. Thus, the following circuit is equivalent to the circuit that swaps an unknown qubit state $|\psi\rangle$ and the qubit state $|0\rangle$.

$$\tag{5.54}$$

Although it is not required to read control bits during the application of a controlled quantum gate, still we may do so if we want to. Typically, a quantum state is prepared and then it is fed to a quantum circuit that evolves the quantum state, and in the end, one measures the output qubits. However, it is possible to proceed differently. One can choose to move the final measurement on control bits to earlier parts of the circuit, but this will force us to use the resulting classical bits to find out which operation to apply to the corresponding target qubits. This methodology will change the final state produced by the circuit, but it will not change its *statistical* properties. Thus, a quantum controlled gate can be replaced by a classical controlled gate when the control qubit is measured.

The meter represents the measurement of Z. This measurement projects the measured state onto $|0\rangle$ or $|1\rangle$. The double line connecting U with the meter carries the classical measurement result and U is performed if this result is $|1\rangle$. Using this "equation", we can transform circuit (5.54) to the following one:

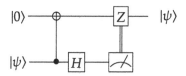

This is called Z *teleportation* and it is definitely something one cannot do by classical means. By replacing $|0\rangle$ with $|+\rangle \equiv \big(|0\rangle + |1\rangle\big)/\sqrt{2}$, where $a \equiv b$ means that a and b are equivalent, we get the following circuit:

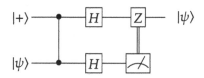

Now this circuit is "equal" to the following one:

Here m is either zero or one and corresponds to the outcome of a measurement of the first qubit. Assume that

$$Z_\theta = R_z(\theta) = \begin{pmatrix} e^{-i\theta/2} & 0 \\ 0 & e^{i\theta/2} \end{pmatrix} \tag{5.55}$$

Then, the following circuit is another example of one-bit teleportation:

$$Z_\theta|\psi\rangle \text{ —●—[} H \text{]—[measure]}$$
$$|+\rangle \text{ ————————— } X^m H Z_\theta |\psi\rangle$$

This circuit is "equal" to the following one:

$$|\psi\rangle \text{ —●—[} Z_\theta H \text{]—[measure]}$$
$$|+\rangle \text{ —●—————— } X^m H Z_\theta |\psi\rangle \tag{5.56}$$

The equality is justified by the fact that it is allowed to change the order of Z_θ and the controlled phase gates.

Imagine a grid on which we are allowed to place qubits on various positions. These qubits are connected by a conceptual wire so that there is a path from any qubit to any other qubit. This means that not all qubits are directly connected. In order to define a cluster state from an arrangement on a grid, we have to do a few things. First, we initialize each qubit in the state $|+\rangle$. Then, we perform a controlled phase gate between qubits that are directly connected. The following "equation" shows exactly how to go from an arrangement on a grid to a cluster state:

$$\bigcirc\!\!-\!\!\bigcirc = \begin{matrix} |+\rangle \text{ ——●——} \\ |+\rangle \text{ ——●——} \end{matrix} \tag{5.57}$$

Now we can see how to use circuit (5.56) in order to understand how cluster-state computation can simulate quantum circuits. Consider the following very simple circuit:

$$|+\rangle \text{—[} HZ_{\theta_1} \text{]—[} HZ_{\theta_2} \text{]—} \tag{5.58}$$

This almost trivial circuit exhibits all the important features that are used in the general case. Note that although the qubit starts in state $|+\rangle$ and the single qubit gates are HZ_α gates, this setup does not cause any loss of generality. The following is the cluster-state computation that simulates circuit (5.58):

$$\overset{1}{\left(HZ_{\theta_1}\right)}\!\!-\!\!\overset{2}{\left(HZ_{\pm\theta_2}\right)}\!\!-\!\!\bigcirc \tag{5.59}$$

The qubits that are labeled with the numbers 1 and 2 will be measured while the third one will remain as the output of the computation when the various measurements will be completed. The labels indicate the order by which qubits will be measured. Qubits labeled with the same number will be measured in any order or simultaneously. The $\pm$ symbol shows that the sign depends on the outcomes of earlier measurements. It is possible to fix the system so to have either a purely quantum output or a purely classical output. In the first case, one assumes that the computation yields a quantum state, which is the state of the qubits that remain when the sequence of processing measurements is over. In the second case, we merely add a sequence of single-qubit measurements that applies to the qubits that remain when the processing measurements have been terminated. The output of this cluster-state computation is equal to the output of the quantum circuit that follows:

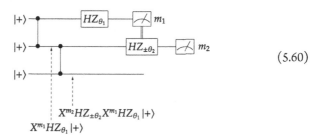

$$(5.60)$$

where m_1 and m_2 are the outputs of the measurements on the first and the second qubits. In addition, it is a fact that $XZ_\theta X = Z_{-\theta}$. Also, the sign of θ_2 depends on the measurement m_1. In particular, if $m_1 = 1$, then the sign is $+$ and if $m_1 = 0$, then the sign is $-$. The circuits used in cluster-state quantum computing allow measurements and *feedforward* of the measurement results during computation, so later actions may depend on the results of earlier measurements. Now the output of (5.60) is $X^{m_2}HZ_{\pm\theta_2}X^{m_1}HZ_{\theta_1}|+\rangle$ and because of feedforward, we have $Z_{\pm\theta_2}X^{m_1} = X^{m_1}Z_{\theta_2}$. Thus the following holds true:

$$X^{m_2}HZ_{\pm\theta_2}X^{m_1}HZ_{\theta_1}|+\rangle \to X^{m_2}HZ_{(-1)^{m_1}\theta_2}X^{m_1}HZ_{\theta_1}|+\rangle$$
$$= X^{m_2}HZ_{\theta_2}X^{m_1}HZ_{\theta_1}|+\rangle$$
$$= X^{m_2}Z^{m_1}HZ_{\theta_2}HZ_{\theta_1}|+\rangle$$

The $X^{m_2}Z^{m_1}$ part is something "useless". Since we know m_1 and m_2, we can perform teleportation to remove this factor and, of course, $HZ_{\theta_2}HZ_{\theta_1}|+\rangle$ is exactly what we wanted. This method can be used to simulate multi-qubit quantum circuits. For example, the circuit can be simulated using the following cluster-state computation:

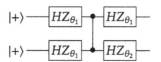

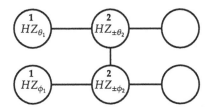

5.6   Topological Quantum Computing

A coffee cup with a single handle and a donut are definitely two different geometric objects, but both have a hole that can be used to hold them. Imagine that the coffee cup and the donut were made by plasticine. Then, it would be possible to deform the coffee cup to a donut and vice versa. Thus a coffee cup and a donut are in this sense equivalent. However, a coffee sleeve and a donut are not equivalent in the previous sense since it is not possible to deform the coffee sleeve to a donut because the coffee sleeve has no hole. The systematic study of properties of geometric objects that are equivalent under certain deformations is called *topology*. *Knot theory* is a subfield of topology that studies simple closed curves in three-dimensional space, known as knots, in order to determine whether two such curves can be rearranged (without cutting) to be exactly alike. Of course, one may wonder what topology, in general, and knot theory, in particular, have to do with quantum computing.

A topological quantum computer is built using a system in a *non-Abelian topological phase*. This simply means that a topological quantum computing is performed in an environment where observable properties do not depend on what space–time coordinates we opt to use. In addition, one has to create *quasiparticles*,[11] braid them, and measure their final state in order to perform a computation.

The *perfect gas* is an idealization of a gas of identical non-interacting particles in which the potential energy of interaction between the particles is unimportant compared to their kinetic energy (e.g., energy of motion). Assume that such a gas exists and its particles may be in discrete single-particle states $1, 2, \ldots, r, \ldots$, having energies $\varepsilon_1 \leq \varepsilon_2 \leq \cdots \varepsilon_r \leq \cdots$. A gas of N particles is in a state that is completely determined by the set of *occupation numbers*

$$n_1, n_2, \ldots, n_r, \ldots \qquad (5.61)$$

---

[11]Quasiparticles are imaginary particles that correspond to excitations (i.e., energy elevations) and transport spin, charge, momentum, and energy. In metals, quasiparticles and quasiholes are "realized" by electrons and holes equivalent to the absence of electrons, correspondingly. Richard D. Mattuck In *A Guide to Feynman Diagrams in the Many-Body Problem*, likens a particle to a horse, and a quasiparticle to a galloping horse plus the dust cloud created by it. Thus, in an electrolyte solution, a positively charged ion will temporarily attract negatively charged ions and all these particles together will make up a quasiparticle.

where n_i is the number of particles in the single-particle state i. An important question regarding this gas is the following: What values can these occupation numbers assume? Without going into any detail, according to quantum mechanics, there are two different situations that correspond to two mutually exclusive classes. In the first situation an occupation number can assume any integer value (i.e., $n_i = 0, 1, 2, ...$) while in the second situation, at most one particle can be in any state (e.g., $n_7 = 0, 1$). The first situation is known as *Bose–Einstein statistics* while the second one as *Fermi–Dirac statistics*. Examples of *bosons*, that is, particles obeying the Bose–Einstein statistics, are photons and π mesons. Examples of *fermions*, that is, particles obeying the Fermi–Dirac statistics, are electrons, positrons, and protons.

Although we live in three spatial dimensions, it is possible to construct a two-dimensional quantum system whose wavefunction splits to a two-dimensional and a one-dimensional part. How is this possible? Roughly, some functions $f(x, y, z)$ but not all of them can be written as $f_{xy}(x, y)f_z(z)$. This is exactly the idea that one can use in order to rewrite a wavefunction. And by suppressing motion in two spatial dimensions, we get a two-dimensional system that is described by the Ψ_{xy} part of the wavefunction. Now suppose that we have two identical bosons in two spatial dimensions whose combined wavefunction is $\psi(\mathbf{r}_1, \mathbf{r}_2)$. Then, if we interchange the positions of these particles twice, the resulting wavefunction would be $e^{i\theta}\psi(\mathbf{r}_1, \mathbf{r}_2)$, where θ is called *exchange phase*. Note, that in three dimensions, there is only one way to perform this swap, however, this is not true when we are in two dimensions [see Figure 5.3(a)]. Obviously, the same remarks apply to the case where the two particles are fermions. In general, when "working" in two dimensions θ can be any rational multiple of 2π

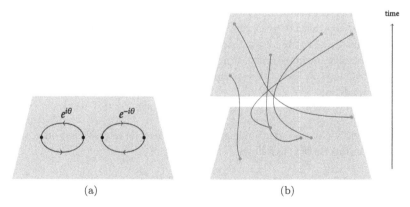

(a)   (b)

Figure 5.3: Interchanging positions in two dimensions. (a) The difference between right-handed and left-handed switching may result to a quantum phase factor $e^{\pm i\theta}$ which is different from ±1. (b) If many particles interchange positions, the collection of particle paths can be viewed as a braid.

(e.g., $3/2\pi$, $2/3\pi$, but not $\sqrt{2}\pi$). The particles whose exchange phase is different from 0 (bosons) and π (fermions) are called *anyons*.

Figure 5.3(b) depicts anyons that change position in the plane. The curly lines show the positions of these specific particles on the plane in the course of time (they are called *worldlines*). Now, these trajectories are not arbitrary but, provided we have n such trajectories, they are in one-to-one correspondence with the elements of the *braid group* $\mathcal{B}_n$. In order to explain what the braid group is, we need to know the basics of braids, which are special kinds of knots. Let me start with a definition of what a braid is.

Assume that $\mathbb{D}$ is a unit cube, that is, each of its 12 edges have unit length. On the top face of the cube, we place n points, P_1, P_2,..., P_n. Also, we place n points on the bottom face, Q_1, Q_2,..., Q_n. The next thing to do in the construction is to join the n points Q_1, Q_2,..., Q_n with P_1, P_2,..., P_n by means of n polygonal segments d_1, d_2,..., d_n (i.e., each d_i is a connected series of line segments). However, there are restrictions on how these segments can join the points:

(i)   The segments d_1, d_2,..., d_n do not intersect each other (i.e., they have no common points).

(ii) Segments are not allowed to connect two points P_i and P_j (or Q_i and Q_j).

(iii) Each *level plane* (i.e., a plane that is parallel to the plane that extends the top face and lies between the top and the bottom face) contains exactly *one and only point* of each d_i.

Each of the n segments d_1,..., d_n including the end points P_1,..., P_n, Q_1,..., Q_n is called a *(braid) string* and the totality of the n strings is called an *n-braid*, or a *braid with n strings*. In order to see whether two braids are equivalent, one needs to introduce the notion of elementary move.

Again, assume that $\mathbb{D}$ is a unit cube that contains a number of strings. Also, suppose that AB is an edge of a string d and that C is a point of $\mathbb{D}$ such that the triangle $\triangle ABC$ does not intersect any other string. In addition, suppose that $AC \cup CB$ is a string that consists of AC and CB. Then, this substring should intersect all level planes at most one point and we define:

$$\Omega \equiv \text{replace } AB \text{ by } AC \cup CB \tag{5.62}$$

Similarly, if $AC \cup CB$ is a part of a string and $\triangle ABC$ does not intersect any other string, we define the inverse of Ω as follows:

$$\Omega^{-1} \equiv \text{replace } AC \cup CB \text{ by } AB \tag{5.63}$$

Both Ω and Ω^{-1} are called *elementary moves*. Thus an n-braid β is *equivalent* (or *equal*) to another n-braid β', written as $\beta \sim \beta'$, if β can be transformed or deformed into β' by applying a finite series of elementary moves.

It is possible to "multiply" braids, but we should not confuse this operation with multiplication between numbers. Braid multiplication is an operation that has some of the characteristics of number multiplication. In order to keep things simple, we will work with elements of $\mathcal{B}_4$, the set of all 4-braids. Given two braids β_1 and β_2, their product $\beta_1 \beta_2$ is a new braid produced by stacking the second atop the first one. For example, consider the following three braids.

σ_1 σ_2 σ_3

Then, $\sigma_1 \sigma_2$ and $\sigma_2 \sigma_1$ are defined as follows:

$\sigma_1 \sigma_2$ $\sigma_2 \sigma_1$

From these drawings, it is easy to deduce that $\sigma_1 \sigma_2 \neq \sigma_2 \sigma_1$. However, $\sigma_1 \sigma_3 = \sigma_3 \sigma_1$ as the following braid diagram reveals:

$\sigma_1 \sigma_3$ $\sigma_3 \sigma_1$

There is a special braid called the *identity* braid, which is denoted by $\mathbf{1}_n$. A form of this braid is shown in the braid diagram that follows.

The identity braid is such that for any braid β, it holds that $\beta \mathbf{1}_n \sim \mathbf{1}_n \beta$. For example, the multiplication in the diagram below verifies that $\mathbf{1}_4 \sigma_2 \sim \sigma_2 \mathbf{1}_4$.

$$1_4\sigma_2 \qquad \sigma_2 1_4$$

From, any braid β, one can construct a braid β^{-1} such that $\beta\beta^{-1} \sim 1_n \sim \beta^{-1}\beta$. How can we construct such a braid? Think again the cube $\mathbb{D}$ and the braid β inside. Now create a new cube $\mathbb{D}'$ and place it under the bottom face of $\mathbb{D}$. By assuming that the bottom face of $\mathbb{D}$ or the top face of $\mathbb{D}'$ is the reflection "line", we create the new braid β^{-1}. The following pictorial representation shows the result of this construction.

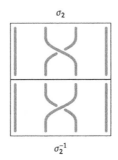

$$\sigma_2$$
$$\sigma_2^{-1}$$

Now it is easy to verify that, for example, $\sigma_2\sigma_2^{-1} \sim 1_4$:

$$\sigma_2\sigma_2^{-1} \qquad\qquad 1_4$$

In general, it holds that $\sigma_i(\sigma_j\sigma_k) = (\sigma_i\sigma_j)\sigma_k$. This property of the braid product is called *associativity*. The set of n-braids equipped with braid multiplication, the special element 1_n, and the inverse braid form what is called a *group*. Roughly, an operation between elements of a set (e.g., braids or numbers) combines two of them and yields another element of some other set, in the most general case. A group is a set together with an operation that yields elements that belong to this set. However, not all sets equipped with an operation are groups. The group should contain an identity element and for each element, it should contain its inverse. Also, the operation must be associative (i.e., it should not matter in what order we perform the operation). For example, the set of integers and addition between integers forms a group. Zero is the identity, the inverse of a is $-a$ and obviously $a + (b + c) = (a + b) + c$. Similarly, it is easy to conclude that the set of all n-braids, $\mathcal{B}_n$, is a group.[12] Because $\sigma_i \sigma_j \neq \sigma_j \sigma_i$ is in general true, $\mathcal{B}_n$ is called *non-Abelian*.

So far, I have used specific braids to demonstrate the various properties. Apart from $\mathbf{1}_m$ I have used braids σ_i and σ_i^{-1}. It is quite possible that the reader may have concluded that there is something special about these braids. Indeed, any braid β in $\mathcal{B}_n$ can be written as a product of the braids $\sigma_1,..., \sigma_n, \sigma_1^{-1},..., \sigma_1^{-n}$. These braids are known as *Artin braids* to honor Emil Artin who introduced the braid group in 1925. Figure 5.4 shows the Artin braids for $\mathcal{B}_4$. Note that for each $\mathcal{B}_n$, the number of σ_i braids is $n - 1$ and the number of σ_i^{-1} is also $n - 1$.

The worldlines of two anyons can be exchanged. This leads to the braiding of worldlines. Two anyons can be created from the vacuum. Quantum vacuum fluctuations (i.e., roughly a temporal variation in the amount of energy at a point in space that allows the creation of particles) should be held responsible for the creation of an anyon and its anti-anyon (i.e., its anti-particle). A third possibility is to have two anyons that are fused to create a new anyon. Figure 5.5 is a pictorial representation of these events.

Different types of anyons have different fusion rules. There are three different *Ising* anyons: $\mathbf{1}$, σ, and ψ. The fusion rules for these anyons are:

$$\sigma \times \sigma = \mathbf{1} + \psi, \quad \sigma \times \psi = \sigma, \quad \psi \times \psi = \mathbf{1},$$
$$\mathbf{1} \times x = x \quad \text{for } x = \mathbf{1}, \sigma, \psi$$

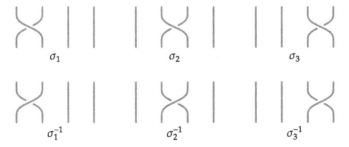

$$\sigma_1 \qquad \sigma_2 \qquad \sigma_3$$

$$\sigma_1^{-1} \qquad \sigma_2^{-1} \qquad \sigma_3^{-1}$$

Figure 5.4: The Artin braids for $\mathcal{B}_4$.

---

[12] Strictly speaking, $\mathcal{B}_n$ is not a group because it includes braids that are equivalent (the set of integers does not include equivalent numbers). The set $\mathcal{B}_n/\sim$ (i.e., the set of all *equivalence classes* of $\sim$, see Section 6.4), which, in a sense, is the set $\mathcal{B}_n$ after removing all "duplicate" elements, is a group.

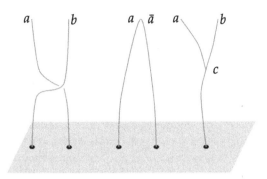

Figure 5.5: Worldlines of particles "living" on a plane with time flowing downwards. An exchange of two particles is depicted on the left; creation of a pair from the vacuum is depicted in the middle; and fusion of two particles is depicted on the right.

Here, the notation $a \times b = c + d$ means that the two particles a and b are fused and can yield either particle c or particle d. For the *Fibonacci* anyons, there is only one fusion rule:

$$1 \times \tau = \tau, \quad \tau \times 1 = \tau, \quad \text{and} \quad \tau \times \tau = 1 + \tau \qquad (5.64)$$

The fusion rules are very important since we create anyons and then either exchange them or fuse them in order to compute. For example, for Ising anyons when the outcome is 1, the qubit is in state $|0\rangle$ and when the outcome is ψ, the qubit is in state $|1\rangle$. However, we will continue discussing only Fibonacci anyons, mainly because it seems to be the most promising direction in topological quantum computing.

A computer can be initialized by creating pairs of anyons. Technically, these pairs consist of a quasiparticle and a quasihole. Note that here quasiholes are anyons having opposite electric charge and both of them have a special spin called *q-spin*. The state of each such pair will be designated by $(\bullet, \bullet)_n$. In a way, one may think of this designation as a cross-section of world-lines. Now, n indicates the total q-spin number and means that both anyons are in q-spin state n. In order to encode a qubit, one has to create two pairs of pairs. Thus $|0\rangle = ((\bullet, \bullet)_1, (\bullet, \bullet)_1))_1$ and $|1\rangle = ((\bullet, \bullet)_\tau, (\bullet, \bullet)_\tau))_1$. However, one may consider to use three anyons, instead of four, to encode a qubit. In this case, qubits are represented as follows:

$$|0\rangle = ((\bullet, \bullet)_1, \bullet)_\tau$$
$$|1\rangle = \left((\bullet, \bullet)_\tau, \bullet\right)_\tau$$
$$|N\rangle = \left((\bullet, \bullet)_\tau, \bullet\right)_1$$

The last one corresponds to a single non-computable state. Now when it comes to braiding, the Artin braids are expressed as operators that act on qubits. For example, here is the definition of σ_1 and σ_2:

$$\sigma_1 = \left(\begin{array}{cc|} \mathrm{e}^{-\mathrm{i}4\pi/5} & 0 \\ 0 & \mathrm{e}^{\mathrm{i}3\pi/5} \\ \hline & \mathrm{e}^{\mathrm{i}3\pi/5} \end{array} \right), \ \sigma_2 = \left(\begin{array}{cc|} -\varphi^{-1}\mathrm{e}^{-\mathrm{i}\pi/5} & \sqrt{\varphi^{-1}}\mathrm{e}^{-\mathrm{i}3\pi/5} \\ \sqrt{\varphi^{-1}}\mathrm{e}^{-\mathrm{i}3\pi/5} & -\varphi^{-1} \\ \hline & \mathrm{e}^{\mathrm{i}3\pi/5} \end{array} \right) \quad (5.65)$$

where $\varphi = \frac{1+\sqrt{5}}{2}$ is the *golden ratio*[13] and the upper left 2×2 parts of these matrices act on computational qubits while the lower right matrix element is a phase factor that is applied to the state $|N\rangle$. Also, the reader must bear in mind that since we have three anyons, there are three worldlines and so the braids are part of $\mathcal{B}_3$. Braided worldlines correspond to quantum gates. At the end of the computation, if anyons fuse to 1, the result of computation is $|0\rangle$; otherwise it is $|1\rangle$. The definition of two qubit gates is more complicated so I will say nothing on this subject.

So far, I have presented anyons and how they can be used to compute, however, I have not explained how these quasiparticles can been observed. Obviously, anyons is not something a casual observer will encounter in any quantum system. On the contrary, anyons are encountered in the environment where the quantum Hall effect is realized.

Before giving an overview of the quantum Hall effect (QHE), it would be beneficial to introduce the plain Hall effect. Consider a thin plate of a conductive material (e.g., a material that allows electric current to flow, such as copper). Electric current is supplied by a battery and flows through this plate. Also, we position a pair of probes connected to a voltmeter opposite each other along the sides of the plate. Initially, the voltmeter shows no voltage difference. However, when a magnetic field perpendicular to the current flow is applied to the plate, the voltmeter shows a small voltage difference. By reversing the direction (polarity) of the magnetic field, the polarity of the voltage will also reverse. This phenomenon is called the Hall effect, named after Edwin Hall.

In 1980, Klaus von Klitzing discovered the QHE, which is a very important achievement in condensed matter physics. For this discovery, he was honored with the Nobel Prize in Physics in 1985. Von Klitzing found that at low temperatures and in strong magnetic fields, the Hall resistance of a two-dimensional electron system assumes quantized values that depend only on fundamental constants and integer numbers. In particular, the Hall resistance $R_H = h/(je^2)$, where e is the elementary

---

[13] Take a line segment and divide it into two parts so that when the length of the longer part (a) is divided by the length of the smaller part (b) is equal to the length of the line segment divided by the length of longer part, or in symbols:

$$\frac{a}{b} = \frac{a+b}{a} = 1.6180339887498948420...$$

This number is an irrational one and has been used extensively in ancient architecture.

charge (i.e., the electric charge carried by a single electron), and $j = 1, 2, 3, \ldots$. The constants h and e combine to form the quantum resistance $h/(e^2) \approx 25812$ Ω, which is used as the international reference standard for resistance. Currently, there are some experimentally verified two-dimensional electron systems. One such system is the surface of liquid helium.

5.7   Adiabatic Quantum Computing

Light up a candle and hold it with your hand. Then start walking fast through your house. Most probably the candle will snuff out. Now, hold the candle and walk slowly. The candle will not snuff out. Of course, the difference lies in the gradual and not sudden change of position. An *adiabatic invariant* is a physical quantity that remains constant when the parameters of a system are *adiabatically* (slowly) changing. A simple example of such a system is a pendulum having a weight of mass m attached to the end of it, whose string has length L, and which is oscillating with energy E and period τ. By gradually decreasing L, E gradually increases and τ decreases, but the product $E\tau$ remains constant. Thus, this product is an adiabatic invariant. Now consider a mass m attached to a string that passes through a small hole in the plane where this mass slides. The string has length R and we can reduce it by pulling the string that is under the hole. In this case, E/ω, where $E = \frac{1}{2}mR^2\omega^2$, is the adiabatic invariance.[14]

Adiabatic systems are not unique to classical mechanics. In fact, there is a theorem that describes the evolution of a quantum adiabatic system. In particular, the *adiabatic theorem* refers to cases where the initial Hamiltonian H_i of the system is gradually changing into a final Hamiltonian H_f. Roughly speaking, the theorem states that if a particle was initially in the nth eigenstate of H_i, then it will be carried into the nth eigenstate of H_f. The basic idea behind adiabatic quantum computing is to employ the Schrödinger equation

$$i\hbar \frac{d|\psi(t)\rangle}{dt} = \hat{H}(t)|\psi(t)\rangle \tag{5.66}$$

If $\hat{H}(t)$ is slowly varying, we can use the adiabatic theorem to see how $\hat{H}(t)$ will evolve. This capability was initially utilized by Edward Farhi, Jeffrey Goldstone, Sam Gutmann, and Michael Sipser to devise a quantum algorithm for solving instances of the *satisfiability problem*,[15] which will be explained in the next paragraph. The idea behind their solution is to find the *ground state* (i.e., the lowest-energy state) of a Hamiltonian

---

[14] These and other examples of adiabatic invariance are presented in Frank S. Crawford. *Elementary examples of adiabatic invariance.* American Journal of Physics, 58, pp. 337–344, 1990.

[15] See: Edward Farhi, Jeffrey Goldstone, Sam Gutmann, Joshua Lapan, Andrew Lundgren, and Daniel Preda. *A quantum adiabatic evolution algorithm applied to random instances of an NP-complete problem.* Science, 292, pp. 472–475, April 2001. Also, see: Edward Farhi, Jeffrey Goldstone, Sam Gutmann, and Michael Sipser. *Quantum Computation by Adiabatic Evolution.* arXiv:quant-ph/0001106v1, 2000.

H_P. Unfortunately, finding the ground state of the Hamiltonian of some problem may turn out to be a difficult task, although the specification of the Hamiltonian is straightforward. A solution to this problem is to consider another Hamiltonian H_B that is straightforward to construct and whose ground state is easy to find. The next step involves the deformation of H_B in time T into H_P through a time-dependent process:

$$\hat{H}\left(\frac{t}{T}\right) = \left(1 - \frac{t}{T}\right)\hat{H}_B + \frac{t}{T}\hat{H}_P \qquad (5.67)$$

According to the adiabatic theorem, if the deformation is slow enough, the initial state will evolve with high probability into the desired ground state. The longer it takes for the deformation to take place, the higher is the probability that it will evolve into the desired state.

In Boolean logic, *Boolean variables* $x_1, x_2, \ldots, x_n$ stand for individual statements (e.g., statements like "it is snowing now"), which can be either true or false. Now let X be a finite set of Boolean variables and $\overline{X}$ a set whose elements are the elements of X negated. That is if x is in X, then $\neg x = \overline{x}$ is in $\overline{X}$. Now the elements of both X and $\overline{X}$ are called *literals*, a *clause* C is non-empty set of literals, and a *Boolean formula* F is a set of clauses defined on X.

Example 5.7.1 Suppose that $X = \{x_1, x_2, x_3\}$ and naturally $\overline{X} = \{\overline{x_1}, \overline{x_2}, \overline{x_3}\}$. Then a formula F might be

$$F = \left\{\{x_1, \overline{x_2}, x_3\}, \{\overline{x_1}\}, \{x_2, \overline{x_2}\}\right\} \qquad (5.68)$$

It is customary to write each element of F as a disjunction between its elements. Remember that $\vee$ is the corresponding operator. Thus $\{x_1, \overline{x_2}, x_3\}$ is written as $x_1 \vee \overline{x_2} \vee x_3$.

A *truth assignment* for F is a mapping from X to the set $\{1, 0\}$. A truth assignment T *satisfies* F if for each clause C in F there is at least one variable x_i such that

— $T(x_i) = 1$ and x_i is in C or
— $T(x_i) = 0$ and $\overline{x_i}$ is in C.

F is called *satisfiable* if there is a truth assignment that satisfies it. In the literature, this is called the SAT problem.

Example 5.7.2 Assume that $G = \left\{\{x_1, \overline{x_2}\}, \{\overline{x_1}, x_2\}\right\}$ and that $T(x_1) = T(x_2) = 1$. Then, G is satisfiable.

The 3-SAT problem is a special case of SAT where each clause has exactly three elements. An n-bit instance of 3-SAT is a formula that is specified by a set of three-element clauses.

This problem belongs to a large class of problems that can be solved by the equivalent problem of finding a variable assignment that minimizes an "energy" function, which has the following form for each clause C:

$$h_C(z_{i_C}, z_{j_C}, z_{k_C}) = \begin{cases} 0, & \text{if } (z_{i_C}, z_{j_C}, z_{k_C}) \text{ satisfies clause } C \\ 1, & \text{if } (z_{i_C}, z_{j_C}, z_{k_C}) \text{ does not satisfy clause } C \end{cases} \tag{5.69}$$

The total energy h is

$$h = \sum_C h_C \tag{5.70}$$

It should be clear that $h \geq 0$ whereas $h(z_1, z_2, ..., z_n) = 0$ if and only if $(z_1, z_2, ..., z_n)$ satisfies all the clauses. Thus, in order to see whether a formula has a truth assignment that satisfies it, we need to see if there is a minimum energy configuration of h.

In a quantum mechanical setting, bits are replaced by qubits. Thus bit z_i is replaced by qubit $|z_i\rangle$. For the states $|z_i\rangle$ it holds that

$$\frac{1}{2}(1 - Z)|z_i\rangle = z_i|z_i\rangle \tag{5.71}$$

In order to solve this problem quantum mechanically, we consider an n-dimensional Hilbert space with the vectors $|z_1\rangle, |z_2\rangle, ..., |z_n\rangle$ as its basis. A clause C is associated with the operator $H_{P,C}$:

$$\hat{H}_{P,C}\left(|z_1\rangle|z_2\rangle|z_n\rangle\right) = h_C(z_{i_C}, z_{j_C}, z_{k_C})|z_1\rangle|z_2\rangle|z_n\rangle \tag{5.72}$$

The Hamiltonian associated with all these clauses are:

$$\hat{H}_P = \sum_C H_{P,C} \tag{5.73}$$

$\hat{H}_P$ is non-negative, which means that $\langle\psi|\hat{H}_P\psi\rangle \geq 0$ for all $|\psi\rangle$ and $\hat{H}_P|\psi\rangle = 0$ if and only if $|\psi\rangle$ is a superposition of states of the form $|z_1\rangle|z_2\rangle \cdots |z_n\rangle$ where $z_1, z_2, ..., z_n$ satisfy all clauses.

In general, for some problem, Π it might be difficult to find the ground state of H_P although it is not difficult to specify H_P. Thus, we consider an n-bit Hamiltonian H_B that is easy to construct and whose ground state is simple to find. Assume that $\hat{H}_B^{(i)}$ is a one-bit Hamiltonian that acts on the ith bit:

$$\hat{H}_B^{(i)} = \frac{1}{2}(1 - X) \quad \text{so } \hat{H}_B^{(i)}|x_i = x\rangle = x|x_i = x\rangle \tag{5.74}$$

where

$$|x_i = 0\rangle = \frac{1}{\sqrt{2}}\begin{pmatrix} 1 \\ 1 \end{pmatrix} \quad \text{and} \quad |x_i = 1\rangle = \frac{1}{\sqrt{2}}\begin{pmatrix} 1 \\ -1 \end{pmatrix} \tag{5.75}$$

Now a clause C is associated with the three bits $i_C, j_C,$ and k_C. Next we define

$$H_{B,C} = H_B^{(i_C)} + H_B^{(j_C)} + H_B^{(k_C)} \quad \text{and} \quad H_B = \sum_C H_{B,C} \qquad (5.76)$$

The ground state of H_B is $|x_1 = 0\rangle|x_2 = 0\rangle \cdots |x_n = 0\rangle$ and is a superposition of the basis vectors:

$$|x_1 = 0\rangle|x_2 = 0\rangle \cdots |x_n = 0\rangle = \frac{1}{2^{n/2}} \sum_{z_1} \sum_{z_2} \cdots \sum_{z_n} |z_1\rangle|z_2\rangle \cdots |z_n\rangle \qquad (5.77)$$

A basic characteristic of H_B is that its ground state is easy to find. This particular H_B leads to an $\hat{H}(t)$ that takes the following form:

$$\hat{H}(t) = \hat{H}_{C_1}(t) + \hat{H}_{C_2}(t) + \cdots + \hat{H}_{C_m}(t) \qquad (5.78)$$

where $\hat{H}_{C_i}(t)$ is a Hamiltonian associated with clause C_i, which is what we were looking for. The final solution involves some quite complicated calculations that are not important for this discussion. What matters is that one can use the adiabatic theorem to solve computational problems.

5.8   Programmable Quantum Computers

Any atom has a nucleus that may consist of a number of protons and neutrons and a number of electrons that, figuratively speaking, orbit the nucleus. In fact, these orbits are not arbitrary but are quite specific. Each such orbit is called an *electron shell*. These shells are called K_1, L_1, L_2, L_3, M_1 and so on. Each proton has a positive charge and each electron has a negative charge. Both charges are equal. Typically, in any atom the number of electrons is equal to the number of protons. Thus an atom has no charge. However, there are atoms that do not have an equal number of electrons and protons and so have some charge. Such atoms are called *ions*. There are natural phenomena that produce ions. For example, the atoms in the ionosphere (i.e., the part of the Earth's upper atmosphere from about 60 to 1000 km) are ionized by solar radiation. Ions are interesting to quantum computing because they are used to realize qubits. And this is exactly the reason why we need to trap them. Thus it is necessary to devise an ion trap.

An ion trap is a device that uses both electric and magnetic fields to trap ions. In particular, a rf-Paul trap (named after the Nobel laureate Wolfgang Paul) uses direct current (e.g., current produced by ordinary batteries) and radio frequency (rf) oscillating electric fields to trap ions. The ions of the chemical element ytterbium (Yb) are especially attractive because electrons can go from electron shell L_1 to the shell L_3 or from L_3 to L_1 and this allows the use of optical fibers. In turn, this makes feasible the coupling of atomic qubits to photonic qubits. And this is exactly the reason why an ion trap that uses ytterbium ions is particularly interesting.[16] Ions are trapped between four rods that make up the trap. This trap is mounted inside vacuum chamber (usually made of stainless steel). Ytterbium ions are loaded into the trap by photoionization of an atomic beam of neutral ytterbium. This beam is produced by heating a tube made of stainless steel that is filled with ytterbium and which is directed toward the trap. The ytterbium atoms are photoionized by laser beams once inside the trap. Laser beams are also used to stabilize the ions: the ions "crash" with laser beam and so they stop.

When a body rotates, then it has something we call *moment of inertia*. We use the letter I to symbolize this quantity. The moment of inertia depends on the mass of the body and its geometry. Thus, for a point mass (an idealized object that has no width and no height but has some mass) having mass m, its moment of inertia is $I = mr^2$, where r is the distance from the axis of rotation. Also, for a sphere, the moment of inertia is $2/5\,mr^5$ (r is the radius of the sphere) and for a rod that rotates around its center, the moment of inertia is $1/12\,ml^2$, where l is the length of the rod. The *angular momentum* of a body is the product of its moment of inertia and the *angular velocity*. At any given moment, the angular velocity of a body that rotates about an axis is $\omega = v/r$, where v is its speed at that specific moment and r is the distance from the axis of rotation. It has been found that the orbital angular momentum is quantized according to the relationship:

$$L = \sqrt{\ell(\ell + 1)}\hbar$$

where ℓ is the angular momentum quantum number and is a non-negative integer. Using trapped $^{171}\mathrm{Yb}^{+}$ ions it is possible to encode qubits. Qubit $|0\rangle$ is encoded by state $L_1|F = 0; m_f = 0\rangle$ and qubit $|1\rangle$ is encoded by state $L_1|F = 1; m_f = 0\rangle$, where F is the total angular momentum of the atom, m_F is its projection along the quantization axis, and L_1 denotes the energy shell.

All approaches presented so far, assume that we set up a system to solve a specific problem. But when we want to solve another problem, we have to practically build a new computer. However, it seems that trapped $^{171}\mathrm{Yb}^{+}$ ions can be used to design a (small) programmable quantum computer.[17] The computer's qubits are $^{171}\mathrm{Yb}^{+}$ ions. Initially, all qubits are set to state $|0\rangle$. In order to achieve this and other tasks, we use laser beams of different colors. Thus, a laser beam of a specific color illuminates each ion until it reaches the required state. This technique is used to measure the qubits at the end of computation. The quantum gates that are required to solve a particular problem are "built" on the fly. In particular, laser beams of different colors illuminate the ions so to emulate the behavior of gate. This is possible because all gates are "built"

[16]S. Olmschenk, K.C. Younge, D.L. Moehring, D.N. Matsukevich, P. Maunz, and C. Monroe. *Manipulation and detection of a trapped Yb⁺ hyperfine qubit*, Physical Review A, 76(5), p. 052314, 2007.
[17]S. Debnath, N.M. Linke, C. Figgatt, K.A. Landsman, K. Wright, and C. Monroe. *Demonstration of a small programmable quantum computer with atomic qubits.* Nature, 536, pp. 63–66, 2016.

using two "simple" gates: $R_\phi(\theta)$ and $XX(\chi_{ij})$. These gates are described by the following matrices:

$$R_\phi(\theta) = \begin{bmatrix} \cos\left(\frac{\theta}{2}\right) & -i\sin\left(\frac{\theta}{2}\right)e^{-i\phi} \\ -i\sin\left(\frac{\theta}{2}\right)e^{i\phi} & \cos\left(\frac{\theta}{2}\right) \end{bmatrix}$$

and

$$XX(\chi_{ij}) = \begin{bmatrix} \cos(\chi_{ij}) & 0 & 0 & -i\sin(\chi_{ij}) \\ 0 & \cos(\chi_{ij}) & -i\sin(\chi_{ij}) & 0 \\ 0 & -i\sin(\chi_{ij}) & \cos(\chi_{ij}) & 0 \\ -i\sin(\chi_{ij}) & 0 & 0 & \cos(\chi_{ij}) \end{bmatrix}$$

Certainly, there are no real gates involved but the combination of the different lasers, which realize these two gates, have the effect of various quantum gates. For example, the Hadamard quantum gate can be implemented as $H = R_x(-\pi)R_y(\pi/2)$. The technology has been tested with Simon's algorithm, which has been invented by Daniel R. Simon.[18] This algorithm finds how often a given mathematical function repeats and I will say more on this in the next section.

5.9   What Can We Do With a Quantum Computer?

I have tried to present the basic ideas behind the four major approaches to quantum computation, but one may wonder why does quantum computing matter? In different words, is there anything special to quantum computers that makes them so attractive?

First of all, we need to recall that there are easy and difficult problems. Easy problems can be solved with our current hardware with no difficulty. However, it may take centuries to solve a difficult problem with current hardware. A quantum computer should be able to employ massive parallelism to solve difficult problems in speed comparable to that required by ordinary computers to solve easy problems. This simply implies that difficult problems will become easy. Let me give a specific example that will make things clear.

Cryptography[19] is a method by which we store or transmit data in form so that only the people for whom it is intended can read and process it. A very simple method to encrypt plain text is Caesar's cipher. According to this method, each letter is replaced by another letter some fixed number of positions down the alphabet. For example, given here the plain and "cipher" alphabet when we shift by two each letter:

plain: a b c d e f g h i j k l m n o p q r s t u v w x y z
cipher: c d e f g h i j k l m n o p q r s t u v w x y z a b

[18]Daniel R. Simon. *On the power of quantum computation.* SIAM Journal on Computing, 26(5), pp. 1474–1483, 1997.
[19]From Greek kryptos (κρυπτός) "hidden" + graph "process of writing or recording".

Thus, the word "computer" is encrypted as "eqorwvgt". To decrypt the word is easy: just go back two positions. Of course, this method is far too easy to decrypt and that is the reason it is not used today. Nowadays, we need strong encryption techniques that will make it impossible for anyone to crack them.

When we have an integer number, a prime factorization of it is the decomposition of the number into a product of smaller prime numbers. Modern cryptographic algorithms depend on the fact that prime factorization of large numbers takes a long time. In different words, prime factorization is a difficult problem. The encryption method uses the product of two large prime numbers, which is known as "public key", to encrypt a message and a "secret key" consisting of those two primes used to decrypt the message. Typically, the public key is known to everybody so that everyone can encrypt data (e.g., when one sends a credit card number as an encrypted text) but only one of very few should know the secret key. This encryption and decryption method is safe because prime factorization is almost impossible. But is this really true?

In 1994, at the Annual Symposium on Foundations of Computer Science that took place in Santa Fe, New Mexico, Peter Williston Shor presented a quantum algorithm that could perform prime factorization very fast.[20] In principle, *Shor's algorithm* shows that it is possible to solve difficult problems as if they were easy! Second it shows why quantum computing matters: it opens a new vista to computing that may make it possible to make all difficult problems easy. So finally have proved that difficult problems are in fact easy.

Unfortunately, the answer to this question is no! In fact, it is quite interesting to see what Shor himself had to say about this:

> In the history of computer science, however, most important problems have turned out to be either polynomial-time or NP-complete. Thus quantum computers will likely not become widely useful unless they can solve NP-complete ["difficult"] problems. Solving NP-complete problems efficiently is a Holy Grail of theoretical computer science which very few people expect to be possible on a classical computer. Finding polynomial-time algorithms for solving these problems on a quantum computer would be a momentous discovery. There are some weak indications that quantum computers are not powerful enough to solve NP-complete problems, but I do not believe that this potentiality should be ruled out as yet.

---

[20] Peter W. Shor. *Polynomial-time algorithms for prime factorization and discrete logarithms on a quantum computer.* SIAM Journal on Computing, 26(5), pp. 1484–1509, 1997. This paper is also available as arXiv:quant-ph/9508027.

Clearly, this not so optimistic stance. However, Edward Gerjuoy has presented an interesting study where he concluded[21]:

> Suppose we were able to construct a quantum computer which, like the classical computer we hypothesized previously, could factor RSA-309 [i.e., a number with 309 digits] in two weeks time. Then this same quantum computer should be able to factor RSA-617 [i.e., a number with 617 digits] in no more than about nine weeks, in contrast to the 60 million years for the classical computer.

I think this shows, beyond any doubt, the computation speed up we get, when using quantum computers. But what makes quantum computing so appealing? Martin Ziegler has shown that an infinite number of Turing machines operating in parallel can solve most insolvable problems.[22] Although it is impossible to have an infinite number of Turing machines, still this thought experiment shows why parallelism matters. Although I have talked about quantum parallelism, still I have not described a "real" word application of it.

The following is description of Shor's algorithm.[23] In what follows, N is the number whose prime factorization we are looking for. $\gcd(x, y)$ is the greatest common divisor of x and y, $x \bmod y$ denotes the remainder of the integer division of x by y, and $a \equiv b \bmod m$ means that m divides $b - a$.

(i) Input N.
(ii) Select a integer a such that $a < N$.
(iii) Let $h = \gcd(a, N)$.
(iv) If $h \neq 1$, then h is a factor of N and stop; otherwise, continue with step (v).
(v) Find the *period* of the function

$$f(x) = a^x \bmod N$$

that is, the smallest positive integer r such that $f(x+r) = f(x)$. In different words, find the period of the sequence:

$$a \bmod N, \ a^2 \bmod N, \ a^3 \bmod N, \ a^4 \bmod N, \ a^5 \bmod N, \ldots$$

(vi) If r is odd, go to step (ii).
(vii) If $a^{r/2} \equiv -1 \bmod N$, go to step (ii).
(viii) $\gcd(a^{r/2} + 1, N)$ and $\gcd(a^{r/2} - 1, N)$ are the non-trivial factors of N.

---

[21] Edward Gerjuoy. *Shor's factoring algorithm and modern cryptography. An illustration of the capabilities inherent in quantum computers*, American Journal of Physics, 73(6), pp. 521–540, 2005.
[22] Ziegler, M. *Computational power of infinite quantum parallelism.* International Journal of Theoretical Physics, 44(11), pp. 2059–2071, 2005.
[23] The presentation is based on Wikipedia's article "Shor's algorithm" and the entry "Shor's Algorithm — Breaking RSA Encryption" by Stephanie Blanda in the AMS Blogs site.

Note that here we use Euclid's well-documented algorithm to compute the greatest common divisor. The only part of this algorithm that cannot be tackled by classical machine is step (v). This step can be computed by quantum computer only. The machine uses two quantum registers having n qubits. Here, n is large enough so to be able to represent in binary form the number N. Then, the individual qubits of the first register go through a Hadamard gate. Although we have discussed how Hadamard gates can transform single qubits, it is easy to get a similar effect for many qubits. In the next step, we call an oracle, or black-box quantum function, that is actually $f(x)$, where x is what is stored in the first register. The result is stored in the second register. A second Hadamard transformation is applied to the first register and then we measure both registers. This process is repeated a few times and the result is computed.

Another thing that no *conventional* system can do is the computation of random numbers. This means that such systems produce *pseudo-random* numbers that can be predicted. Since random numbers are used in cryptography, it is really important to be able to generate truly random numbers. Deutsch, while introducing quantum Turing machines (i.e., Turing machines capable of holding qubits in their cells), argued that quantum computers should be able to compute truly random numbers.

Annotated Bibliography

- Seiki Akama. *Elements of Quantum Computing*. Springer, Cham, 2015.

  This little book, when compared to others in the field, is one that contains all information required to get a good understanding of quantum computing. The book's linguistic quality is its only downside.

- Jean-Louis Basdevant and Jean Dalibard. *Quantum Mechanics*. 2nd edition, Springer, Berlin, 2005.

  A good introduction to quantum mechanics. In my opinion this book and Griffiths's introduction to quantum mechanics are an ideal combination to learn the physics of quantum mechanics.

- David B. Cook. *Probability and Schrödinger's Mechanics*. World Scientific, Singapore, 2002.

  The book tries to give a "new" interpretation of Schrödinger's Mechanics using Andrey Nikolaevich Kolmogorov (Андрей Николаевич Колмогоров) formulation of probability theory.

- Artur Ekert, Patrick Hayden, Hitoshi Inamori, and Daniel Kuan Li Oi. *What is quantum computation?* International Journal of Modern Physics A, 16(20), pp. 3335–3363, 2001.

This is a very nice review of quantum computation. In fact, I would suggest this article to anyone with a basic understanding of quantum mechanics who just wants to learn the basics of quantum computing.

- G. Falci and E. Paladino. *The physics of quantum computation*. International Journal of Quantum Information, 12(4), pp. 1430003-1–1430003-40, 2014.

In this article, the authors give an overview of the physics involved in quantum computing. However, the paper equates quantum computing with quantum circuits, therefore there is nothing there about topological quantum computing or adiabatic quantum computing.

- David J. Griffiths. *Introduction to Quantum Mechanics*. 2nd edition, Pearson Education Limited, NJ, 2004.

A very accessible introduction to quantum mechanics. The book introduces all relevant mathematical notions and also introduces some very "specialized" subjects such as teleportation, the adiabatic approximation, the no-clone theorem, etc.

- Mika Hirvensalo. *Quantum Computing*. Springer, Berlin, 2001.

One of the earliest textbooks on quantum computing. Still a book that I would suggest to computer science students who want to learn about quantum circuits and quantum algorithms.

- L. Hormozi, G. Zikos, N. E. Bonesteel, and S. H. Simon. *Topological quantum compiling*. Physical Review B, 75, pp. 165310, 2007. Also available as *arXiv:quant-ph/0610111v2*.

This paper describes how one can set up a topological quantum computer to perform a specific task. In particular, it describes how one translate an algorithm so as to work on a quantum topological computer.

- Kunio Murasugi and Bohdan I. Kurpita. *A Study of Braids*. Springer Science and Business Media, Dordrecht, 1999.

A very good and accessible introduction to braid theory. Certainly, this is a book for someone who wants to deepen his understanding of braids and not for someone who just wants to understand more about topological quantum computers.

- Chetan Nayak, Steven H. Simon, Ady Stern, Michael Freedman, and Sankar Das Sarma. *Non-abelian anyons and topological quantum computation*. Reviews of Modern Physics, 80, pp. 1083–1159, 2008. Also available as *arXiv:0707.1889v2* *[cond-mat.str-el]*.

This is the most recent and quite *accessible* presentation of topological quantum computing. Naturally, it is accessible to people who have a good background in physics.

- Jiannis K. Pachos. *Introduction to Topological Quantum Computation*. Cambridge University Press, Cambridge, 2012.

Currently, the only book-length presentation of topological quantum computing. The book is written for theoretical physicists. Thus, computer scientists with no background in physics will have great difficulty following it.

- Roger Penrose. *The Road to Reality: A Complete Guide to the Laws of the Universe*. Alfred A. Knopf, New York, 2004.

An excellent and lengthy volume that presents modern physics. In a sense, the book is self-contained since it introduces many required ideas from mathematics, computer science and of course physics.

- Colin P. Williams. *Explorations in Quantum Computing*. 2nd edition, Springer, London, 2011.

A very good and modern introduction to quantum computing. The emphasis is on quantum gates and quantum circuits but it includes a brief presentation of other approaches to quantum computing.

Chapter 6

Vague Computing

Typically, computing is perceived as a precise activity. For example, the operations of the Turing machine are precisely defined. Even the scanning head is assumed to accurately recognize what is printed on any cell while printing to cells never fails. Clearly, this is not what happens in reality where many different operations fail for various reasons (e.g., printers fail to print because of a paper jam). Of course, this happens because computing is a pure mathematical theory that does not take into account *imprecision, ambiguity, uncertainty,* and *vagueness.* It is a fact that vagueness is so pervasive in language and in the way we understand things that led many thinkers and philosophers to devote time and energy on understanding it. But vagueness has a role to play in computing and its role will be described in this chapter.

6.1 What is Vagueness?

It is widely accepted that a term is vague to the extent that it has borderline cases, that is, cases in which it seems impossible either to apply or not to apply a vague term. The Sorites Paradox (σόφισμα τοῦ σωρείτη), which was introduced by Eubulides of Miletus (Εὐβουλίδης ὁ Μιλήσιος), is a typical example of an argument that shows what it is meant by borderline cases. The term "sorites" (σωρείτες) derives from the Greek word for heap: "soros" (σωρός). No one can say for sure how many grains of wheat make a heap and this is a paradox. In particular, all agree that a single grain of wheat does not comprise a heap. The same applies for two, three, or four, etc. grains of wheat as they do not comprise a heap. However, there is a point where the number of grains becomes large enough to be called a heap, but there is no general agreement as to which number this is.

Bertrand Arthur William Russell[1] was perhaps the first thinker who has given a definition of vagueness:

> Per contra, a representation is vague when the relation of the representing system to the represented system is not one-one, but one-many.

Mathematically speaking, a representation is vague when it is not characterized by a function but by a relation (Section 6.4 introduces mathematical relations). According to Russel, a photograph which is so smudged that it might equally represent Smith or Jones or Robinson is vague. Building on Russell's ideas, Max Black[2] had argued that most scientific theories, which should definitely include a theory of computation, are "ostensibly expressed in terms of objects never encountered in experience". In different words, one could argue that the Turing machine is an idealization of some real-world system and as such does not correspond to anything real! Black proposed as a definition of vagueness the one given by Charles Sanders Peirce:

> A proposition is vague when there are possible states of things concerning which it is intrinsically uncertain whether, had they been contemplated by the speaker, he would have regarded them as excluded or allowed by the proposition. By intrinsically uncertain we mean not uncertain in consequence of any ignorance of the interpreter, but because the speaker's habits of language were indeterminate.

According to Black, the word chair demonstrates the suitability of this definition. But it is the "variety of applications to objects differing in size, shape and material" that "should not be confused with the vagueness of the word". In different words, vagueness should not be confused with generality. In addition, vagueness should not be confused with ambiguity. A term or phrase is ambiguous if it has at least two specific meanings that make sense in context. For example, consider the phrase he ate the cookies on the couch. Obviously, one can say that this means that someone brought his cookies, sat on the couch and ate them there or that someone ate the cookies that were on the couch. In conclusion, vagueness, ambiguity, and generality are entirely different notions.

It is widely accepted that there are three different expressions of vagueness:

Many-valued Logics and Fuzziness Borderline statements are assigned truth-values that are between absolute truth and absolute falsehood.
Supervaluationism The idea that borderline statements lack a truth value.

---

[1] Bertrand Russell, Vagueness. Australasian Journal of Philosophy, 1(2), pp. 84–92, 1923.
[2] Max Black. Vagueness. An exercise in logical analysis. Philosophy of Science, 4(4), pp. 427–455, 1937.

Contextualism The truth value of a proposition depends on its context (i.e., a person may be tall relative to American men but short relative to NBA players).

In this chapter, I am only interested in many-valued logics and fuzziness so I will not further discuss supervaluationism and contextualism.

It seems that Aristotle was the first thinker who recognized that there are propositions that cannot be classified as either true or false. In particular, in Chapter IX of his treatise *De Interpretatione* (Περὶ Ἑρμηνείας, On Interpretation), which is part of his *Organon*, he ponders about *future contingents* and their truth values. He concludes that[3]

ὥστε δῆλον ὅτι οὐκ ἀνάγκη πάσης καταφάσεως καὶ ἀποφάσεως τῶν
ἀντικειμένων τὴν μὲν ἀληθῆ τὴν δὲν ψευδῆ εἶναι· οὐ γὰρ ὥσπερ ἐπὶ
τῶν ὄντων οὕτως ἔχει καὶ ἐπὶ τῶν μὴ ὄντων, δυνατῶν δὲ εἶναι ἢ μὴ εἶναι,
ἀλλ' ὥσπερ εἴρηται.[4]

In a sense, Aristotle's work influenced the development of many valued logics by Jan Łukasiewicz and Post. In a few words, a many-valued logic is a logic where propositions may assume more than two truth values. For example, a typical three-valued logic may have true (T), false (F), and undecided (U) as truth values. The following is the truth table for the logical conjunction of a three-valued logic:

$$T \wedge T = T \quad T \wedge U = U \quad T \wedge F = F$$
$$U \wedge T = U \quad U \wedge U = U \quad U \wedge F = F$$
$$F \wedge T = F \quad F \wedge U = F \quad F \wedge F = F$$

One can define logics with a finite number n of truth values. It is convenient to represent these n truth values as fractions:

$$\frac{0}{n-1}, \frac{1}{n-1}, \cdots, \frac{n-2}{n-1}, \frac{n-1}{n-1}$$

Thus, a three-valued logic would have the numbers 0, 1/2, and 1 as truth values. It is even possible to define an infinite-valued logic where the truth values are the numbers 0, 1, 2,.... A special form of infinite-valued logic is fuzzy logic. However, this logic was a "byproduct" of fuzzy set theory, which will be discussed in the rest of this section.

Sets occupy a key position in mathematics. Indeed, one approach to the foundations of mathematics is based on the idea that sets are the most fundamental objects of mathematics. According to the established view, given an element x and a set A, then x either belongs to the set, denoted by $x \in A$, or does not belong to the set, denoted by $x \notin A$. By relaxing this requirement, one gets generalizations of the concept of a set.

---

[3] Aristotle. *Organo: Categoriae and De Interpretatione*. Kaktos Editions, Athens, 1994.

[4] Translation: *It is clear then that it is not necessary for every affirmation or negation taken from among opposite propositions that the one be true, the other false. For what is non-existent but has the potentiality of being or not being does not behave after the fashion of what is existent, but in the manner just explained.*

In different words, by generalizing the membership relation, one gets a generalization of sets. For example, we have encountered multisets. In a *fuzzy* set, an element belongs to some degree to it. This degree is usually assumed to be a number that is greater or equal to zero and less than or equal to one, where zero denotes falsehood and one denotes truth. Fuzzy sets have been introduced by Lotfi Asker Zadeh.[5] Of course, it is not enough to propose a generalization of some structure. In addition, it is necessary to explain why this generalization matters and how it leads us to a better understanding of things. Thus, in the rest of this section, I will try to address these matters.

Given some ordinary set X, one can define many fuzzy subsets of X by assigning to each element of X a membership degree. For example, if X is a set of students, then it makes perfectly sense to define the fuzzy subset of tall students, short students, thin or fat students and so on. However, one should be aware that there is no automatic or mechanical way to say that Aylin is tall to a specific degree. In most cases, this degree depends on many things. For instance, if Aylin is 1.75 meters tall and her friends are basketball players, who are definitely tall people, and we are asked to form a fuzzy set of tall people, clearly her membership degree will be rather low. On the other hand, if she spends her free time with people whose height is close to the *average*, then the corresponding membership degree will be probably high. Interestingly, even if the membership degree of some element is zero, still this element belongs to the fuzzy subset with this membership degree.

Before presenting an interesting objection to the very idea behind fuzzy sets, let me stress that there are a number of scholars who believe that vagueness should be equated with lack of information. A typical manifestation of this "lack of information" is any measurement. And this is something I have learned during my first days as a university student. At that time, I and my team-mates had to perform our first laboratory exercise, which involved the calculation of the volume of a wooden cube. We were surprised by the *simplicity* of the assignment, yet we were also puzzled by the instructor's demand to measure the edge of the cube ten times and perform the same calculations each time. When we proceeded with the actual measurements, we realized that not all of them were the same! But let me continue with the objection against fuzzy set theory.

A reader who has not bought the idea of fuzzy sets may think that instead of saying that Aylin is tall to a degree that is equal to 0.70, we would state that *Aylin is 70% tall* and, thus, we would have transformed a vague statement into an *exact* one! Because of this (invalid) "transformation", it has been advocated that the need for fuzzy sets is just an "elementary mistake of logic". To begin with, the statement *Aylin is 70% tall* can be either true or false. On the other hand, the statement *Aylin is tall to a degree that is equal to 0.70* is actually a "compound" statement that consists of the proposition *Aylin is tall* and its denotation that happens to be the number 0.70 (remember 1 denotes truth

[5]Lotfi Asker Zadeh. *Fuzzy sets*, Information and Control, 8, pp. 338–353, 1965.

while 0 denotes falsehood). So these two statements are different things and, of course, there is no "elementary mistake of logic".

The great Canadian physician William Osler stated that "Medicine is a science of uncertainty and an art of probability". Statements like this are based on the traditional view that probability theory is the most important, if not the only, facet of uncertainty. Although it has been argued that fuzziness is another facet of *uncertainty*, and I will say more on this in a moment, still today there are researchers who work (?) in the area of fuzzy set theory and assume that fuzziness and probability theory are the same! Unfortunately, I have learned this the hard way. A few years ago, I submitted a paper to a prestigious journal devoted to the international advancement of the theory and application of fuzzy sets. The paper described a model of computation built on the idea that vagueness is a fundamental property of our world. To my surprise, the paper was rejected mainly because three (!) reviewers insisted that it is a "fact that there is an equivalence between fuzzy set theory and probability theory". Obviously, I was shocked with what the reviews stated, but I thought that if reviewers and editors of journals, which are supposed to be devoted to the advancement of fuzzy set theory, express and endorse, respectively, such ideas, then people who are not convinced that fuzzy set theory has anything to offer, should dismiss fuzzy set theory as almost nonsense! Of course, just because some people have not clarified their thoughts, to say the least, it does not mean fuzzy set theory is nonsense. On the contrary, the advent of fuzzy set theory has brought a new way of looking at the world that surrounds us.

Zadeh has repeatedly advocated the idea that fuzzy set theory and probability theory are complementary theories and not competitive. In particular, Zadeh presented a number of reasons why probability theory cannot be used to tackle all problems that are encountered in an environment of uncertainty. Some points that demonstrate his thesis are given below:

(i) One cannot express in the language of probability theory judgments like *tomorrow will be a warm day* or *there will be a strong earthquake in the near future*, etc. According to Zadeh these propositions involve *fuzzy events*.

(ii) One cannot express certain fuzzy quantifiers like *many, most, few,* etc. in the language of probability theory.

(iii) It is not possible to perform estimations that involve fuzzy probabilities expressed as *likely, unlikely, not very likely,* etc.

(iv) It is difficult to analyze problems in which data are described in fuzzy terms.

Personally, I think these points are staying at the linguistic level but vagueness is not just a linguistic phenomenon. Otherwise, the whole discussion is pointless. A better approach is the one advocated by Bart Kosko, another prominent fuzzy set theorist, who defended the superiority of fuzzy set theory when compared to probability theory by saying that fuzziness "measures the degree to which an event occurs, not whether it occurs. Randomness describes the uncertainty of event occurrence".[6] Still this does not answer the previous question: Does vagueness exist in nature?

If vagueness is not just part of our everyday expression, then there should be vague objects. But are there such objects? I will not give a "yes" or "no" answer but instead I would like to ponder about the length of the UK coastline. The British Cartographic Society does not give an exact answer on their web page. Instead, they give this answer: *The true answer is: it depends! It depends on the scale at which you measure it.* Benoit Mandelbrot gave exactly this answer in 1967. So, in a sense, it is not exactly known what is inside the UK and what is outside. And, of course, it is quite possible that some objects may lie somewhere in the middle. Thus, one could say that the UK is actually a vague object since its boundaries are not rigid. Similarly, clouds are vague objects for exactly the same reasons. On the other hand, there are objects that appear to be genuine vague objects (e.g., think of heaps of grain or men with few hair), still most of them are classified as such because the terms that describe them are vague. However, there is a third approach to the problem of finding vague objects in nature. In quantum mechanics, the "standard" view is that elementary particles are indistinguishable, nevertheless, not everybody shares this view. More specifically, Edward Jonathan Lowe[7] has argued against this view thus demonstrating that vagueness exists in the subatomic level:

Suppose (to keep matters simple) that in an ionization chamber a free electron a is captured by a certain atom to form a negative ion which, a short time later, reverts to a neutral state by releasing an electron b. As I understand it, according to currently accepted quantum-mechanical principles there may simply be no objective fact of the matter as to whether or not a is identical with b. It should be emphasized that what is being proposed here is not merely that we may well have no way of telling whether or not a and b are identical, which would imply only an epistemic indeterminacy. It is well known that the sort of indeterminacy presupposed by orthodox interpretations of quantum theory is more than merely epistemic—it is ontic. The key feature of the example is that in such an interaction electron a and other electrons in the outer shell of the relevant atom enter an 'entangled' or 'superposed' state in which the number of electrons present is determinate but the identity of any one of them with a is not, thus rendering likewise indeterminate the identity of a with the released electron b.

The idea behind this example is that "identity statements represented by 'a = b' are 'ontically' indeterminate in the quantum mechanical context".[8] In other words, in

[6] Bart Kosko. *Fuzziness vs. probability*. International Journal of General Systems, 17(2), pp. 211–240, 1990.

[7] Edward Jonathan Lowe. *Vague identity and quantum indeterminacy*. Analysis 54(2), pp. 110–114, 1994.

[8] Steven French and Décio Krause. *Quantum vagueness*. Erkenntnis, 59, pp. 97–124, 2003.

the quantum mechanical context a is equal to b to some degree, which is one of the fundamental ideas behind fuzzy set theory.

6.2   Fuzzy Sets and Fuzzy Logic in a Nutshell

Fuzzy set theory was introduced by Lotfi Askar Zadeh as an extension of ordinary set theory. The central idea behind fuzzy set theory is that an element x belongs to some fuzzy subset A to a degree, which is usually a number $0 \le i \le 1$ (i.e., $i \in [0,1]$). Thus, one writes $A(x) = i$ to mean that x belongs to A with degree equal to i. More generally, given some ordinary or *crisp* set X (called universe), then a fuzzy subset of X is *characterized* by a function that maps elements of X to numbers that are greater or equal to zero and less than or equal to one. Some researchers insist that i should be a computable number. This demand implies that i cannot be an irrational number. A weird consequence of this demand is that numbers like $\pi/8$, which is a computable irrational number, cannot be used as membership degrees.

If A and B are two crisp sets, then one can define some operations between them. In particular, the intersection of A and B, denoted $A \cap B$, is a set consisting of all the elements that are common to both sets; their union, denoted $A \cup B$, is a set consisting of the common and non-common elements of both A and B. These operations can be easily extended to handle fuzzy sets. If A and B are two functions that characterize two fuzzy subsets of the same universe, then

$$(A \cup B)(x) = \max\{A(x), B(X)\}$$

and

$$(A \cap B)(x) = \min\{A(x), B(X)\}$$

In words, the membership degree of x when it is a member of the union of A and B is equal to the maximum membership degree. In the case of the intersection , it is equal to the minimum membership degree. Given some universe U, and a set A that draws elements from U, then the complement of A is the set of all element in U that are not in A. Also, this notion can be easily extended in the case of fuzzy sets. Assume that $\bar{A}$ is the complement of the fuzzy subset A. Then, $\bar{A}(x) = 1 - A(x)$.

There are certain extensions of the notion of fuzzy subset and its operations. The set $[0,1]$ has certain properties and, of course, there are other sets that have exactly the same properties. For example, the set of all pairs (a, b), where $a, b \in [0,1]$, is such a set. Thus, one can use these sets to define different types of fuzzy subsets. Whether these sets are more expressive or not should not be concern to us here since we are not going to use them. In addition, it is quite possible to use functions other than min and max to define the intersection and the union of fuzzy subsets. In general, min and max belong to a wide class of functions called *t-norms* and *t-conorms*, respectively. A *t*-norm is a binary operation $* : [0,1] \times [0,1] \rightarrow [0,1]$ that satisfies at least the following conditions for all $a, b, c \in [0,1]$:

Boundary condition $a * 1 = a$ and $a * 0 = 0$.
Monotonicity $b \leq c$ implies $a * b \leq a * c$.
Commutativity $a * b = b * a$.
Associativity $a * (b * c) = (a * b) * c$.

A *t*-conorm is a binary operation $\star : [0,1] \times [0,1] \rightarrow [0,1]$ that satisfies at least the following conditions for all $a, b, c \in [0,1]$:

Boundary condition $a \star 0 = a$ and $a \star 1 = 1$.
Monotonicity $b \leq c$ implies $a \star b \leq a \star c$.
Commutativity $a \star b = b \star a$.
Associativity $a \star (b \star c) = (a \star b) \star c$.

Fuzzy set theory gave birth to the so-called *fuzzy logic*, that is, a logic where propositions usually assume values in the unit interval (i.e., the set $[0,1]$). As for the case of membership degrees, it has been argued that truth values should assume values that are rational numbers between 0 and 1. A proposition whose truth value is equal to zero is one that is definitely false and, similarly, when a proposition has a truth value equal to one, the proposition is absolutely true. One could say that fuzzy logic is an infinite-valued logic, since the unit interval has an infinite number of elements. Assume that T is function that returns the truth value of a fuzzy proposition or expression. Also, assume that p and q are two fuzzy propositions. Then,

$$T(\neg p) = 1 - T(p),$$
$$T(p \wedge q) = \min\left(T(p), T(q)\right)$$

and

$$T(p \vee q) = \min\left(T(p), T(q)\right)$$

Since $p \veebar q$ is equivalent to the expression $(p \vee q) \wedge (\neg p \vee \neg q)$, one can define a fuzzy version of it using these definitions as follows:

$$T(p \veebar p) = \min\left(\max\left(T(p), T(q)\right), \max\left(1 - T(p), 1 - T(q)\right)\right)$$

By comparing these operations with the ones in Equation (1.1) on page 14, one can easily verify that the fuzzy operations are pure extensions of the non-fuzzy operations. More generally, it is possible to use any *t*-norm and the corresponding *t*-conorm to define logical operations. In addition, one should note that in fuzzy logic, proofs are symbol manipulations, but the meaning of a logical operation is evaluated algebraically. For example, if the truth value of "John's sweater is pink" is 0.50 and the truth value of "Carol's shirt is blue" is 0.60, the truth value of their conjunction is min(0.50, 0.60) = 0.50. Closing this section, let me stress that there is no algorithm or no method by which one assigns truth values to vague statements. Typically, people employ some heuristic technique in order to assign these truth values.

6.3   Fuzzy Computing

In general, the term *fuzzy computation* describes fuzzy arithmetic, fuzzy databases, fuzzy web searches, etc. However, these can be considered as applications of fuzzy computation, but they are not exactly...fuzzy. For example, a fuzzy database operates in a non-vague environment and is supposed to handle vague data. Clearly, this is quite useful, but it is far from being a vague computation. In fact, to say that operations on a fuzzy database are some sort of vague computing is like saying that a simulator of a quantum computer can achieve exactly what a real quantum computer can do. Of course, if one is sure that quantum computers are just a bit faster than ordinary computers, then obviously a computer simulation of a quantum computer is the real thing albeit a bit slower. Of course, Feynman would not agree with this approach, but then Feynman was a physicist and not a...computer scientist!

A theory of fuzzy computation should propose methods to compute in a vague environment (e.g., conceptual computing devices that operate in an environment, where, for instance, one cannot precisely measure the position of particles, and their operations are vague) that "realize" vagueness using fuzzy set theory. A theory of fuzzy computation could be also used to examine whether there are limits to what can be computed. Since Turing machines are the archetypal conceptual computing device, they have been used as a basis to define fuzzy conceptual computing devices.

A fuzzy Turing machine is a kind of vague conceptual computing device. In order to define a fuzzy Turing machine, one can introduce vagueness in different parts of a machine. As was noted above, one can say that the scanning head recognizes what is printed on a cell to some degree. Alternatively, one can say that what is printed on the cell is a letter to some degree and the scanning head makes some sort of assessment using this degree to deduce what is printed on a cell (something that most optical character recognition tools are supposed to do). For example, assume that the following is a part of the tape of some Turing machine.

Then, the scanning head can only deduce to some degree that each of these letters is an "E". In fact, a fuzzy Turing machine does not have to recognize similar symbols, instead it goes from one state to another with some degree, since it has entered a particular state to some degree. Thus, in the end, it delivers a computational result to some degree. What is really interesting is that there is no universal fuzzy Turing machine. One way to view this fact is to recognize that there is something problematic about universal machines and, of course, another way to view it is to recognize that there is something problematic about fuzzy computing, in general.

Although fuzzy Turing machines are supposed to be really powerful, still I am not convinced that they are a natural model of fuzzy computation—vagueness is also about similarity and here there is no use of it. In a sense, the Turing machine is a natural model of computation of the very specific model of computation that Turing had on mind. More natural models of fuzzy computation are fuzzy versions of P systems and a fuzzy version of the chemical abstract machine.

A fuzzy P system is a P system that "processes" fuzzy multisets and/or has fuzzy multiset processing rules. In a way, fuzzy rules are similar to the fuzzy states of a fuzzy Turing machine. Thus, fuzzy membrane computing is about systems whose compartments contain fuzzy multisets. Recall that a multiset may contain multiple copies of any element. Since these are copies, they are identical. But what if they are imperfect copies of some prototype or just similar objects? Then, we say that each elements belongs to the fuzzy multiset to some degree. Thus one can say that there are n copies of x that belong to the fuzzy multiset to degree equal to r_1 and at the same time there are m copies of x that belong to the fuzzy multiset to degree equal to r_2, and so on. If the elements of the fuzzy multiset A are drawn from some crisp set $X = \{x_1, x_2, \ldots\}$, then its MITSOS cardinality given by the following equation:

$$|A| = A_\pi(x_1) \cdot A_\sigma(x_1) + A_\pi(x_2) \cdot A_\sigma(x_2) + \cdots + A_\pi(x_n) \cdot A_\sigma(x_n)$$
$$= \sum_{a \in X} A_\pi(a) \cdot A_\sigma(a) \tag{6.1}$$

where $A_\pi(a)$ is the number of a's in the multiset and $A_\sigma(a)$ the membership degree of these a's. Clearly, this means that it is possible to have a fuzzy multiset whose cardinality is a rational number or even a real number, provided that membership degrees can be irrational numbers. As was noted above, people insist that membership degrees should be rational number since irrational numbers are not physically representable. However, this is not true! The English mathematician John Wallis derived the following formula that can be used to compute the number π:

$$\frac{\pi}{2} = \frac{2 \cdot 2}{1 \cdot 3} \frac{4 \cdot 4}{3 \cdot 5} \frac{6 \cdot 6}{5 \cdot 7} \cdots \tag{6.2}$$

Recently, Tamar Friedmann and Carl Richard Hagen[9] made an amazing discovery: using a variational computation of the spectrum of the hydrogen atom they managed

---

[9]Tamar Friedmann and C. R. Hagen. *Quantum mechanical derivation of the Wallis formula for* π. Journal of Mathematical Physics, 56, 112101, 2015.

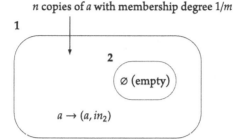

n copies of a with membership degree $1/m$

Figure 6.1: A simple P system with fuzzy data.

to derive Wallis formula! This clearly proves that irrational numbers can be physically represented and therefore it does make sense to say that some membership degree is, say, equal to $\pi/6$. Consider the fuzzy P system that is depicted in Figure 6.1. The result of the computation is a rational number. Turing machines are not able to "directly" compute rational numbers, but, of course, they can compute rational numbers indirectly. Since fuzzy P systems can directly compute rational and possibly irrational numbers, they are strictly more expressive than Turing machines.

A chemical abstract machine, or just cham, is a model of a computer system that is based on the chemical reaction metaphor. When one speaks metaphorically, then she uses words like mother, go, and night not in their normal everyday sense. Thus, in the case of the chemical reaction metaphor, we speak about molecules and reactions, but we actually mean data and alteration of data through specific reaction rules. In addition, it is assumed that a magic hand stirs the solution so that molecules that float inside it can come together and react. The solution is realized by a multiset while the reaction rules are realized by multiset rewriting rules. This model can be extended so to be a model of a vague computer system. Since the cham processes multisets, a vague model of the cham should process vague molecules. But what is a vague molecule?

Given some chemical compound, say water, the established view is that all molecules of this compound are identical. Of course, it is possible to form similar molecules using isotopes of some chemical element. For example, ^2H_2O or just D_2O is called heavy water and is a variety of the water molecule. Another variety of this molecule is the super heavy water molecule (i.e., ^3H_2O or just T_2O). Note that super heavy water is a corrosive substance (i.e., a substance that behaves like a strong acid). In addition, there are more water varieties: HDO, HTO, and DTO. Naturally, all these substances can be found in ordinary water, however, their quantities are very small. If we go back to our metaphor, then the different molecule varieties can be viewed as molecules that are similar to H_2O to some degree. In different words, one can assume that we have a fuzzy multiset and the various "water" molecules belong to it to some degree. If this does not seem vague enough, then one may try to imagine that elementary particles are not indistinguishable as we are taught in high school and university. If these particles are different, then one can imagine that there is some sort of ideal particle and all others are similar to it to some degree. Thus, a hydrogen molecule is actually a vague entity and, consequently, any water molecule is definitely vague. However, I will say more on this in Section 6.5.

There are four different types of multiset rewriting rules. The first type is the fuzzy reaction rule. Suppose that the following is a general reaction rule between ideal molecules:

$$m_1, \ldots, m_k \underset{\lambda}{\to} m'_1, \ldots, m'_l \qquad (6.3)$$

where λ is number that describes how likely is this reaction. Furthermore, assume that

$$M_1, \ldots, M_k \underset{\lambda}{\to} M'_1, \ldots, M'_l \qquad (6.4)$$

is a fuzzy reaction between molecules M_i that are similar to the ideal molecule m_i to some degree equal to λ_i. Then, reaction (6.4) is feasible if the minimum of all λ_i is greater than or equal to λ.

The fuzzy chemical rule is about mixing two solutions in order to yield a new solution. Suppose that

$$S_1 \underset{\lambda}{\to} S_2$$

that is, solution S_1 evolves into solution S_2. Also, suppose that solution S_3 consists of molecules whose likelihood degrees are greater or equal to λ. Then, the mixture of S_1 and S_3 will evolve to the mixture of S_2 and S_3 with plausibility degree equal to λ.

The fuzzy airlock rule is about the creation of new molecules from a single molecule and an entire solution. In order to allow an instance of the rule to happen, we need to make sure that the plausibility degree of the instance allows the operation. Thus, we estimate the likelihood degree of the solution by finding the minimum of the likelihood degrees of all molecules that make up the solution. Then, we compute the minimum of the likelihood degree of the solution and the lone molecule. Provided this is greater or equal to some plausibility degree, the operation can take place.

When $S \underset{\lambda}{\to} S'$, then we can insert S into some greater solution and the same process should take place in this new context. Of course, the only limitation to the applicability of this rule comes from the likelihood degrees of S and its new context. If these degrees are greater or equal to λ, then the rule is applicable.

A fuzzy neural network is a form of neural network where its key components can be fuzzy. In fact, there are seven different types of fuzzy neural networks:

Fuzzy neural net	Weights	Inputs	Outputs
Type 1	crisp	fuzzy	crisp
Type 2	crisp	fuzzy	fuzzy
Type 3	fuzzy	fuzzy	fuzzy
Type 4	fuzzy	crisp	fuzzy
Type 5	crisp	crisp	fuzzy
Type 6	fuzzy	crisp	crisp
Type 7	fuzzy	fuzzy	crisp

The various equations now use t-norms and t-conorms. For example, the equation

$$y_j = \bigvee_{i=1}^{n} \{x_i \wedge w_{ij}\}, \quad j = 1,\dots,m$$

is used to compute the output of a neuron y_j that is presented with input x_i and where w_{ij} are some sort of synaptic efficacies.

From the discussion so far, it should be clear that computing is about many things and not only about calculating numbers or function values. And these many things are not exact or precise. Thus, one should be able to find many applications of vague computing as described so far. In addition, there have been efforts to build fuzzy hardware while it seems that analog computing and vague computing are somehow related.

6.4   Rough Sets and Computing

Fuzzy set theory is not the only way to describe vagueness mathematically. *Rough* sets have been introduced by Zdzisław Pawlak[10] as an alternative mathematical model of vagueness. Rough set theory is based on the idea that one can approximate a vague object with two crisp sets: one that contains the vague object and one that is contained in the vague object. Figure 6.2 is graphical representation of this idea. Let me now give a more formal description of rough sets.

---

[10]Zdzisław Pawlak. *Rough sets.* International Journal of Computer and Information Sciences, 11(5), pp. 341–356, 1982.

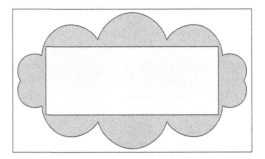

Figure 6.2: A vague set and a rough set approximation of it.

In mathematics, a binary relation R is a set that consists of pairs (x, y), where each x and y are members of some universe X. Typically, we write $x \, R \, y$ if x and y are related through relation R while we write $x \not\!R y$ if x and y are not related. As an example of a relation, consider the set of students of some class. Then, a possible relation, R, between students would be one that includes the all students zx and y that satisfy the phrase "x likes y". Thus, if *John likes Mary*, then (John, Mary) would be an element of R. A relation R is called *reflexive* if $x \, R \, x$ for all possible (values of) x. For example, the relation "$=$" is reflexive since $x = x$ for all x. A relation R is *symmetric* whenever $x \, R \, y$ means that $y \, R \, x$. For example, the relation "is married to" is reflexive because whenever "x is married to y", then obviously "y is married to x". A relation R is *transitive* if $x \, R \, y$ and $y \, R \, z$ means that $x \, R \, z$. For example, the relation "$\leq$" is transitive since, for example, $3 \leq 4$ and $4 \leq 5$ imply that $3 \leq 5$. Any relation that has all these three properties is called an *equivalence relation*. The relations "$=$" and "$\leq$" are equivalence relations. Assume that $X = \mathbb{Z}$, where $\mathbb{Z}$ is the set of all integers. Next, define a relation S such that $x \, S \, y$ if and only if $x - y$ is divisible by 4, then S is an equivalence relation on $\mathbb{Z}$ (verify this!). Because S a special significance in mathematics, it is customary to write $x \equiv y$ (mod 4) instead of $x \, S \, y$. This new relation is known as congruence modulo 4. More generally, $x \equiv y$ (mod n) is called congruence modulo n.

Given some equivalence relation R, which is defined over a universe X, an *equivalence class* is a subset of X of the following form:

$$\left\{ x \mid (x \text{ is an element of } X) \text{ and } (a \, R \, x) \right\}$$

For each a, the corresponding equivalence class is written as $[a]$. Assume that R is congruence modulo 4. Then, $[2]$ would be the set of all s such that $2 \equiv s$ (mod 4). Because the relation is transitive, $2 \equiv s$ (mod 4) can be written as $s \equiv 2$ (mod 4). This implies that $s - 2 = 4l$, where l is an integer. Thus, $s = 4l - 2$ and so

$$[2] = \left\{ \ldots, -14, -10, -6, -2, 2, 6, 10, 14, \ldots \right\}$$

Similarly, one can find the equivalence class [6]:

$$[6] = \left\{\ldots, -22, -18, -14, -10, -6, -2, 2, 6, 10, \ldots\right\}$$

It is not difficult to see that [2] = [6].

An *approximation space* is a pair (X, R) where X is finite universe and R is an equivalence relation on X. When x R y, then x and y are indistinguishable in (X, R). Consider the set of all different equivalence classes of X, which is denoted by X/R and called a *quotient* set. This set partitions the set X into sets those elements share some property. Any element E_i of X/R is called an *elementary set*. If A is a subset of X, its *lower approximation*, $\underline{A}$, is a set of objects x that belong to the elementary sets contained in A or in symbols:

$$\underline{A} = \bigcup_{E_i \subseteq A} E_i = \left\{x \mid (x \in X) \wedge ([x]_R \subseteq A)\right\}$$

The *upper approximation* of A, $\overline{A}$, is the union of these elementary sets that have a non-empty intersection with A or in symbols:

$$\overline{A} = \bigcup_{E_i \cap A \neq \varnothing} E_i = \left\{x \mid (x \in X) \wedge ([x]_R \cap A \neq \varnothing)\right\}$$

An element x of X definitely belongs to A when x belongs to $\underline{A}$. The same element possibly belongs to A when x belongs to $\overline{A}$. The *boundary* of A, denoted by $\mathrm{Bnd}(A)$, is the set $\overline{A} \setminus \underline{A}$.[11] A set A that is a subset of X is said to be *definable* in (X, R) if and only if $\mathrm{Bnd}(A) = \varnothing$, where $\varnothing$ is the empty set (i.e., a set with no elements).

Given an approximation space (X, R), a rough set is a pair (L, U) such that L and U are definable sets, L is a subset of U, and if any R-equivalence class is a singleton $\{s\}$ and $\{s\}$ is an element of U, then $\{s\}$ is an element of L. The membership function for rough sets is defined by employing the relation R as follows:

$$\mu_A^R(x) = \frac{\left|A \cap [x]\right|}{\left|[x]\right|}$$

where $|B|$ is the cardinality of B. It follows that $0 \leq \mu_A^R(x) \leq 1$.

A *rough finite semi-automaton* is characterized by a quadruple (Q, R, S, δ). Here Q is a finite set of internal states, R is an equivalence relation on Q, S is the set of input symbols, $\mathbf{D}$ is the class of all definable sets in the approximation space (Q, R), and δ : $Q \times S \to \mathbf{D} \times \mathbf{D}$ is the transition function and it holds that for all q that are elements of Q and all σ that are elements of S, $\delta(q, \sigma) = (D_1, D_2)$, where both D_1 and D_2 are elements

---

[11]Note that given two sets A and B, the set $A \setminus B$ is the set that consists of all x that belong to A but do not belong to B.

of D and D_1 is a subset of D_2. Obviously, $\delta(q, \sigma)$ is a rough set having as lower and upper approximations the sets D_1 and D_2, respectively, that is,

$$D_1 = \underline{\delta(q, \sigma)} \quad \text{and} \quad D_2 = \overline{\delta(q, \sigma)}$$

Also, the transition function of this automaton yields a rough set of states. Moreover, if for all q that are elements of Q and σ that are elements of S

$$\delta(q, \sigma) = ([q'], [q'])$$

where q' is an element of Q and $[q'] = \{q'\}$, then this automaton is actually a finite state automaton.

A sextuple $A = (Q, R, S, \delta, I, H)$ characterizes a *rough finite automaton*[12] if the quadruple (Q, R, S, δ) characterizes a rough finite state semi-automaton, I is a definable set in the approximation space (Q, R) that is called the *initial configuration*, and H, which is a subset of Q, is the set of *accepting states* of A.

6.5   Vagueness and Quantum Mechanics

The *Schrödinger's cat paradox* is a thought experiment devised by Schrödinger in the 1930s. In this mind experiment, a cat is placed in a sealed box along with a radioactive sample, a Geiger counter and a bottle of poison. If there is decay, it is detected by the Geiger counter. This will trigger a mechanism that breaks the bottle of poison and the cat will be killed. According to the Copenhagen interpretation of quantum mechanics (I will say more on this in Section 5.3), a particle exists in all possible states until someone will perform some measurement. This means that the radioactive material is decayed and not decayed at the same time and so the cat is dead and alive at the same time. This can be expressed mathematically as follows:

$$\psi = \frac{1}{\sqrt{2}} \psi_{\text{alive}} + \frac{1}{\sqrt{2}} \psi_{\text{dead}} \tag{6.5}$$

Schrödinger regarded this as patent nonsense, however, I do not agree with this conclusion. The equation clearly specifies that cat is as much alive as much it is dead. However, one can say that the cat is partially dead or partially alive. And this is exactly the essence of vagueness: things are usually neither black nor white. Thus, a patient who is in coma is not exactly alive and not exactly dead. Regardless of any objections, superposition is what makes quantum computing really interesting.

The standard interpretation of $\alpha|0\rangle + \beta|1\rangle$ is that a particle is in states $|0\rangle$ or $|1\rangle$ with probability that depends on α and β. Of course, according to a layman's interpretation

---

[12] Sumita Basu. *Rough finite-state automata*. Cybernetics and Systems: An International Journal, 36(2), pp. 107–124, 2005.

of probability theory, these two numbers express the change that a particle is in one of these states. A fuzzy theoretic interpretation of this state is that the particle is in both states but with some degree. In fact, one can define a fuzzy set as follows:

$$\Psi(|0\rangle) = |\alpha|^2 \qquad (6.6)$$
$$\Psi(|1\rangle) = |\beta|^2 \qquad (6.7)$$

However, here there is no reason to demand that $|\alpha|^2 + |\beta|^2 = 1$. In fact, there is no reason to impose any restriction other than $|\alpha|^2 \leq 1$ and $|\beta|^2 \leq 1$. One may argue that these two restrictions are not that different, however, the fuzzy theoretic approach assumes that the particle is, in fact, in a state that is partly $|0\rangle$ and partly $|1\rangle$. In other words, $\alpha|0\rangle + \beta|1\rangle$ is like a shade of gray, where, for instance, $|0\rangle$ is like black and $|1\rangle$ is like white.

Assume that Ψ describes the state of a quantum particle in superposition. Then, the superposition collapses upon a measurement, but the question is why this happens. Perhaps, the measurement forces a defuzzification of Ψ, that is, a process by which one gets bivalent data from multivalued data (in this case a vague state is transformed into a crisp one). But if defuzzification is possible, then one might expect that fuzzification is also possible. Recall that the Hadamard gate is a mechanism that creates "vague" states as follows:

$$H|0\rangle = \frac{1}{\sqrt{2}}|0\rangle + \frac{1}{\sqrt{2}}|1\rangle \qquad (6.8)$$

$$H|1\rangle = \frac{1}{\sqrt{2}}|0\rangle - \frac{1}{\sqrt{2}}|1\rangle \qquad (6.9)$$

Thus, superposition corresponds to the fuzzification of a quantum system by means of the H operator, while measurement is a "natural" defuzzification process. Why these processes happen and what is their deep meaning is something we do not know yet!

The following is an example of a typical entangled state:

$$|\Psi\rangle = \frac{1}{\sqrt{2}}\left(|\alpha_1\rangle \otimes |\beta_1\rangle + |\alpha_2\rangle \otimes |\beta_2\rangle\right) \qquad (6.10)$$

Lowe proposed a thought experiment that showed that entanglement is vague.[13] Assume that there are two determinately distinct electrons. One of them (call it a) is determinately absorbed by an atom and then becomes entangled with a single electron (call it a^*) determinately already in the atom. Because these electrons exist in an entangled state inside the atom, they are not determinately distinct but, of course, we know that there are two of them. At some moment, one electron is emitted and so one

---

[13] Edward Jonathan Lowe. *Vague identity and quantum indeterminacy: further reflections.* Analysis, 59(4), pp. 328–330, 1999.

electron is still inside the atom and one is outside the atom. Since these two electrons were in an entangled state, it is impossible to tell which electron left the atom. In a nutshell, this is the root of vagueness in entanglement.

Quantum computing is so attractive because it is harnessing both superposition and entanglement to achieve its exponential computational power. Since both superposition and entanglement are vague in their nature, this means that quantum computers operate on vague data using vague operations.

Annotated Bibliography

• Steven French and Décio Krause. *Identity in Physics: A Historical, Philosophical, and Formal Analysis.* Oxford University Press, Oxford, 2006.

A philosophical book that deals with the problem of identity of elementary particles. The authors provide arguments in favor of the distinguishability of elementary particles contra to the "established" view. It is a very interesting book.

• George J. Klir and Bo Yuan. *Fuzzy Sets and Fuzzy Logic: Theory and Applications.* Prentice Hall, NJ, 1995.

This is a classical introduction to the theory of fuzzy sets and fuzzy logic. The book presents the mathematical theory of fuzzy sets and logic, evidence theory, etc. In addition, it covers a good number of applications of fuzzy set theory. It is a bit dated now but still a book worth reading.

• Apostolos Syropoulos. *Theory of Fuzzy Computation.* Springer, New York, 2014.

This is the first and to date the only book that presents the field of fuzzy computation. It is a book that describes the various conceptual computing devices (fuzzy P systems, fuzzy Turing machines, etc.) as well as other related ideas (e.g., fuzzy recursion theory, etc.).

Chapter 7

Physical Reality and Computation

Do we know the laws that govern the universe we are living in? Having an answer to this question means that one can fully determine the capabilities of the *ultimate* computing device. Thus, progress in our understanding of the physical world will help us better understand computation. Or is it the other way around? That is, a better understanding of computation will make it easier to better understand the world we live. In this chapter, I examine this and other similar questions.

7.1   The Universe as a Computer

A few years ago, the Greek government was practically trying to oust computer education, not computer literacy, from Greek upper-high schools. This was a really sad situation that was triggered by the economic crisis and was seen as a measure to reduce public servants. Fortunately, this did not happen; however, in an effort to prevent this from happening, a prominent computer scientist of Greek origin wrote an open letter to the then government. In this letter, he tried to explain why, in his opinion, the actions of the Greek government are in the wrong direction. One of his arguments, in favor of the necessity of inclusion of computer education in upper-high schools, was that information is pervasive. In particular, he mentioned John Archibald Wheeler's "it from bit" slogan as an indication that information, therefore information processing, plays an important role in Nature. But what is this "it from bit" and why is it so important? Here is how Wheeler described the essence of "it from bit":[1]

> It from bit symbolizes the idea that every item of the physical world has at bottom—at a very deep bottom, in most instances— an immaterial source and explanation; that what we call reality arises in the last analysis from the posing of yes–no questions and the registering of equipment-evoked responses; in short, that all things physical are information-theoretic in origin and this is a *participatory universe.*

Physicists have theorized that the surface area of the event horizon of any black hole measures the *entropy* of the black hole.[2] Entropy is the amount of "randomness" in a chosen region of space. An increase of entropy means that things are becoming more and more random. More specifically, entropy is proportional to the logarithm of the number of different ways the atoms and the molecules in a specific region can be distributed without changing the macroscopic appearance of the region. The surface of the event horizon can be divided into tiny tiles each having an area of $4\hbar \ln 2$. Each such tile is a quantum container that contains information (i.e., a binary digit), which is used to assemble the black hole. Thus, the entropy of a black hole is connected to the number of these tiny tiles.

I am sure that the prominent computer scientist wanted to do good, but I think his example was rather unfortunate mainly because "it from bit" is not a scientific fact but rather an hypothesis. If "it from bit" is true, then one can easily deduce that the universe is a computer. From there, it is almost obvious to conclude that there is some super-being, or just god, that operates this computer. Note that this conclusion is *obvious* only if we accept that computation is a natural phenomenon.

Any theory should be proved or at least verified in order to gain credibility. In fact, this is the cornerstone of what we call science. According to the Austrian philosopher of science Karl Raimund Popper, a theory is *scientific* only if it is *falsifiable.* Otherwise, a theory is considered unscientific. In different words, Popper suggested that a theory is scientific only if we can test it. A "scientific" theory makes predictions or one can use the theory to make predictions. If all these predictions can be tested, then the theory is scientific. One way to test a theory is by setting up an experiment. Another way is by using a computer simulation. The crucial question is: Can we simulate everything with a computer?

---

[1]John Archibald Wheeler. Information, physics, quantum: The search for links. In Wojciech Hubert Żurek, editors, *Complexity, Entropy and the Physics of Information*, pp. 3–28, Westview Press, Tennessee, 1990.

[2]The following book contains a good and not so technical description of entropy, in particular, and black holes, in general: Kip Stephen Thorne. *Black Holes and Time Warps: Einstein's Outrageous Legacy.* W. W. Norton, New York, 1994.

By definition, a simulation is an imitation of the functionality of a system or a process by means of the functionality of another system. In the case of a computer simulation, the "other system" is a computer. Today there are many computational models of global weather that are quite accurate in certain cases. Also, there are computer models of galaxies, stars, etc. Thus simulations of physical systems are quite possible. However, a physical system includes living beings, and some of them happen to be intelligent. This, of course, does not prevent us from simulating minds. Just like one can simulate quantum computers on conventional hardware. Clearly, one cannot realize a quantum computer on conventional hardware, and this is something we do not need to explain. Going one step further, can we realize nature on conventional hardware? For the moment pretend that Feynman's objections as discussed in Section 5.4 are pointless. Then, if the mind is a "device" that goes beyond the capabilities of conventional hardware, then obviously it is impossible to realize nature in today's hardware. But is nature computable?

Marian Boykan Pour-El and Jonathan Ian Richards have managed to discover non-computability in ordinary physical systems, such as wave propagation (i.e., any of the ways in which waves travel). In general, the following equation describes the wave propagation phenomenon in three spatial dimensions:

$$\nabla^2 \psi = \frac{\partial^2 \psi}{\partial x^2} + \frac{\partial^2 \psi}{\partial y^2} + \frac{\partial^2 \psi}{\partial z^2} = \frac{1}{v^2} \frac{\partial^2 \psi}{\partial t^2} \tag{7.1}$$

where v is the velocity of the wave and ψ is a function that depends on the three spatial coordinates $(x, y, \text{and } z)$ and time (t). Suppose that v is equal to 1 and let us consider the equation with initial conditions

$$\nabla^2 \psi - \frac{\partial^2 \psi}{\partial t^2} = 0$$

$$\psi(x, y, z, 0) = f(x, y, z) \tag{7.2}$$

$$\frac{\partial \psi}{\partial t}(x, y, z, 0) = 0$$

Pour-El and Richards considered the wave equation on *compact spaces* (a rectangular parallelepiped is a typical example of such a space). These subspaces must be large enough so that "light rays" from the outside cannot reach any point in the subspace in any time considered. Let us now define two cubes (i.e., special cases of rectangular parallelepiped):

$$D_1 = \left\{ (x, y, z) \mid -1 \le x \le 1, -1 \le y \le 1, -1 \le z \le 1 \right\}$$

$$D_2 = \left\{ (x, y, z) \mid -3 \le x \le 3, -3 \le y \le 3, -3 \le z \le 3 \right\}$$

That is, D_1 is a cube where all of its points have coordinates in the range from -1 to 1. Similarly, D_2 is a cube where all of its points have coordinates in the range from -3 to 3. Now consider the wave Equation (7.1). Then, there exists a computable *continuous* function $f(x, y, z)$ in D_2 (i.e., a function whose graph has no gaps) such that the solution $u(x, y, z, t)$ of (7.2) at time $t = 1$ is not a computable function there. But what are the consequences of such a discovery?

First of all, this discovery means that in an otherwise "computable" world, there are things that are not computable. Therefore, even if one could have the resources to build a computer to realize the physical world, it would be impossible to do it. Second, it rules out various hypotheses about physical reality. For example, Niklas Boström (who has "simplified" his name to Nick) published a paper where he advocated the idea that the human race will be able to reach the "posthuman" stage if and only if we are living in a computer simulation![3] More specifically, he argued that

(i) it is very probable that humanity will vanish before reaching a "posthuman" stage;

(ii) it will not be possible to run a significant number of simulations of the evolution of any posthuman civilization; and

(iii) it very probable that we live in a computer simulation.

Here the word *simulation* means *realization*. Personally, I cannot buy the idea that we are living in a computer simulation. In fact, I consider this idea absurd. However, it seems that I am somehow part of some minority! Indeed, some years ago, I was invited to contribute a talk to a workshop. There I met someone who turned out to be a strong supporter of this idea. When I told her that I find absurd the idea that we live in a computer simulation, she told me that I am solipsists (i.e., "I think that I am the only mind that exists"). What is really astonishing is that this person was considered a leading figure in her scientific discipline in her country!

If we ignore the "importance" of the survival of the human race, then Boström is unfortunately not alone. Some years ago, Brian Hayes wrote an article[4] in which he "investigated" the possibility of constructing a computer program written in some ordinary computer programming language (e.g., Java or C) capable of simulating the Universe, without specifying what he meant by this. After examining all "relevant" parameters, he had reached the conclusion that although this is a particularly difficult task, nevertheless, it is a feasible one! So it is possible to construct a simulation of the entire universe but it is absurd to think about a computer that flies near a black hole…!

For the sake of the argument, let us assume that we actually live in a computer simulation. Obviously, at a certain moment, someone will discover how to build a

[3] Nick Boström. *Are we living in a computer simulation?* The Philosophical Quarterly, 53(211), pp. 243–255, 2003.

[4] Brian Hayes. *Debugging the universe.* International Journal of Theoretical Physics, 42(2), pp. 277–295, 2003.

simulation of some universe. An intelligent being that some day will emerge in this simulation will start wondering about their existence. Then, someone might come with the idea that they are actually living in a computer simulation. Obviously, they would like to find a way to check the validity of this idea. The natural question is: How can one check whether they live in a computer simulation? After all, in this case, "reality" is another simulation! Moreover, it would be really interesting to get to know what reality is? But if our world is not computable, does this rule out the possibility of living in a computer simulation? No, but I do not think that people who put forth the idea that our world is a simulation accept that the CTT is false! For them, it is reasonable to accept that we live in a computer simulation but unreasonable to accept that the CTT might be wrong...Another problem with the computer simulation idea is that computers occasionally fail or even if they do not fail, certain processes fail. Thus, if we were living in a computer simulation, we should be able to witness some manifestations of these failures. For example, we should be able to see a person stop functioning while being in upright position or even we could see an airplane standing still in the air. Fortunately or unfortunately, no one has reported such an event till today and I am sure no one will report anything like this anytime soon.

The idea that the universe is some sort of computer is not a new one. First, Zuse had put forth the idea that the universe is a computer in his book *Rechnender Raum* (Calculating Space). There he proposed that the laws of the universe are discrete, and that the entire universe is a giant cellular automaton computing its next state. Lee Smolin in an article that was published in the June 2009 issue of the *Physical World* (the article is free available on the magazine's web site) argued against cosmological views that insist that time does not exist. He coined the term *Newtonian Schema* to refer to such universe. Ken Wharton[5] used the Newtonian Schema to argue against the view that the world is a computer. His argument is based on the remark that quantum mechanics does not allow one to make predictions about many things (e.g., the uncertainty principle ensures that we cannot know with precision the position and momentum of a moving particle), while according to the Newtonian Schema time is reversible and so predictions are quite possible. The fact that we cannot make predictions means that the universe is not a computer. One may argue that there are probabilistic algorithms but they operate on conventional hardware...

The digital universe is another idea closely related to the idea that the universe is a computer. Edward Fredkin[6] and other notable researchers are proponents of the digital universe and advocate that all quantities in nature are finite and discrete. A direct consequence of this idea is that any quantity can be representable by an integer. Moreover, this means that in Nature there are no infinities, infinitesimals,

---

[5]Ken Wharton. *The Universe is not a computer.* arXiv:1211.7081v2 [quant-ph], 2015.
[6]For example, see Edward Fredkin. *An introduction to digital philosophy.* International Journal of Theoretical Physics, 42(2), pp. 189–247, 2003.

discontinuities, or locally determined random variables. This implies that both time and space are discrete. But are they? I will say more on this in the next section.

The *holographic principle* is an idea that was proposed by the Nobel laureate Gerardus 't Hooft.[7] In simple words, this principle states that the volume of a space has nothing to do with the amount of "information" it may contain, what really matters is the area of a region's boundary. This means that one needs only the information "stored" in the surface of some space in order to explain all that happens inside the space (compare this principle with the entropy of a black hole). Note that the principle is called holographic because a hologram is a two-dimensional image containing all the three-dimensional information of an object. Thus, one can say that one can fully understand what goes on in the universe provided they have access to the information stored at the boundaries of the universe. For this reason, many say that "our universe is a hologram", which is clearly wrong. So far, so good, but the "problem" starts from here! There is an idea called *anti-de Sitter/conformal field theory correspondence* which very roughly states that our universe is a four-dimensional (three spatial dimensions and one time dimension) boundary of a five-dimensional (four spatial dimensions and one time dimension) space. And these two spaces contain exactly the same information. It was argued that this correspondence may help us to understand black holes. Whether the holographic principle has anything to do with reality is something that should not concern us here. What really matters is that the universe is not a holograph!

An idea not completely alien to the idea that the universe is a computer is Max Erik Tegmark's *mathematical universe hypothesis* (MUH).[8] This hypothesis states that the physical world is an abstract mathematical structure. Certainly, if this hypothesis is correct, then automatically the CTT is true! Why? Simply because according to this hypothesis, only computable and decidable structures exist. In physics, we use mathematics to describe what we see in Nature. Thus, mathematics is a language that we use to express things about Nature not the opposite way as this hypothesis suggests. This hypothesis may sound surprisingly similar to mathematical platonism, that is, the idea that there are mathematical objects whose existence is independent of us and our language, thought, and practices. According to platonism, mathematical truths are discovered, not invented. Mathematical platonism assumes that there is a world of mathematical structures in addition to our physical world while the MUH assumes that the world we live is a mathematical structure. And this is exactly the main difference between the two approaches. In a way, mathematical platonism is about our belief that somehow we will manage to solve a problem and not about a world where mathematical objects exist. Thus the MUH shows, in a negative way, how our understanding of the world dictates what can be computed.

---

[7] Gerardus 't Hooft. *Dimensional reduction in quantum gravity.* arXiv:gr-qc/9310026, 1993.
[8] Max Tegmark. *The mathematical universe.* Foundations of Physics, 38(2), pp. 101–150, 2007.

Recently, Stephen William Hawking posted on his Web site the transcript of a talk he gave. The posting is titled *Gödel and the End of the Universe*. The posting is about the connection between Gödel's incompleteness theorems and models of the physical world. According to Hawking's view, the mathematical description of the physical world should be identified with the world itself. Moreover, he assumes that each model of the physical world is some sort of formal system. Since formal systems are incomplete, so he must be any model of the physical world. This simply means that there are things in any model of the physical world that we see but we cannot prove their existence. And this explains why string theory was replaced by supergravity, which was later replaced by M-Theory, according to Hawking. Clearly, Hawking defends MUH!

I have two objections to this line of thought. First, Hawking is sure that string theory is correct. And his argument is actually defending the validity of the theory (I will say more about string theory in the next section). On the other hand, there are physical theories that work like charm. For example, Einstein's General Theory of Relativity is one such theory where all of its predictions have been totally confirmed. The second objection is about the role of mathematics in physics. Naturally, physicists use mathematics to create models that describe the world around us. However, these models are not the world itself but a mathematical model of the world!

7.2   Is Space–Time Discrete or Continuous?

One of the most important problems of modern physics is whether time and space are granular or not. The Ancient Greek philosopher Democritus (Δημόκριτος), known as the Laughing Philosopher, introduced the idea that matter consists of very tiny indivisible *atoms*. In fact, the word atom (ἄτομος) means indivisible. Today, of course, the term atom refers to something that has structure and it is divisible yet the general idea is that there are elementary particles that are undividable. Moreover, the granularity of space–time is important to most theories that have introduced the idea of a universe-as-a-gigantic-computer.

Equation (5.9) (i.e., the time-dependent Schrödinger equation for one spatial dimension) assumes that both space and time are continuous. Even the Klein–Gordon equation

$$\frac{1}{c^2}\frac{\partial^2 \Psi}{\partial t^2} - \nabla^2 \Psi + \frac{m^2 c^2}{\hbar}\Psi = 0 \tag{7.3}$$

which is a relativistic version of the Schrödinger equation, assumes that space–time is continuous. However, it is a fact that of the four fundamental forces (or interactions as they are also known) only gravity has not been quantized. The strong force, which keeps protons and neutrons in nuclei of atoms together, the electromagnetic force, and the weak force, which is responsible for radioactive decay, have all been quantized. Strictly speaking, there is no reason to quantize gravity as general relativity explains all phenomena related to gravity. Nevertheless, a good proportion of the scientific community sees it as a challenge to quantize gravity. For this reason, a number of physicists have proposed different versions of quantum gravity. String theory and quantum loop theory are the most popular theories and it is interesting to see what they *predict*.

A popular account of string theory is that matter does not consist of particles that are more or less like ultratiny spheres but rather of tiny closed strings loops, which can either break into open strings or cannot break into open strings. In a sense, one can say that these strings produce elementary particles just like the strings of guitar produce notes. For example, just like a guitar player may push or pull a string sideways across the fret to raise the pitch of a note, a string may excite to produce different *excitation modes* that eventually correspond to elementary particles. However, this is not quite true since a string vibrates by consuming energy. This energy is determined by the tension of the string. The strings of string theory demand a lot of energy to vibrate since they are under a lot of tension. But the particles induced in such cases are really heavy ones that are not the familiar particles researchers encounter in their experiments. Instead nature "uses" supersymmetry to create those ordinary particles. According to string theory, supersymmetry relates different types of particles to each other. Thus, when there is a vibration that goes higher and higher, there are also vibrations of low energy. This means that particles are generated in pairs. In fact, these pairs consist of a fermion and a boson.

Strings are one-dimensional objects that cannot solve all possible problems. This led researchers to add D-branes to later versions of string theory. These are objects that are supposed to exist in p geometrical dimensions. Thus when $p = 0$, point particles are D-branes, when $p = 1$, a string is a D-brane, when $p = 2$, membranes are D-branes, etc. The term *brane* drives from the word membrane. Also, the "D" in D-brane comes from Johann Peter Gustav Lejeune Dirichlet, a German mathematician whose relationship to the D-brane comes from a special type of boundary condition, called the Dirichlet boundary condition, which the D-branes exhibit.

Quantum mechanics is about quanta, that is, discrete quantities of energy. This implies that any quantization of gravity should involve a quantum for gravity and of course quantization of space and time. According to string theory, a string should have a length that is about the size of the so called Planck length, which is defined by the following equation:

$$\ell_P = \sqrt{\frac{\hbar G}{c^3}} \cong 1.61622837 \times 10^{-35} \text{ meters} \qquad (7.4)$$

According to string theory, any length shorter than ℓ_P would make no physical sense. Similar to Planck length, there is also a Planck time, which is the time required by photon traveling with the speed of light to cover a distance that is equal to the Planck length:

$$t_P = \frac{\ell_P}{c} \cong 5.39121 \times 10^{-44} \text{ seconds} \qquad (7.5)$$

But what happens if we could observe things happening in distances less than the Planck length and at time intervals less than the Planck time? Wheeler speculated that space–time is like a foam at these scales. He based this on the generalized uncertainty principle, which can be stated as follows:

$$\sigma_A^2 \sigma_B^2 \geq \left(\frac{1}{2i}\langle[\hat{A}, \hat{B}]\rangle\right) \tag{7.6}$$

where A and B are two observables and $[\hat{A}, \hat{B}] = \hat{A}\hat{B} - \hat{B}\hat{A}$. For example, the uncertainty principle for time and space takes the following form:

$$\sigma_X \sigma_T > \ell_s^2 \tag{7.7}$$

where ℓ_s^2 can be thought of as the typical size of strings. As was pointed out, it was initially assumed that $\ell_s^2 = \ell_P$ but since string theory allows extra dimensions that are extremely small, the string length ℓ_s is taken to be of the order of 10^{-20} meters. The theory evolves and so everything should evolve. The quantum foam idea is a way to say that there is no empty space just quantum foam. This reminds me of the ether of the 19th century physics...

If string theory is correct, then of course space and time are granular. Consequently, there is no way to actually disprove all these wild speculations about the computational nature of the universe, parallel universes, etc. However, there is a little problem here. So far Nature has steadily continued to say "No" to all predictions of string theory. It is not enough to have a theory that is mathematically elegant. It is necessary to provide experimental data that show the validity of its predictions. As was pointed out in a comment to nature magazine,[9] there are aspects of string theory that can be tested experimentally. For example, according to string theory, there is a symmetry between fermions and bosons that predicts that each boson is related to some fermion. The problem is that none of these hypothetical particles have been detected yet by the Large Hadron Collider (LHC) at CERN. Because of this failure, string theorists revise the theory and "predict" that the LHC must probe at even higher energies. The LHC is configured to probe at these higher energies but nothing comes up again and that is the way life goes on!

String theory has an archival theory. This is the so-called loop quantum gravity (LQG) theory. As noted above, this theory is also based on the assumption that space and time are granular. According to LQG, space is like a grid where each node is a grain of space. The lines that go through these grains are like the "lines of force" of an electric field, that is, a path followed by an electric charge free to move in an electric field. When such "lines of force" are curved and closed, they are the *loops* in LQG. The gravitational field is the space–time and the quantum "lines of force" form the texture of the space.

[9]George Ellis and Joe Silk. *Defend the integrity of physics*. Nature, 516, pp. 321–323, 2014.

In other words, they are not in space but they are the space itself. This is the basic idea of LQG. In a sense, both string theory and LQG are based on the same idea developed in completely different ways.

It seems that LQG is far more promising than string theory mainly because LQG makes some testable predictions. For example, Carlo Rovelli and his colleagues have found strong evidence that LQG predicts that two balls will attract each other in exactly the way classical mechanics predicts![10] However, the theory is far from being complete and needs further development and/or modification.

So is space and time granular? I do not know! Perhaps quantization of gravity is impossible because gravity is something entirely different or even because quantum mechanics is not the final theory. After all, both approaches to quantum gravity assume that quantum mechanics is absolutely correct while all other physical theories are just approximations of physical reality. Of course, it is rather interesting that general relativity, which assumes that both space and time are continuous, has made a lot of predictions and all of them turned out to be true. The only prediction that was not experimentally verified was the existence of gravitational waves. However, quite recently, the Laser Interferometer Gravitational-Wave Observatories (LIGO) has been used to actually detect gravitational waves.[11] Thus, all predictions of relativity theory have been verified, which make it a correct theory.

Stochastic effects occur by chance while deterministic effects that are the result of a direct effect. If the quantum foam exists, then the structure of space–time at short distances would allow stochastic effects to take place. For example, two massless particles of equal energy would travel the exact same distance in different times. This is actually what is expected to happen! In a recent paper,[12] the authors examined the "characteristic" of the space–time foam. In particular, they observationally examined a bunch of photons of equal energy E emitted simultaneously from a distant astrophysical source. According to the theory, these photons should propagate with different speeds and arrive at different times. Note that this stochastic variation of the speed of the light directly violates relativity theory (this "phenomenon" is known in the literature as the Lorentz invariance violation). Interestingly, the authors did not observe anything that would support the idea of stochastic variation of the speed of light. Does this mean that the quantum foam does not behave the expected way? Does this mean that space–time is not granular? Yes and no, but all those that work on quantum gravity should seriously take under consideration these findings in order

[10]Carlo Rovelli. *Graviton propagator from background-independent quantum gravity.* Physical Review Letters, 97, p. 151301, 2006.

[11]B. P. Abbott *et al.* Observation of gravitational waves from a binary black hole merger. Physical Review Letters, 116, p. 061102, 2016.

[12]Vlasios Vasileiou, Jonathan Granot, Tsvi Piran, and Giovanni Amelino-Camelia. *A Planck-scale limit on spacetime fuzziness and stochastic Lorentz invariance violation*, Nature Physics, 11, pp. 344–346, 2015.

to develop a theory consistent with experimental findings. So gain, is space–time granular? My personal opinion is that space and time is not granular or better our capabilities to measure both space and time at very small intervals determine their "granularity". Also, I do not think that stochastic effects happen beyond the point that determines our measuring capabilities. At that level, space and time are becoming vague as it is not clear what belongs to the past or to the future and if something is in the south or the north of something else. Although there is no theory of a vague universe, still it would be really nice to see the emergence of a new theory that would be based on thoughts like these.

7.3   Ultimate Computing Devices

As Carlo Rovelli and Francesca Vidotto explain in their book (see the annotated bibliography at the end of the chapter), what we know about the elementary physical world is described by the following theories:

— Quantum mechanics.
— The standard model of particle physics describing all matter we have so far observed directly, without its gravitational interactions.
— General relativity that describes gravity, space and time.

More generally, our understanding of the universe is based on these theories. However, as was explained in the previous section, there is no theory to "reconcile" quantum mechanics and general relativity. Thus, we have no idea what is actually going on inside a black hole. Of course, the obvious question is whether this has anything to do with computing.

In 2001, Y. Jack Ng published a paper[13] where he described the computational capabilities of "simple" computers. There, he argued that the number v of operations per unit time and the number I of bits of information in the memory space of a "simple" computer are limited by the inequality

$$Iv^2 \leq t_P^2 \cong 10^{86} \text{ seconds}^2 \tag{7.8}$$

In addition, he concluded that the total running time T over which a simple clock can remain accurate and the smallest time interval t that the clock is capable of resolving are limited by the inequality

$$T \leq t\left(\frac{t}{t_P}\right)^2 \tag{7.9}$$

[13]Y. Jack Ng. *From computation to black holes and space–time foam.* Physical Review Letters, 86(14), pp. 2946–2949, 2001

Ng correctly remarks that it is physics that sets the limits to computation, nevertheless, he adds that the physics that dictates these limits is the one that governs the quantum fluctuations of space–time. In other words, Ng assumes that space and time are granular as the major approaches to quantum gravity predict and based on this assumption gives an estimation of the limits of computation. Ng goes one step further and advocates the idea that in a sense black holes can be regarded as the ultimate simple computers and ultimate simple clocks. Here the term *simple* is used to denote clocks and computers that do not have components. If a black hole is a simple computer, one should be able to demonstrate, at least in principle, how they compute. Note that the idea is identical to the idea that the universe is a computer. If we have black hole that has a mass of 1 kilogram, then its radius would be 10^{-27} meters. The computational input is matter that somehow encodes a problem and is dropped in to the hole. We do not know what happens inside the hole (!), yet we assume that computation takes place...The accepted view is that black holes emit thermal radiation as was proposed by Hawking in 1974. This means that any black hole will vanish sometime in the future. Initially, it was assumed that the radiation corresponded to no information but later it was proposed that it corresponds to processes that take place inside the hole. Thus, one can assume that the radiation carries the result of the computation...

Seth Lloyd has presented a similar approach to the definition of the ultimate computing device.[14] Lloyd's *ultimate laptop* is a computing device whose mass is exactly 1 kilogram and its volume is exactly liter. Again, this machine should operate at the limits set by physics. Thus the ultimate laptop can perform:

$$\frac{2mc^2}{\pi\hbar} = 5.4258 \times 10^{50}$$

logical operations per second on roughly 10^{31} bits. It has been estimated that the internal temperature of such a machine would be roughly 1,000,000,000°C! But what is really striking is the difference in the two estimations. For example, if we assume that $I \cong 10^{16}$ bits, then $\nu \cong 10^{35}$ seconds^{-1}. Whether these calculations are justified and/or "meaningful" is another problem that I will not even touch here. I have already put some arguments against these "theories" and there is absolutely no reason to say more about it.

Annotated Bibliography

- Jim Baggott. *Farewell to Reality: How Modern Physics Has Betrayed the Search for Scientific Truth*. Constable, London, 2013.

---

[14] Seth Lloyd. *Ultimate physical limits to computation*. Nature, 406, pp. 1047–1054, 2000.

A book that critically discusses "modern" physics. In a sense this is a polemic against string theory and related ideas. I think this is a very interesting book.

• Andrew Zimmerman Jones and Daniel Robbins (contributor). *String Theory For Dummies*. Wiley Publishing, Hoboken, NJ, 2010.

A book for people who want to understand what string theory is about without going into the mathematical details. I have read a couple of chapters in this book and I think the presentation is excellent.

• Klaus Mainzer and Leon Chua. *The Universe as Automaton: From Simplicity and Symmetry to Complexity*. Springer, Heidelberg, 2002.

A book that thoroughly discusses the idea that the universe is a computer. It is a book worth the trouble especially if you are a proponent of the idea that the universe is a computer. Even if you think this is nonsense, the book is interesting.

• Carlo Rovelli and Francesca Vidotto. *Covariant Loop Quantum Gravity: An Elementary Introduction to Quantum Gravity and Spinfoam Theory*. Cambridge University Press, Cambridge, 2014.

This is the best book presenting loop quantum gravity. The book is ideal for self-study. What I liked about this book is that the authors do not think their book is a sort of Bible or Quran but rather a report of ongoing research.

• Lee Smolin. *The Trouble With Physics: The Rise of String Theory, The Fall of a Science, and What Comes Next*. Penguin Books, London, 2006.

This book is by one of the creators of loop quantum gravity and as such it contains many arguments against string theory. What I did not like with this book is the author's insistence on the universe as a computer "metaphor"...

• Peter Woit. *Not Even Wrong: The Failure of String Theory and the Search for Unity in Physical Law*. Basic Books, New York, 2006.

To the best of my knowledge, this book is the one that started the "string wars", that is, the "war" between proponents and rivals of string theory and related theories (e.g., multi-verse, etc.). I think that even proponents of string theory should read this book.

• Barton Zwiebach. *A First Course in String Theory*. 2nd edition, Cambridge University Press, Cambridge, 2009.

One of the best books on string theory. It is recommended to anyone willing to understand the theory as well as its implications.

Author Index

Subject Index

Printed in the United States
By Bookmasters